Teach Yourself
VISUALLY™
Flash™ 5

Sherry Willard Kinkoph

Visual

From
maranGraphics™

&

 IDG BOOKS
IDG Books Worldwide, Inc.
An International Data Group Company
Foster City, CA • Chicago, IL • Indianapolis, IN • New York, NY

Teach Yourself VISUALLY™ Flash™ 5

Published by
IDG Books Worldwide, Inc.
An International Data Group Company
919 E. Hillsdale Blvd., Suite 300
Foster City, CA 94404
www.idgbooks.com (IDG Books Worldwide Web Site)

Library of Congress Control Number: 00-109997
ISBN: 0-7645-3540-4
Printed in the United States of America

10 9 8 7 6 5 4 3 2 1

1K/RZ/RR/QR/MG

Distributed in the United States by IDG Books Worldwide, Inc.
Distributed by CDG Books Canada Inc. for Canada; by Transworld Publishers Limited in the United Kingdom; by IDG Norge Books for Norway; by IDG Sweden Books for Sweden; by IDG Books Australia Publishing Corporation Pty. Ltd. for Australia and New Zealand; by TransQuest Publishers Pte Ltd. for Singapore, Malaysia, Thailand, Indonesia, and Hong Kong; by Gotop Information Inc. for Taiwan; by ICG Muse, Inc. for Japan; by Intersoft for South Africa; by Eyrolles for France; by International Thomson Publishing for Germany, Austria and Switzerland; by Distribuidora Cuspide for Argentina; by LR International for Brazil; by Galileo Libros for Chile; by Ediciones ZETA S.C.R. Ltda. for Peru; by WS Computer Publishing Corporation, Inc., for the Philippines; by Contemporanea de Ediciones for Venezuela; by Express Computer Distributors for the Caribbean and West Indies; by Micronesia Media Distributor, Inc. for Micronesia; by Chips Computadoras S.A. de C.V. for Mexico; by Editorial Norma de Panama S.A. for Panama; by American Bookshops for Finland.
For corporate orders, please call maranGraphics at 800-469-6616.
For general information on IDG Books Worldwide's books in the U.S., please call our Consumer Customer Service department at 800-762-2974. For reseller information, including discounts and premium sales, please call our Reseller Customer Service department at 800-434-3422.
For information on where to purchase IDG Books Worldwide's books outside the U.S., please contact our International Sales department at 317-572-3993 or fax 317-572-4002.
For consumer information on foreign language translations, please contact our Customer Service department at 1-800-434-3422, fax 317-572-4002, or e-mail rights@idgbooks.com.
For information on licensing foreign or domestic rights, please phone 1-650-653-7098.
For sales inquiries and special prices for bulk quantities, please contact our Order Services department at 800-434-3422 or write to the address above.
For information on using IDG Books Worldwide's books in the classroom or for ordering examination copies, please contact our Educational Sales department at 800-434-2086 or fax 317-572-4005.
For press review copies, author interviews, or other publicity information, please contact our Public Relations department at 650-653-7000 or fax 650-653-7500.
For authorization to photocopy items for corporate, personal, or educational use, please contact Copyright Clearance Center, 222 Rosewood Drive, Danvers, MA 01923, or fax 978-750-4470.
Screen shots displayed in this book are based on pre-released software and are subject to change.

Trademark Acknowledgments

Permissions

maranGraphics

U.S. Corporate Sales

Contact maranGraphics
at (800) 469-6616 or
Fax (905) 890-9434.

U.S. Trade Sales

Contact IDG Books
at (800) 434-3422
or (650) 653-7000.

ABOUT IDG BOOKS WORLDWIDE

Welcome to the world of IDG Books Worldwide.

IDG Books Worldwide, Inc., is a subsidiary of International Data Group, the world's largest publisher of computer-related information and the leading global provider of information services on information technology. IDG was founded more than 30 years ago by Patrick J. McGovern and now employs more than 9,000 people worldwide. IDG publishes more than 290 computer publications in over 75 countries. More than 90 million people read one or more IDG publications each month.

Launched in 1990, IDG Books Worldwide is today the #1 publisher of best-selling computer books in the United States. We are proud to have received eight awards from the Computer Press Association in recognition of editorial excellence and three from Computer Currents' First Annual Readers' Choice Awards. Our best-selling ...For Dummies® series has more than 50 million copies in print with translations in 31 languages. IDG Books Worldwide, through a joint venture with IDG's Hi-Tech Beijing, became the first U.S. publisher to publish a computer book in the People's Republic of China. In record time, IDG Books Worldwide has become the first choice for millions of readers around the world who want to learn how to better manage their businesses.

Our mission is simple: Every one of our books is designed to bring extra value and skill-building instructions to the reader. Our books are written by experts who understand and care about our readers. The knowledge base of our editorial staff comes from years of experience in publishing, education, and journalism — experience we use to produce books to carry us into the new millennium. In short, we care about books, so we attract the best people. We devote special attention to details such as audience, interior design, use of icons, and illustrations. And because we use an efficient process of authoring, editing, and desktop publishing our books electronically, we can spend more time ensuring superior content and less time on the technicalities of making books.

You can count on our commitment to deliver high-quality books at competitive prices on topics you want to read about. At IDG Books Worldwide, we continue in the IDG tradition of delivering quality for more than 30 years. You'll find no better book on a subject than one from IDG Books Worldwide.

John Kilcullen
Chairman and CEO
IDG Books Worldwide, Inc.

Eighth Annual Computer Press Awards ≥1992

Ninth Annual Computer Press Awards ≥1993

Tenth Annual Computer Press Awards ≥1994

Eleventh Annual Computer Press Awards ≥1995

IDG is the world's leading IT media, research and exposition company. Founded in 1964, IDG had 1997 revenues of $2.05 billion and has more than 9,000 employees worldwide. IDG offers the widest range of media options that reach IT buyers in 75 countries representing 95% of worldwide IT spending. IDG's diverse product and services portfolio spans six key areas including print publishing, online publishing, expositions and conferences, market research, education and training, and global marketing services. More than 90 million people read one or more of IDG's 290 magazines and newspapers, including IDG's leading global brands — Computerworld, PC World, Network World, Macworld and the Channel World family of publications. IDG Books Worldwide is one of the fastest-growing computer book publishers in the world, with more than 700 titles in 36 languages. The "...For Dummies®" series alone has more than 50 million copies in print. IDG offers online users the largest network of technology-specific Web sites around the world through IDG.net (http://www.idg.net), which comprises more than 225 targeted Web sites in 55 countries worldwide. International Data Corporation (IDC) is the world's largest provider of information technology data, analysis and consulting, with research centers in over 41 countries and more than 400 research analysts worldwide. IDG World Expo is a leading producer of more than 168 globally branded conferences and expositions in 35 countries including E3 (Electronic Entertainment Expo), Macworld Expo, ComNet, Windows World Expo, ICE (Internet Commerce Expo), Agenda, DEMO, and Spotlight. IDG's training subsidiary, ExecuTrain, is the world's largest computer training company, with more than 230 locations worldwide and 785 training courses. IDG Marketing Services helps industry-leading IT companies build international brand recognition by developing global integrated marketing programs via IDG's print, online and exposition products worldwide. Further information about the company can be found at www.idg.com.   1/26/00

**maranGraphics is a family-run business
located near Toronto, Canada.**

At **maranGraphics**, we believe in producing great computer books — one book at a time.

maranGraphics has been producing high-technology products for over 25 years, which enables us to offer the computer book community a unique communication process.

Our computer books use an integrated communication process, which is very different from the approach used in other computer books. Each spread is, in essence, a flow chart — the text and screen shots are totally incorporated into the layout of the spread.

Introductory text and helpful tips complete the learning experience.

maranGraphics' approach encourages the left and right sides of the brain to work together — resulting in faster orientation and greater memory retention.

Above all, we are very proud of the handcrafted nature of our books. Our carefully-chosen writers are experts in their fields, and spend countless hours researching and organizing the content for each topic. Our artists rebuild every screen shot

to provide the best clarity possible, making our screen shots the most precise and easiest to read in the industry. We strive for perfection, and believe that the time spent handcrafting each element results in the best computer books money can buy.

Thank you for purchasing this book. We hope you enjoy it!

Sincerely,

Robert Maran
President
maranGraphics
Rob@maran.com
www.maran.com
www.idgbooks.com/visual

CREDITS

Acquisitions, Editorial, and Media Development

Project Editor:
Maureen Spears

Acquisitions Editor:
Martine Edwards

Product Development Supervisor:
Lindsay Sandman

Copy Editors:
Tim Borek, Paula Lowell

Proof Editors:
Maureen Spears, Lindsay Sandman

Technical Editor:
Kyle Bowen

Editorial Manager:
Mary Corder

Media Development Manager:
Laura Carpenter

Permissions Editor:
Carmen Krikorian

Editorial Assistants:
Candace Nicholson, Sarah Shupert

Production

Book Design:
maranGraphics™

Production Coordinator:
Judy Maran

Layout:
Sean Johannesen, Treena Lees

Illustrators:
Russ Marini, Sean Johannesen,
Steven Schaerer, Suzana G. Miokovic,
Dave Thornhill, Natalie Tweedie,
Ronda David-Burroughs,
Jill Johnson

Indexer:
Raquel Scott

Permissions Coordinator:
Jennifer Amaral

Post Production:
Robert Maran

ACKNOWLEDGMENTS

General and Administrative

IDG Books Worldwide, Inc.: John Kilcullen, CEO; Bill Barry, President and COO; John Ball, Executive VP, Operations & Administration; John Harris, CFO

IDG Books Technology Publishing Group: Richard Swadley, Senior Vice President and Publisher; Mary Bednarek, Vice President and Publisher; Walter R. Bruce III, Vice President and Publisher; Joseph Wikert, Vice President and Publisher; Mary C. Corder, Editorial Director; Andy Cummings, Publishing Director, General User Group; Barry Pruett, Publishing Director

IDG Books Manufacturing: Ivor Parker, Vice President, Manufacturing

IDG Books Marketing: John Helmus, Assistant Vice President, Director of Marketing

IDG Books Online Management: Brenda McLaughlin, Executive Vice President, Chief Internet Officer; Gary Millrood, Executive Vice President of Business Development, Sales and Marketing

IDG Books Packaging: Marc J. Mikulich, Vice President, Brand Strategy and Research

IDG Books Production for Branded Press: Debbie Stailey, Production Director

IDG Books Sales: Roland Elgey, Senior Vice President, Sales and Marketing; Michael Violano, Vice President, International Sales and Sub Rights

The publisher would like to give special thanks to Patrick J. McGovern, without whom this book would not have been possible.

ABOUT THE AUTHOR

Sherry Willard Kinkoph has written over 40 books over the past 8 years covering a variety of computer topics ranging from software to hardware, from Microsoft Office programs to the Internet. Sherry's on-going quest is to help users of all levels master the ever-changing computer technologies. No matter how many times they — the software giants and hardware conglomerates — throw out a new version or upgrade, Sherry vows to be there to make sense of it all and help computer users get the most out of their machines.

AUTHOR'S ACKNOWLEDGMENTS

Special thanks go out to the following people; to Publishing Director Barry Pruett and Acquisitions Editor Martine Edwards for allowing me this unique opportunity to write a visual book on Flash, to my Project Editor Maureen Spears who tirelessly worked with me to create a great book under a tight schedule, to Copy Editors Tim Borek and Paula Lowell for making sure all the i's were dotted and the t's were crossed, to Technical Editor Kyle Bowen for checking everything over for technical accuracy, and to the production folks at maranGraphics and IDG for putting together such a good-looking book.

To my husband, Greg, for his patience while I was sequestered away in my office with strict instructions for no interruptions during the writing of this book.

TABLE OF CONTENTS

Chapter 1

Chapter 2

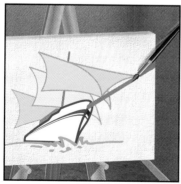

Chapter 3

Chapter 4

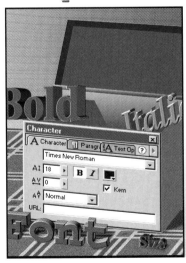

TABLE OF CONTENTS

Chapter 8

Chapter 9

TABLE OF CONTENTS

Chapter 10

CREATING INTERACTIVE BUTTONS

Chapter 11

ADDING SOUNDS

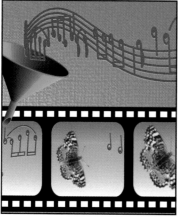

Chapter 12

ADDING FLASH ACTIONS

Chapter 13

DISTRIBUTING FLASH MOVIES

Appendix A

WEB GRAPHIC AND ANIMATION TERMS

CHAPTER 1

Flash Fundamentals

*Are you ready to start using Flash?
In this Chapter, you will learn all
the basics.*

WELCOME
to
Flash 5

INTRODUCING FLASH

Flash is an innovative program that enables users to create all kinds of animation effects and interactive features for the Web. Flash 5 is a compilation of tools for drawing and animating graphics, designing interactive elements, and generating the HTML code needed to display such creations on Web pages.

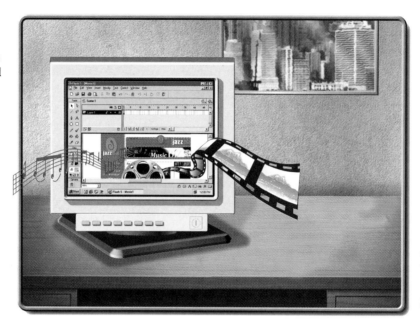

For more helpful definitions, see the Appendix "Web Graphic and Animation Terms."

GRAPHICS ON THE WEB

Most graphics on the Web are raster graphics, such as JPEGs and GIFs. Raster graphics, due to their size, take longer to display on a Web page. Every Web surfer has experienced the frustration of waiting for raster graphics to display.

VECTOR-BASED GRAPHICS

Vector-based graphics, such as those you can create in Flash, are much smaller in file size. They display much faster on a downloading Web page. Vector graphics are a more efficient method of delivering images over the Internet.

DRAWING GRAPHICS WITH FLASH

The ability to draw vector-based graphics is one of the reasons Flash is such a popular program. Flash comes with numerous tools you can use to quickly draw scalable artwork ranging from simple objects to complex graphics.

ANIMATE GRAPHICS

Another reason Flash is so widely used is its animation tools. Flash frames let you animate graphics you create with Flash or any other graphic-editing program.

ADD SOUNDS

Flash also has controls for adding and manipulating sound files. You can include sound effects or music files with an animation for added pizzazz and interest.

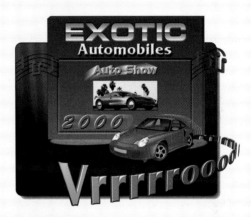

CREATE INTERACTIVE ELEMENTS

You can create interactive Web page features using Flash, such as a button that performs an action as soon as the user moves the mouse pointer over it.

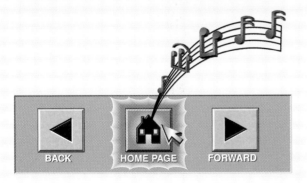

PLAY MOVIES

Flash has features for playing back movies you create and fine-tuning how the animations display.

NAVIGATE THE FLASH WINDOW

The Flash program window has several components for working with graphics and movies. Take time to familiarize yourself with the on-screen elements.

Title Bar

Displays the name of the open file.

Menu Bar

Displays Flash menus which, when clicked, reveal commands.

Main Toolbar

The Main, or Standard, toolbar contains shortcut buttons for common commands, such as creating a new file.

Timeline

Contains all the frames, layers, and scenes that make up a movie.

Drawing Toolbar

Contains the basic tools needed to create vector graphics.

Stage or Movie Area

The area where a movie or graphic displays. This area is also called the *Flash Editor*.

Work Area

The area surrounding the Stage. Anything placed on the work area does not appear in the movie.

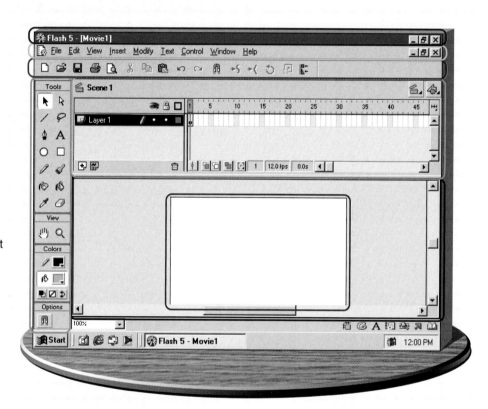

NAVIGATE WITH THE MOUSE

Use the mouse to move around the
Flash window, select tools and activate
menus. To activate a button or menu,
move the mouse pointer over the item
and click it.

NAVIGATE WITH THE KEYBOARD

You can also use the keyboard to select
commands. For example, Windows users
can display the Text menu by pressing and
holding the Alt key and then pressing the
letter T. To activate a command, press the
corresponding underlined character. You
can find keyboard shortcut commands
scattered throughout the menus.

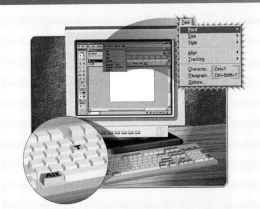

NAVIGATE COMPONENT WINDOWS

Many of the Flash features open into
separate mini-windows onscreen, like
the Library window shown here. To
close an open feature, simply click the
feature's ☒ button. Mac users can
click the Mac Close box (▫).

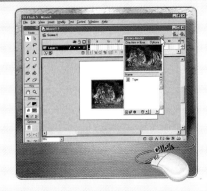

OPEN A FLASH FILE

Flash files are called *documents* or *movies*. When you save a file, you can open it and work on it again. Use the Open dialog box to access Flash files you have saved.

OPEN A FLASH FILE

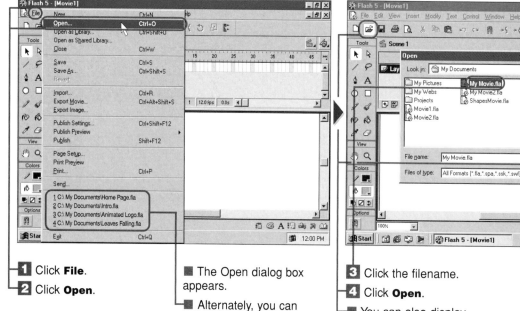

1 Click **File**.

2 Click **Open**.

■ The Open dialog box appears.

■ Alternately, you can reopen one of the last four files you opened by clicking its filename.

3 Click the filename.

4 Click **Open**.

■ You can also display the Open dialog box by clicking 📂 on the Main toolbar.

*Note: If the Main toolbar is not displayed, click **Windows/Toolbar/Main** to open it.*

■ The file opens in the Flash window.

START A NEW FLASH FILE

You can start a new
Flash file at any time,
even if you are currently
working on another file.

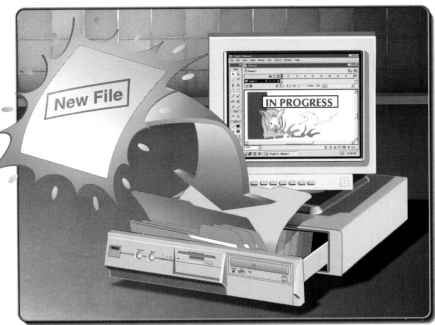

START A NEW FLASH FILE

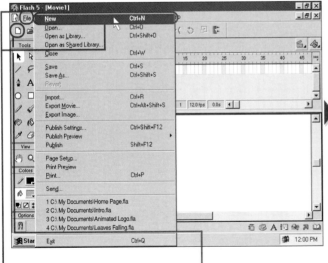

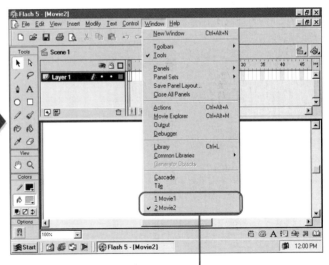

1 Click **File**.

2 Click **New**.

■ Alternately, you
can open a new file
by clicking 🗋.

■ A blank document
appears in the Flash
window.

■ You can have several
Flash files open and
switch between them
via the Window menu.

SAVE A FLASH FILE

As you create movies in Flash, you need to save them in order to work on them again. FLA is the default file format for Flash movies.

Saving graphics, called symbols, to the Flash Library works a bit differently than saving a file. See Chapter 6 for more information about symbols.

SAVE A FLASH FILE

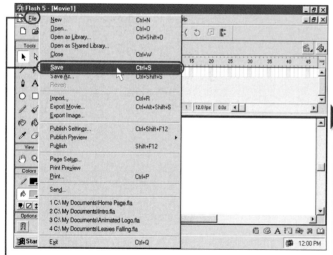

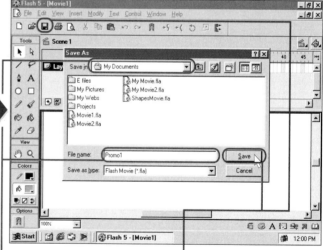

1 Click **File**.

2 Click **Save**.

■ The Save As dialog box appears.

3 Type a unique name for the file.

■ By default, Flash saves your files to the My Documents folder. To save to another folder, click ▾ and select another location.

4 Click **Save**.

■ To quickly save an existing file any time, just click 🖬.

■ Flash saves your file.

CLOSE A FLASH FILE

You can close Flash files
that you are no longer
using to free up memory
on your computer. Be
sure to save your changes
before closing a file.

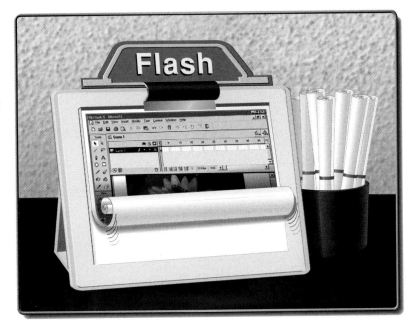

CLOSE A FLASH FILE

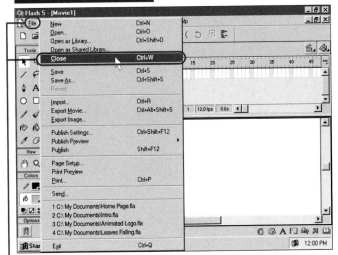

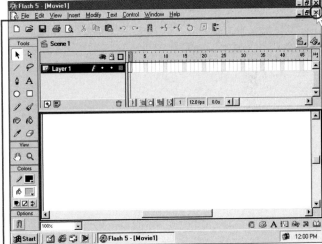

USE THE MENU BAR

1 Save your file
(see the Section
"Save a Flash File").

2 Click **File**.

3 Click **Close**.

■ Flash closes the file
you were working on,
but the program window
remains open.

*Note: If you have not saved your
changes, Flash prompts you to
do so before closing a file.*

USE THE CLOSE BUTTON

1 Save your file
(see the Section
"Save a Flash File").

2 Click ☒ .

*Note: Clicking the program
window's* ☒ *button closes
the Flash application entirely
and might result in lost files.*

*Note: If you have not saved
your changes, Flash prompts
you to do so before closing
a file.*

11

UNDERSTANDING THE FLASH TIMELINE

The Flash Timeline contains the frames, layers, and scenes that make up a movie. You can use the Timeline to organize and control your movies.

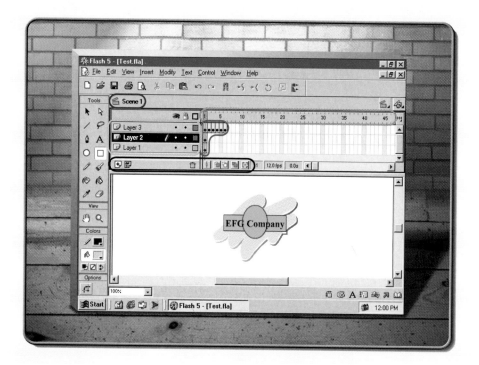

Timeline Buttons

Scattered around the Timeline are buttons for controlling frames, layers, and movies.

See Chapter 8 to learn more about using the Timeline.

Frame Numbers

Frames appear in chronological order in the Timeline, and each frame has a number.

Current Scene

Displays the name of the scene on which you are currently working.

Layers

Use layers to organize artwork, animation, sound, and interactive elements. Layers enable you to keep pieces of artwork separate and combine them to form a cohesive image, such as a company logo that includes a layer of text and another layer with a graphic shape.

Frames

Lengths of time in a Flash movie are divided into *frames*. They enable you to control what appears in animation sequences and which sounds play.

PLAYHEAD AND FRAME DISPLAY

The Playhead, also called the Current Frame Indicator, marks the current frame displayed on the Stage.

Playhead

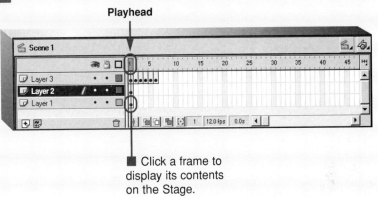

■ Click a frame to display its contents on the Stage.

LAYERS AND LAYERS BUTTONS

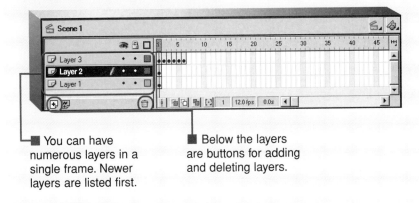

See Chapter 5 to learn more about working with layers.

■ You can have numerous layers in a single frame. Newer layers are listed first.

■ Below the layers are buttons for adding and deleting layers.

MOVE AND DOCK THE TIMELINE WINDOW

You can move the Flash Timeline around the program window or it can be docked to any side of the window.

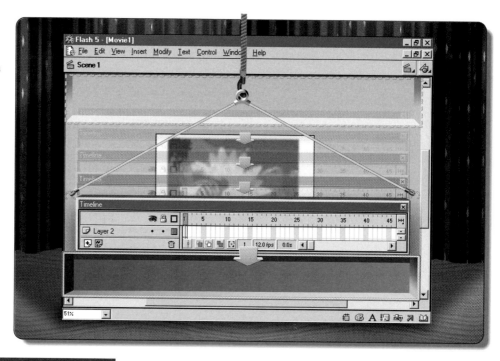

MOVE AND DOCK THE TIMELINE WINDOW

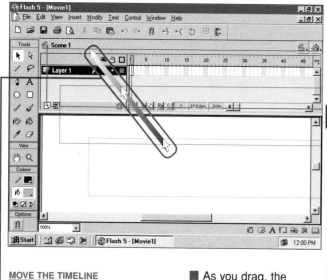

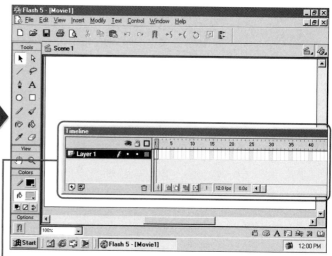

MOVE THE TIMELINE

1 Click and drag the Timeline's top gray bar area.

■ As you drag, the Timeline moves away from its docked position.

2 When you have positioned the Timeline where you want it onscreen, release the mouse button.

Can I hide the Timeline?

If you are drawing vector graphics, you can hide the Timeline to increase your drawing room:

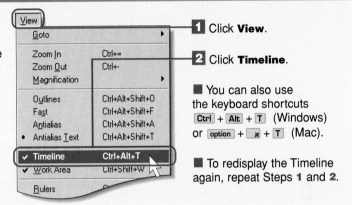

1 Click **View**.

2 Click **Timeline**.

■ You can also use the keyboard shortcuts `Ctrl` + `Alt` + `T` (Windows) or `option` + `⌘` + `T` (Mac).

■ To redisplay the Timeline again, repeat Steps **1** and **2**.

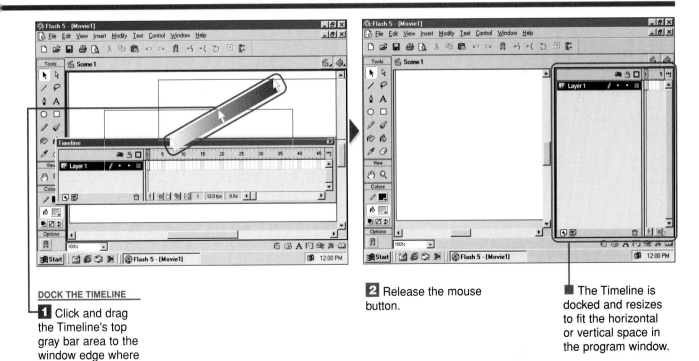

DOCK THE TIMELINE

1 Click and drag the Timeline's top gray bar area to the window edge where you want it docked.

2 Release the mouse button.

■ The Timeline is docked and resizes to fit the horizontal or vertical space in the program window.

SET THE FLASH STAGE

The Stage is the on-screen area where you can view the contents of a frame and draw graphic objects. You can control the size and appearance of the Stage.

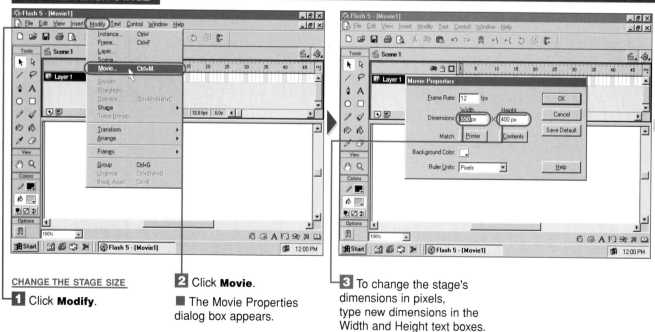

CHANGE THE STAGE SIZE

1 Click **Modify**.

2 Click **Movie**.

■ The Movie Properties dialog box appears.

3 To change the stage's dimensions in pixels, type new dimensions in the Width and Height text boxes.

Can I specify different units of measurement?

You can use inches, points, or even centimeters as size measurements in Flash. To do so, type the correct abbreviation along with the entry in the Dimensions box: **px** for pixels, **mm** for millimeters, **cm** for centimeters, **pt** for points, or **"** for inches.

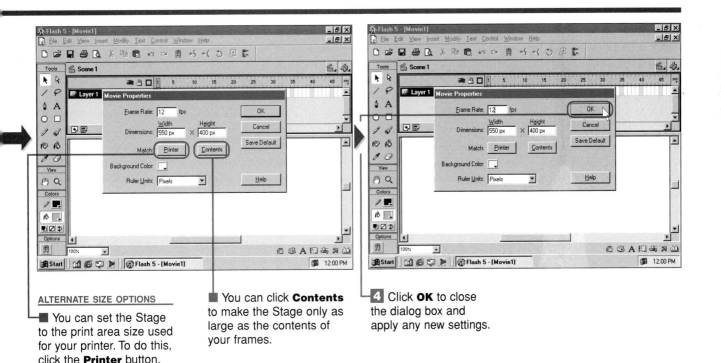

ALTERNATE SIZE OPTIONS

■ You can set the Stage to the print area size used for your printer. To do this, click the **Printer** button.

■ You can click **Contents** to make the Stage only as large as the contents of your frames.

4 Click **OK** to close the dialog box and apply any new settings.

ZOOM OUT OR IN

When working with various elements on the Stage, you can zoom in or out for a better view.

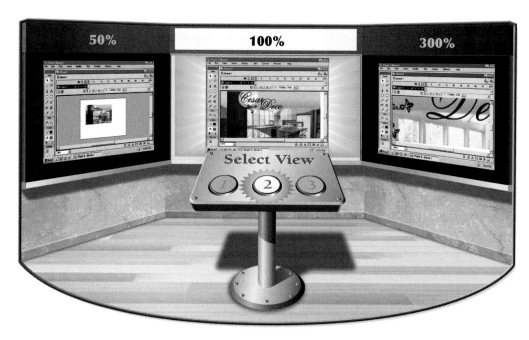

ZOOM OUT OR IN

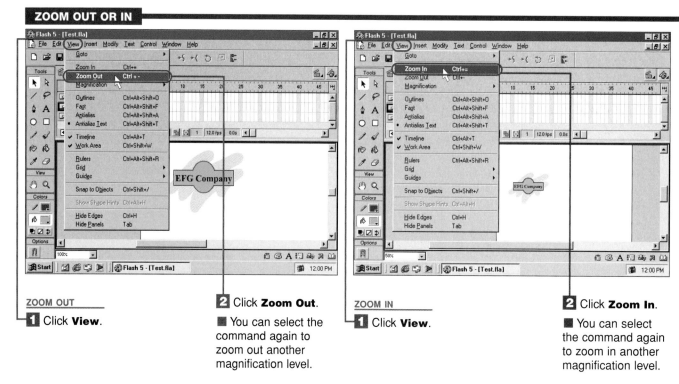

ZOOM OUT

1 Click **View**.

2 Click **Zoom Out**.

■ You can select the command again to zoom out another magnification level.

ZOOM IN

1 Click **View**.

2 Click **Zoom In**.

■ You can select the command again to zoom in another magnification level.

How do I use the Zoom tool button?

The Zoom button on the Drawing toolbar can also be used to change the magnification.

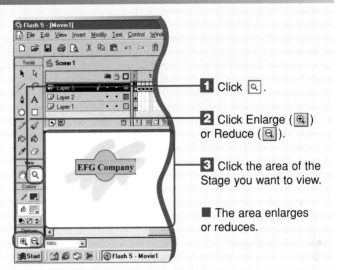

1 Click 🔍.

2 Click Enlarge (🔍) or Reduce (🔍).

3 Click the area of the Stage you want to view.

■ The area enlarges or reduces.

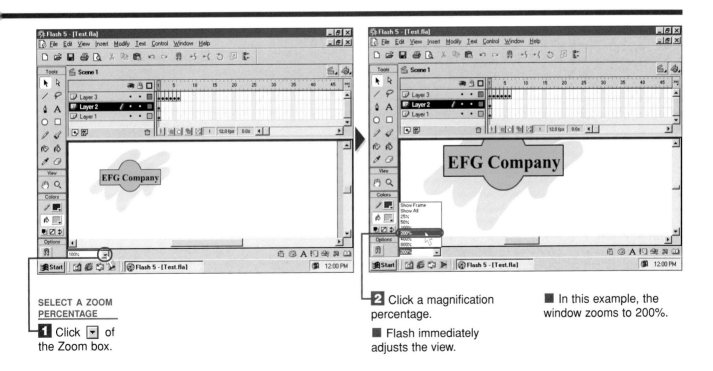

SELECT A ZOOM PERCENTAGE

1 Click ▾ of the Zoom box.

2 Click a magnification percentage.

■ Flash immediately adjusts the view.

■ In this example, the window zooms to 200%.

WORK WITH FLASH TOOLBARS

The Flash toolbars have buttons for quickly activating commands and features. You can hide or display toolbars as you need them, and they can be docked to one side of the screen or appear to float as separate windows.

WORK WITH FLASH TOOLBARS

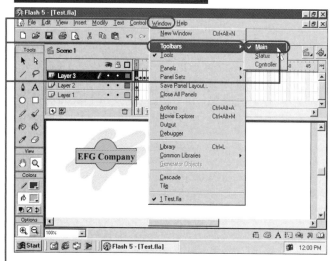

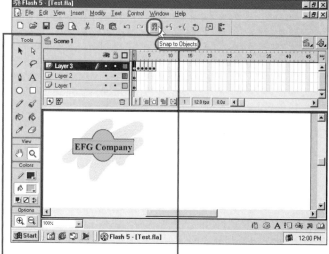

TURN A TOOLBAR ON OR OFF

1 Click **Window**.

2 Click **Toolbars**.

3 Click the name of the toolbar you want to turn on or off.

■ The toolbar turns off or on.

■ A check mark (✔) next to the toolbar name means the toolbar is currently displayed.

VIEW TOOLTIPS

1 To learn the name of any toolbar button, move ⬉ over a button.

2 Pause without clicking the button.

■ A ToolTip box appears with the button name.

Can I move toolbars onscreen?

Flash toolbars can be displayed as floating windows or docked to one side of the screen. To undock a toolbar, drag it away from its docked position. To dock a toolbar, double-click its Title bar.

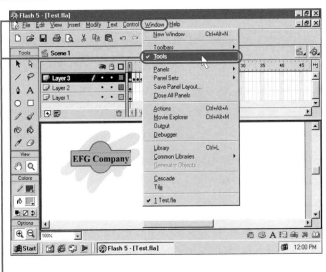

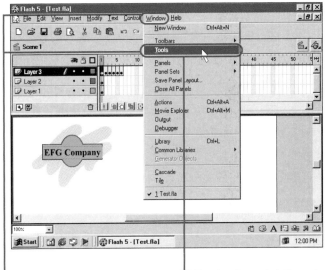

HIDE THE DRAWING TOOLBAR

■ The Drawing toolbar displays by default.

1 Click **Window**.

2 Click **Tools**.

■ A check mark (✔) next to the menu command means the toolbar is currently displayed.

■ The Drawing toolbar hides.

DISPLAY THE DRAWING TOOLBAR

1 Click **Window**.

2 Click **Tools**.

■ No check mark (✔) next to the menu command means the toolbar is currently hidden.

■ The Drawing toolbar appears.

USING RULERS AND GRIDS

To help you draw with more precision, turn on the Flash Rulers and grid lines. Both tools can help you position objects on the Stage.

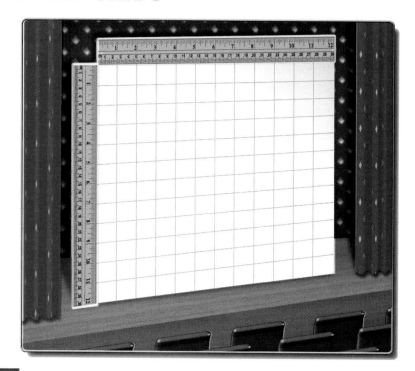

USING RULERS AND GRIDS

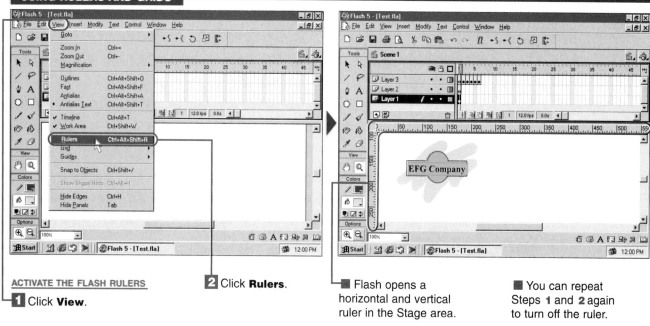

ACTIVATE THE FLASH RULERS

1 Click **View**.

2 Click **Rulers**.

■ Flash opens a horizontal and vertical ruler in the Stage area.

■ You can repeat Steps **1** and **2** again to turn off the ruler.

How can I precisely align objects with the grid?

Use the Snap tool to help you quickly align objects to the grid lines. To activate the tool, click **View**, **Snap** or click 🔟 on the Main toolbar. You can also click **View**, **Grid**, **Snap To Grid**.

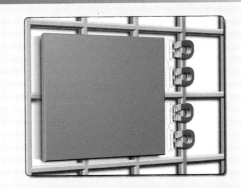

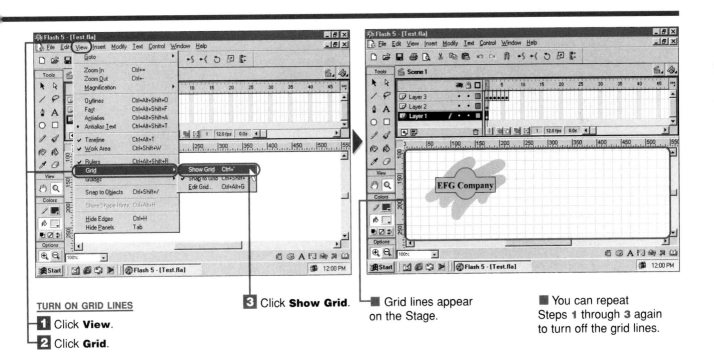

TURN ON GRID LINES

1 Click **View**.

2 Click **Grid**.

3 Click **Show Grid**.

■ Grid lines appear on the Stage.

■ You can repeat Steps **1** through **3** again to turn off the grid lines.

FIND HELP WITH FLASH

When you run across a program feature or technique you do not understand, consult the Flash Help system. Flash comes with Help resources, including lessons to help you better understand Flash capabilities and sample Flash movies to study.

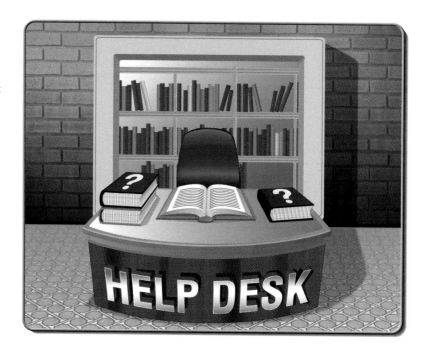

FIND HELP WITH FLASH

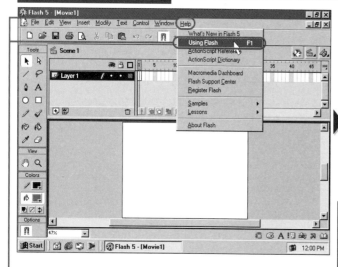

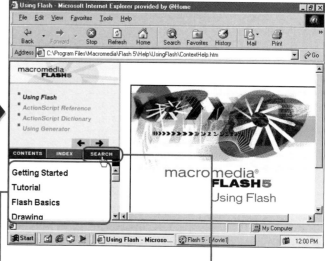

-■1 Click **Help**.

-■2 Click **Using Flash**.

■ Your Web browser immediately launches and displays an offline Web page.

■ You can scroll through the topics and follow links to the information you want.

■3 To search for a specific Flash topic, click the **Search** link.

■ A search window opens.

24

Where else can I find Flash help?

Macromedia's Web site
(www.macromedia.com/support/flash/)
is a good place to start if you are
looking for additional information about
the Flash program. You can also
find numerous sites on the Internet
dedicated to Flash users by performing
a simple search for the keyword *Flash*
using your favorite search engine.
Another way you can find online help
is through the Macromedia Dashboard.
Click **Help, Macromedia Dashboard**.
The site offers news, support, and
Flash resources.

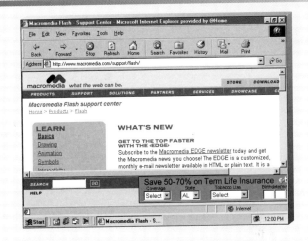

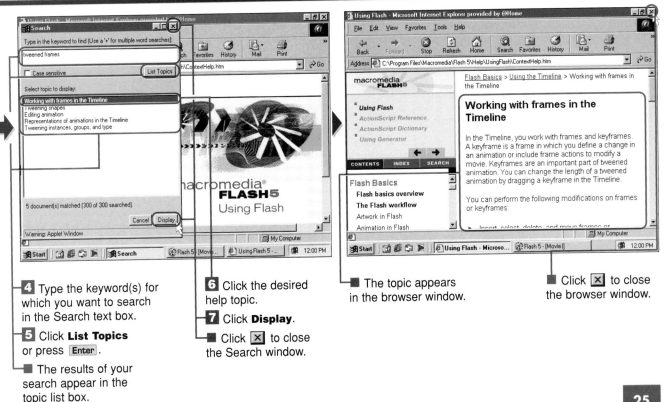

-■4 Type the keyword(s) for
which you want to search
in the Search text box.

-■5 Click **List Topics**
or press Enter.

-■ The results of your
search appear in the
topic list box.

-■6 Click the desired
help topic.

-■7 Click **Display**.

-■ Click ☒ to close
the Search window.

-■ The topic appears
in the browser window.

■ Click ☒ to close
the browser window.

CHAPTER 2

Drawing and Painting Objects

Do you want to draw your own illustrations to animate? Flash offers many tools you can use to make all sorts of illustrations.

INTRODUCING FLASH OBJECTS

Drawings you create in Flash are comprised of fills and lines, called *strokes*. With the tools found on the Drawing toolbar, you can create simple objects, such as shapes, or complex objects that involve layers, grouped elements, and more.

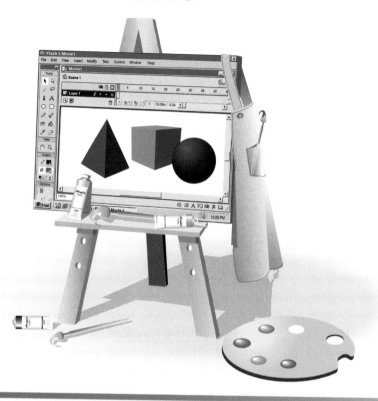

STAGE LEVEL

When working with objects on the Stage, there are two levels: the stage level and the overlay level. The stage level is the bottom level on the stage and any objects you place there can interact. For example, a line and a shape can connect.

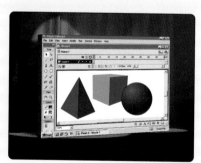

OVERLAY LEVEL

The overlay level is like a transparent sheet of paper on top of the stage level. Any object you place on the overlay level floats on top and does not interact with stage-level objects.

OBJECT TYPES

Stage-level objects include anything you draw with the drawing tools. Overlay-level objects include items you group together to act as a single unit, symbols you create for reuse throughout your movie, text blocks, and imported graphics.

BREAKING APART OBJECTS

Flash makes it easy to break apart overlay-level objects and turn them into stage-level objects you can manipulate and edit. For example, you can turn text into graphic shapes you can resize and rotate.

USING IMPORTED OBJECTS

You do not have to rely on your drawing skills to create objects for your movies. You can also import graphics from other programs and manipulate them with the Flash drawing tools.

MANIPULATING OBJECTS

You can combine simple objects to create drawings, or remove parts to create new shapes. You can change an object's color, scale, and positioning. You can also stack object on top of other objects to give your drawings depth.

SHAPE RECOGNITION

It is not always easy to draw with a computer mouse, but Flash makes it simpler with shape recognition. Draw a rough idea of a shape, and Flash automatically cleans it up for you.

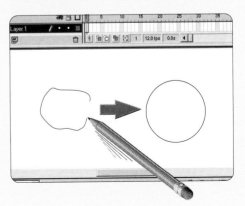

USING THE DRAWING TOOLBAR

The Drawing toolbar is packed with tools that you can use to create and work with graphic objects.

Line

Draws straight lines.

Arrow

Use to grab, select, and move items on the Stage.

Subselect

Displays edit points you can adjust to change a line's shape.

Lasso

Use to select irregularly shaped objects on the Stage.

Pen

Use to draw precise curves.

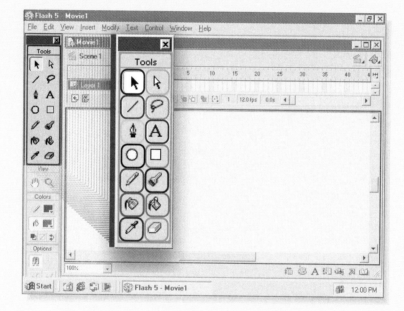

Text

Draws text boxes.

Oval

Draws circle and oval shapes.

Rectangle

Draws square and rectangle shapes.

Pencil

Use to draw freeform lines.

Brush

Draws with a fill color, much like a paintbrush.

Ink Bottle

Use to change the style, thickness, and color of lines.

Dropper

Use to copy the attributes of one object to another.

Eraser

Erases parts of the graphic object.

Paint Bucket

Fills shapes or lines with color.

USING THE VIEW, COLOR, AND OPTIONS BARS

VIEW TOOLS

Hand
Use to move your
view of the objects
on the Stage or
in the work area.

Zoom
Magnifies your
view or zooms
out for a better
look at the Stage.

OPTION TOOLS

Some of the drawing tools you select
might offer modifiers that enable you
to set additional controls for the tool.

See Chapter 1
to learn how to
display or hide
the Drawing
toolbar.

COLOR TOOLS AND CONTROLS

Line Color
Click to display a palette
of colors for lines.

Fill Color
Click to display a palette
of colors for fills.

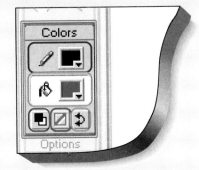

Black and White
Changes the line color to black
and the fill color to white.

No Outline
Use to draw shapes without
outlines or borders.

Toggle Colors
Switches the line color to
the fill color and vice-versa.

DRAW LINE SEGMENTS

You can draw all sorts of objects with lines. The easiest way to draw straight lines in Flash is to use the Line tool. To draw a freeform line, use the Pencil tool. Lines, called *strokes* in Flash, can connect with other lines and shapes to create a drawing.

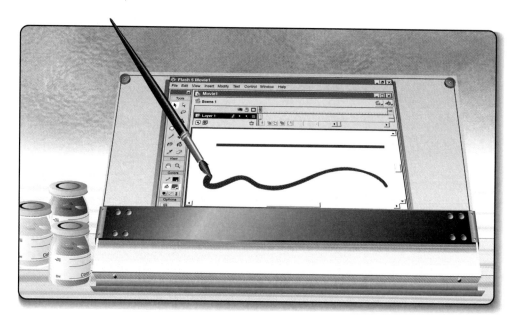

DRAW LINE SEGMENTS

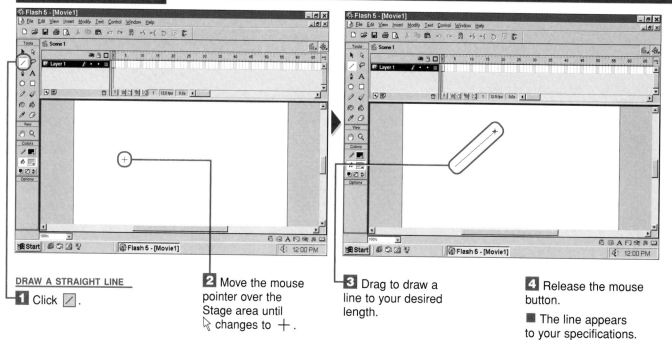

DRAW A STRAIGHT LINE

1 Click ◿.

2 Move the mouse pointer over the Stage area until ▷ changes to ＋.

3 Drag to draw a line to your desired length.

4 Release the mouse button.

■ The line appears to your specifications.

**How do I control
the line thickness?**

You can change the
line thickness after
you draw the line,
or set a thickness
before you start
drawing.

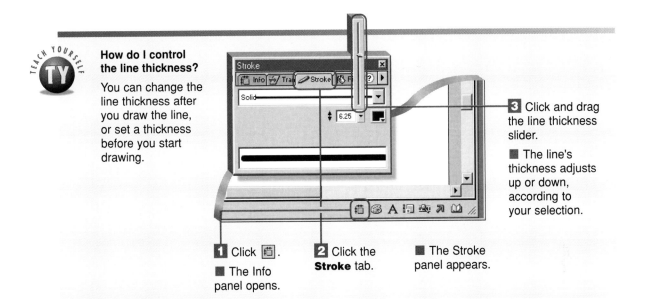

3 Click and drag
the line thickness
slider.

■ The line's
thickness adjusts
up or down,
according to
your selection.

1 Click 📇.

■ The Info
panel opens.

2 Click the
Stroke tab.

■ The Stroke
panel appears.

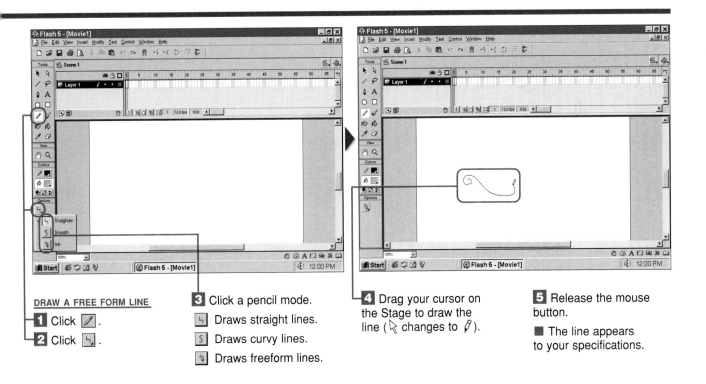

DRAW A FREE FORM LINE

1 Click ✏.

2 Click ↳.

3 Click a pencil mode.

↳ Draws straight lines.

∫ Draws curvy lines.

✎ Draws freeform lines.

4 Drag your cursor on
the Stage to draw the
line (⇖ changes to ✐).

5 Release the mouse
button.

■ The line appears
to your specifications.

FORMAT LINE SEGMENTS

By default, lines you draw on the Stage are solid black lines, 1-point thick. You can control a line's thickness, style, and color using the formatting controls found in the panel window.

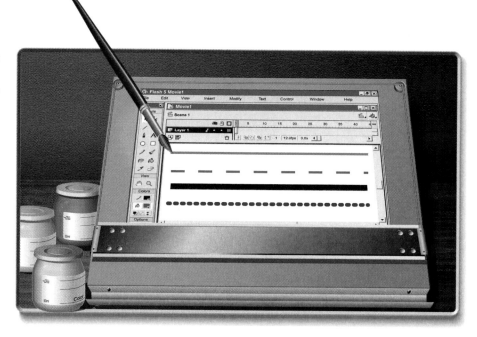

FORMAT A LINE SEGMENT

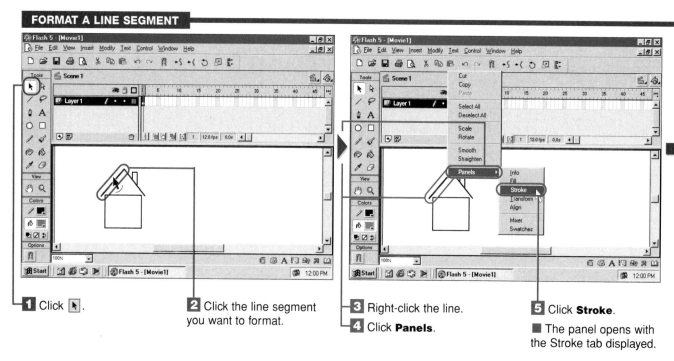

1 Click ▶.

2 Click the line segment you want to format.

3 Right-click the line.

4 Click **Panels**.

5 Click **Stroke**.

■ The panel opens with the Stroke tab displayed.

How do I change the line color?

From the Stroke tab of the panel, click the Line Color box (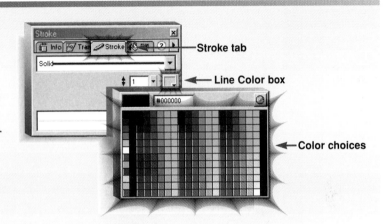) to display a palette of color choices. Then click the color you want to assign.

Stroke tab

Line Color box

#000000

Color choices

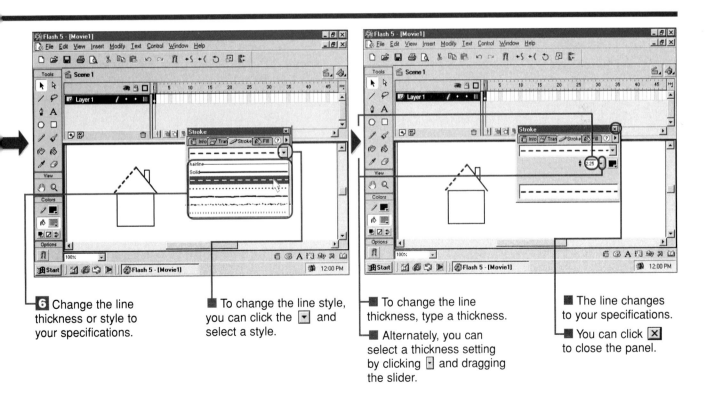

6 Change the line thickness or style to your specifications.

■ To change the line style, you can click the ▾ and select a style.

■ To change the line thickness, type a thickness.

■ Alternately, you can select a thickness setting by clicking ⬚ and dragging the slider.

■ The line changes to your specifications.

■ You can click ✕ to close the panel.

DRAW A CUSTOM LINE

You can select a line style and customize its appearance using the options in the Line Style dialog box. For example, you might want a dotted line with the dots spaced far apart or very tightly together.

DRAW A CUSTOM LINE

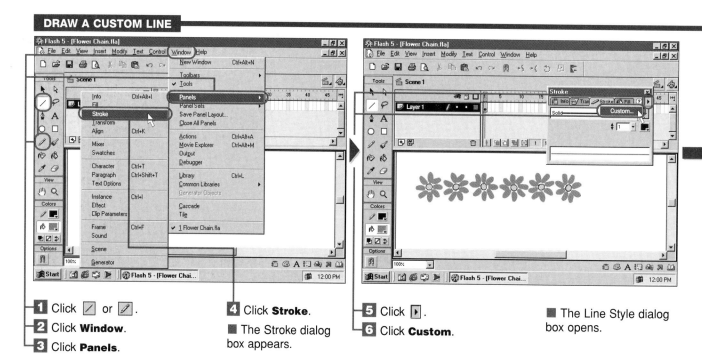

-1 Click ✏ or ✎.

-2 Click **Window**.

-3 Click **Panels**.

4 Click **Stroke**.

■ The Stroke dialog box appears.

5 Click ▶.

6 Click **Custom**.

■ The Line Style dialog box opens.

How do I fix a mistake?

To undo your last action, such as drawing a line segment, just click ↶ on the toolbar. If you change your mind and want the action back, click ↷ .

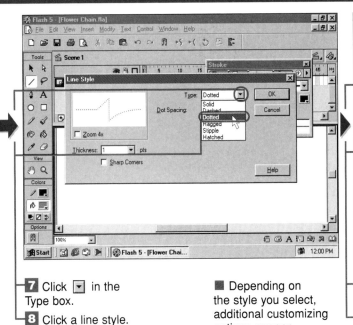

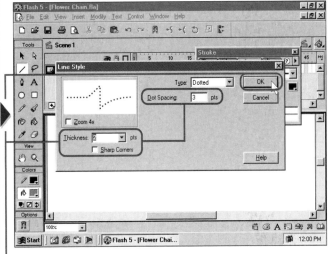

7 Click ▼ in the Type box.

8 Click a line style.

■ Depending on the style you select, additional customizing options appear.

■**9** Set any customizing options you want.

10 Click **OK**.

11 Draw your custom line on the Stage.

■ The line appears with your specifications.

Note: See the Section "Draw Line Segments" to learn more about drawing lines on the Stage.

DRAW CURVES WITH THE PEN TOOL

You can draw precise lines and curves using the Pen tool. Using this tool takes some getting used to, but with a little practice, you can draw curves easily.

DRAW CURVES WITH THE PEN TOOL

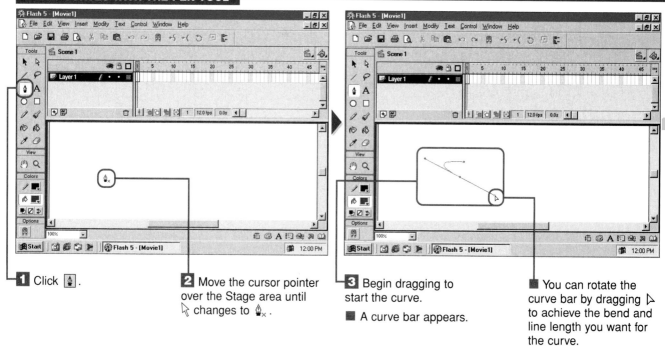

1 Click 🖋.

2 Move the cursor pointer over the Stage area until ▷ changes to 🖋×.

3 Begin dragging to start the curve.

■ A curve bar appears.

■ You can rotate the curve bar by dragging ▷ to achieve the bend and line length you want for the curve.

How can I reshape a curved line?

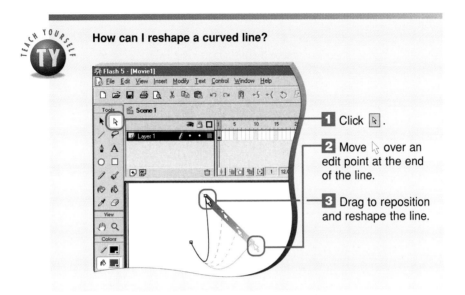

1 Click ▶.

2 Move ▶ over an edit point at the end of the line.

3 Drag to reposition and reshape the line.

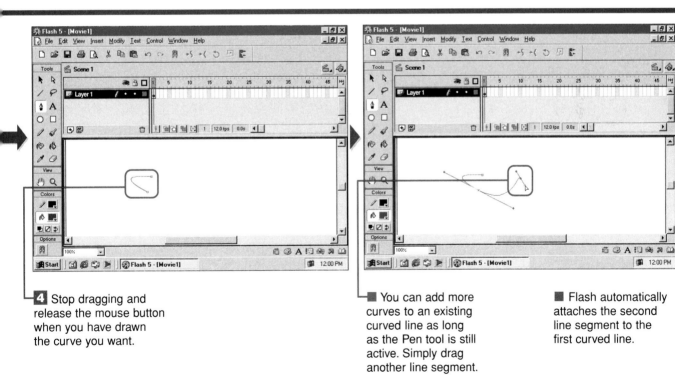

4 Stop dragging and release the mouse button when you have drawn the curve you want.

■ You can add more curves to an existing curved line as long as the Pen tool is still active. Simply drag another line segment.

■ Flash automatically attaches the second line segment to the first curved line.

SMOOTH OR STRAIGHTEN LINE SEGMENTS

Flash has two controls for modifying the appearance of lines you draw. You can smooth or straighten them to create subtle or dramatic changes to your drawing.

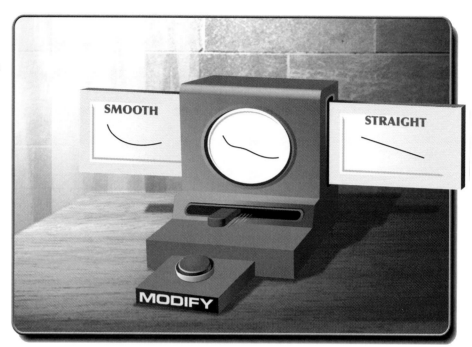

SMOOTH A LINE SEGMENT

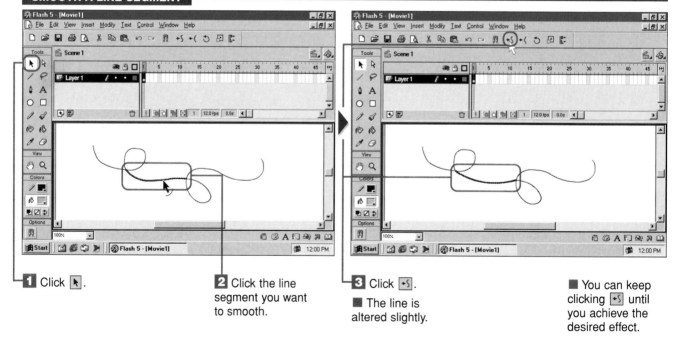

1 Click .

2 Click the line segment you want to smooth.

3 Click.

■ The line is altered slightly.

■ You can keep clicking until you achieve the desired effect.

Can I draw in Smooth or Straighten mode?

Flash can help you with your line-drawing skills. When you click [✎], [↳] appears in the Options tray at the bottom of the Drawing toolbar. Click [↳] and select a mode ([↳], [S] or [✐]) before you begin drawing lines. When you finish drawing a line, Flash smooths or straightens it for you.

STRAIGHTEN A LINE SEGMENT

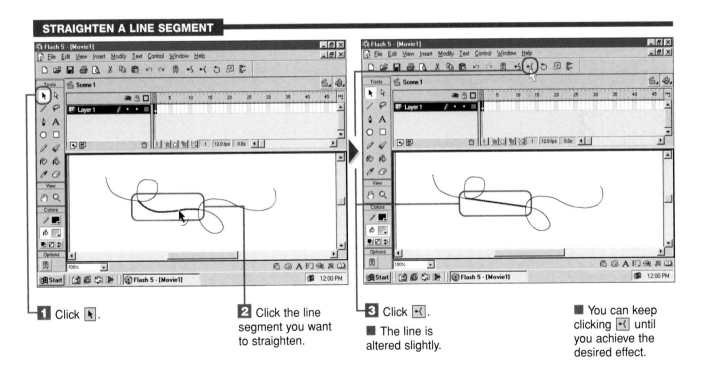

1 Click [↖].

2 Click the line segment you want to straighten.

3 Click [◂].

■ The line is altered slightly.

■ You can keep clicking [◂] until you achieve the desired effect.

DRAW OVAL AND RECTANGLE SHAPES

You can create simple shapes in Flash and then fill them with a color or pattern, or use them as part of a drawing.

DRAW OVAL AND RECTANGLE SHAPES

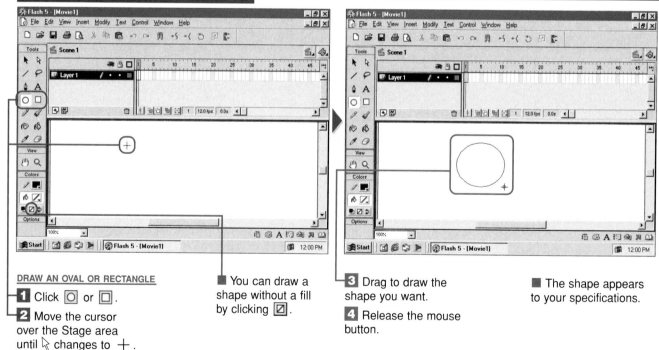

DRAW AN OVAL OR RECTANGLE

1 Click ⬭ or ▭ .

2 Move the cursor over the Stage area until ↖ changes to ✛ .

■ You can draw a shape without a fill by clicking ▨ .

3 Drag to draw the shape you want.

4 Release the mouse button.

■ The shape appears to your specifications.

How do I draw a rectangle with rounded corners?

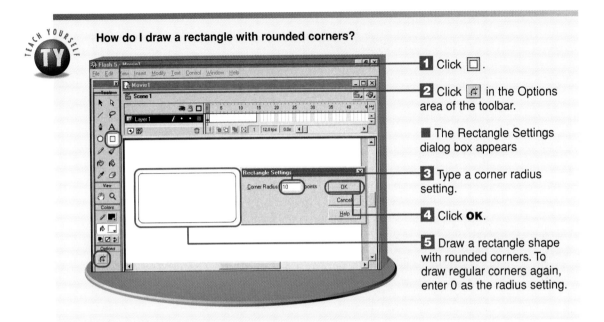

■1 Click ▢.

■2 Click 🔲 in the Options area of the toolbar.

■ The Rectangle Settings dialog box appears

■3 Type a corner radius setting.

■4 Click **OK**.

■5 Draw a rectangle shape with rounded corners. To draw regular corners again, enter 0 as the radius setting.

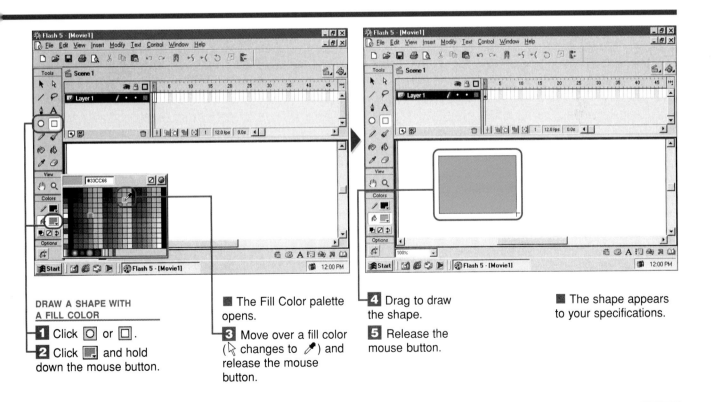

DRAW A SHAPE WITH A FILL COLOR

■1 Click ▢ or ▢.

■2 Click 🔳 and hold down the mouse button.

■ The Fill Color palette opens.

■3 Move over a fill color (↖ changes to ✐) and release the mouse button.

■4 Drag to draw the shape.

■5 Release the mouse button.

■ The shape appears to your specifications.

DRAW OBJECTS WITH THE BRUSH TOOL

You can use the
Brush tool to draw
with brush strokes,
much like a paintbrush.
You can control the
size and shape of the
brush as well as how
the brush strokes
appear on the Stage.

DRAW OBJECTS WITH THE BRUSH TOOL

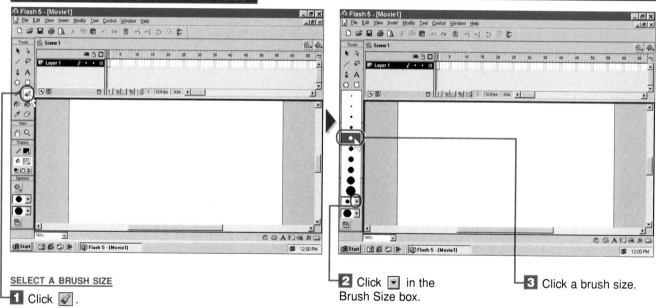

SELECT A BRUSH SIZE

1 Click .

2 Click ▼ in the
Brush Size box.

3 Click a brush size.

What do the Brush modifiers do?

There are five modifiers you can use when drawing with the Brush tool. Paint Normal lets you paint over anything on the Stage. Paint Fills will paint inside fill areas but not on lines. Paint Behind paints beneath any existing objects on the Stage. Paint Selection paints only inside the selected area. Paint Inside begins a brush stroke inside a fill area without affecting any lines.

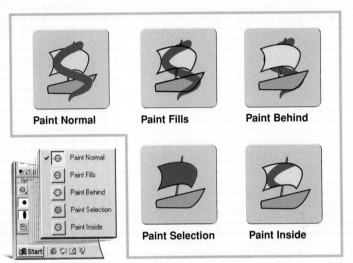

Paint Normal   **Paint Fills**   **Paint Behind**

Paint Normal
Paint Fills
Paint Behind
Paint Selection
Paint Inside

Paint Selection   **Paint Inside**

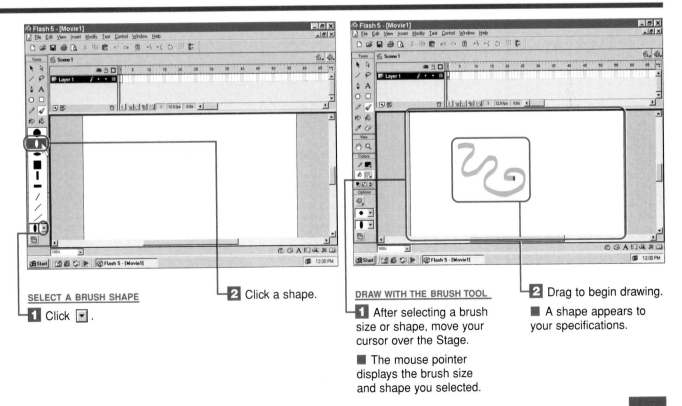

SELECT A BRUSH SHAPE

1 Click ▼.

2 Click a shape.

DRAW WITH THE BRUSH TOOL

1 After selecting a brush size or shape, move your cursor over the Stage.

■ The mouse pointer displays the brush size and shape you selected.

2 Drag to begin drawing.

■ A shape appears to your specifications.

FILL OBJECTS WITH THE PAINT BUCKET TOOL

You can use the Paint Bucket tool to quickly fill in objects, such as shapes. You can fill objects with a color, a gradient effect, or even a picture. The Flash color palette comes with numerous colors and shades, as well as several pre-made gradient effects.

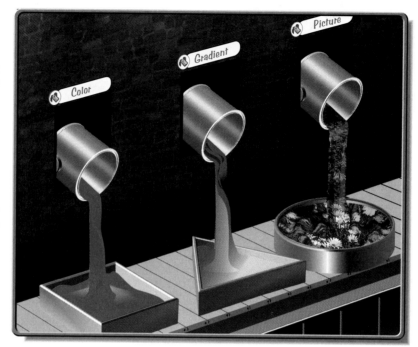

See Chapter 3 to learn more about creating new gradient effects.

FILL OBJECTS WITH THE PAINT BUCKET TOOL

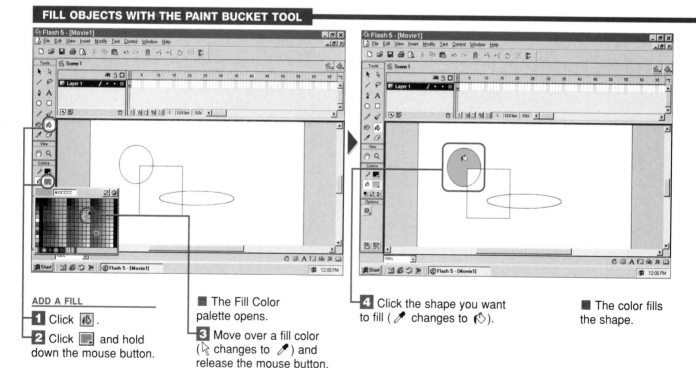

ADD A FILL

1 Click 🪣.

2 Click 🟦 and hold down the mouse button.

■ The Fill Color palette opens.

3 Move over a fill color (🖑 changes to 🖌) and release the mouse button.

4 Click the shape you want to fill (🖌 changes to 🖑).

■ The color fills the shape.

What is a gradient effect?

A gradient effect shows one or several colors of different intensities, creating a three-dimensional effect. With Flash, you can create a linear gradient effect that intensifies color shading from left to right or top to bottom, or create a radial gradient effect that intensifies color shading from the middle to the outer edges or vice versa.

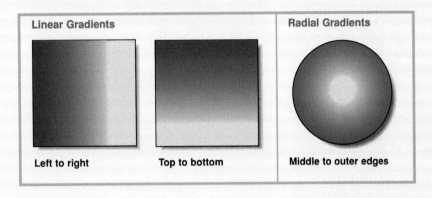

Linear Gradients

Left to right   Top to bottom

Radial Gradients

Middle to outer edges

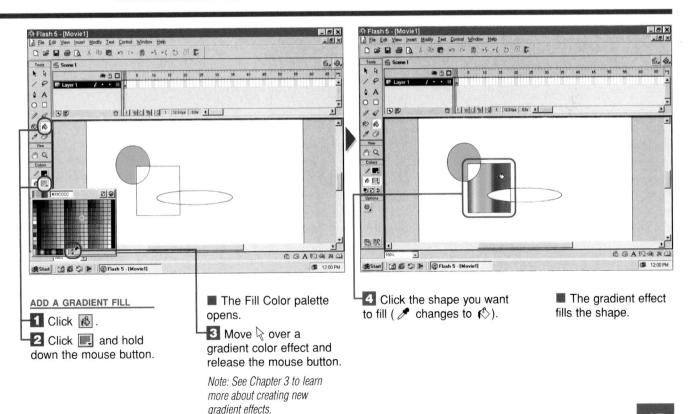

ADD A GRADIENT FILL

1 Click 🖼 .

2 Click 🖼 and hold down the mouse button.

■ The Fill Color palette opens.

3 Move ▷ over a gradient color effect and release the mouse button.

Note: See Chapter 3 to learn more about creating new gradient effects.

4 Click the shape you want to fill (✐ changes to ✑).

■ The gradient effect fills the shape.

Enhancing and Editing Objects

Are you ready to enhance your Flash drawings? This chapter shows you how to manipulate and edit objects you have drawn.

SELECT OBJECTS

To work with objects you draw or place on the Flash stage, you must first select them. The more lines and shapes you place on the Stage, the trickier it is to select only the ones you want. You can use the Arrow tool to quickly select any object.

SELECT OBJECTS

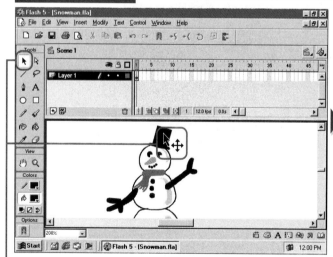

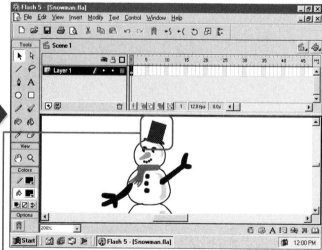

CLICK TO SELECT OBJECTS

1 Click ▶.

2 Move the ▶ over the object you want to select, and then click.

■ You can select a fill and its surrounding line border by double-clicking the fill.

■ Selected objects appear highlighted with a pattern.

■ You can now edit the object.

How do I select multiple objects?

Hold down the **Shift** key while clicking objects when you want to select more than one at a time. For example, if a line is composed of several segments, you can select all of them for editing. Click ▶; then hold the **Shift** key and click each line segment you want to select.

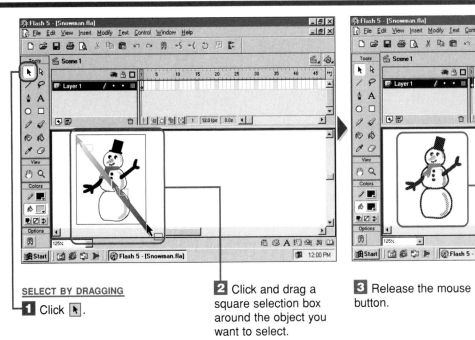

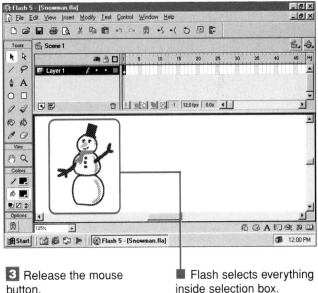

SELECT BY DRAGGING

1 Click ▶.

2 Click and drag a square selection box around the object you want to select.

3 Release the mouse button.

■ Flash selects everything inside selection box.

CONTINUED ▶

SELECT OBJECTS

You can use the Lasso tool to select irregular objects. The Lasso tool draws a freehand "rope" around the item you want to select. This allows you to select an oddly-shaped object or just a small portion of an object.

SELECT OBJECTS (CONTINUED)

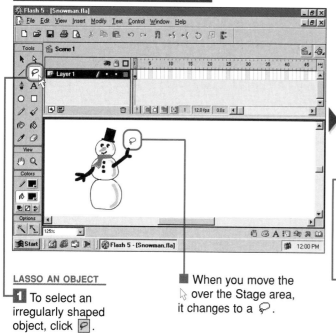

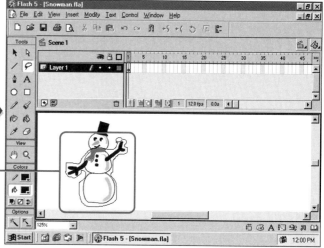

LASSO AN OBJECT

1 To select an irregularly shaped object, click 🔲.

■ When you move the ⟍ over the Stage area, it changes to a ⟁.

2 Click and drag the lasso completely around the object until you reach the point where you started.

3 Release the mouse button.

■ Flash highlights anything inside the lasso shape.

How can I select complex shapes?

Drawing around irregular items with the lasso can be difficult. For additional help, use the Lasso tool's Polygon Mode modifier. Click 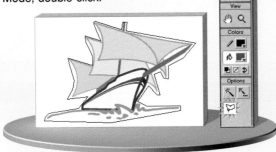 and then click in the Modifier Tray. Now click your way around the object you want to select. Every click creates a connected line to the last click. To turn off the Polygon Mode, double-click.

How do I select just a fill and not its border?

Simply click the fill to select it. To select both the fill and the fill's border, double-click the fill.

Fill   **Fill and border**

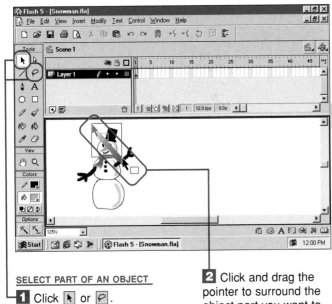

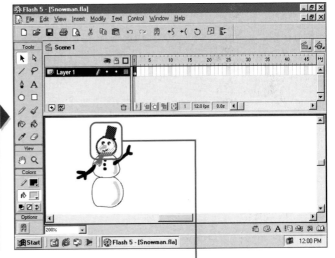

SELECT PART OF AN OBJECT

1 Click ▶ or ⌒.

■ You can click ▶ for simple shapes or lines.

■ You can click ⌒ for irregularly shaped objects.

2 Click and drag the pointer to surround the object part you want to select.

3 Release the mouse button.

■ Everything inside the area you dragged over is selected.

MOVE AND COPY OBJECTS

You can easily reposition objects on the Flash stage. Flash lets you quickly move an object from one area to another, and you can make copies of the original object.

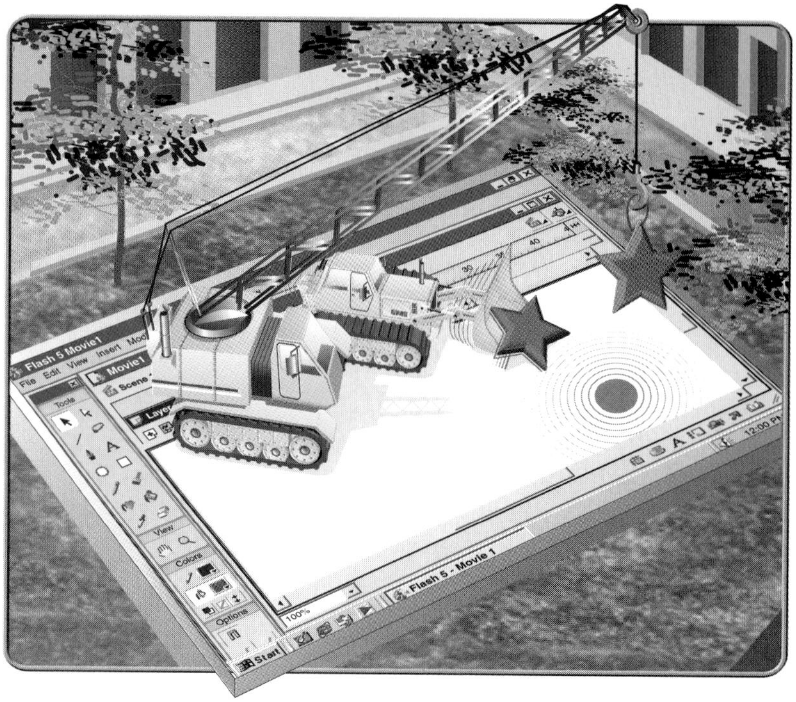

MOVE AN OBJECT

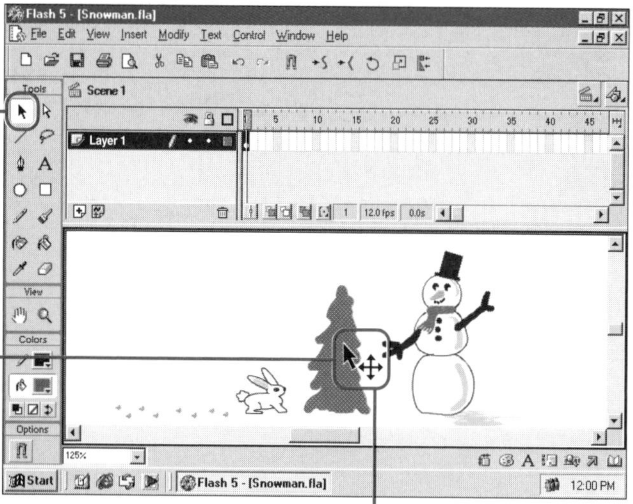

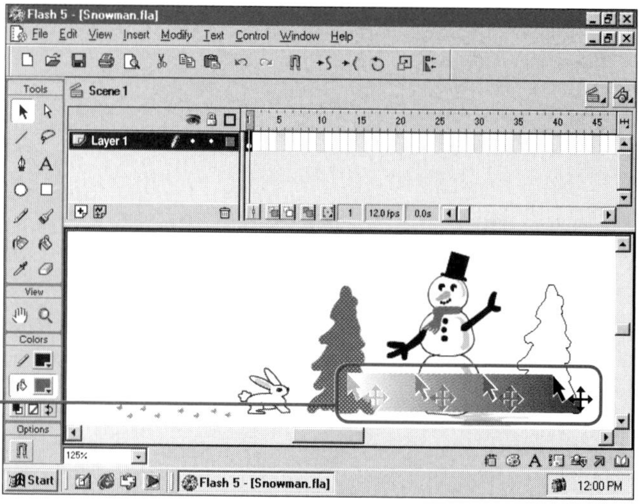

1 Click ↖.

2 Click the object you want to move.

■ A ✥ appears next to the ↖.

3 Click and drag the object to a new position.

4 Release the mouse button.

■ Your object moves to the location you selected.

TEACH YOURSELF

Can I precisely control where an object is positioned?

For more precise positioning controls, open the Align panel. Press Ctrl + K (Windows) or ⌘ + K (Mac), or click [Align button] to open the Align panel where you will find a variety of controls for positioning an object precisely on the Stage. To learn more about using the alignment controls, see the section "Align Objects."

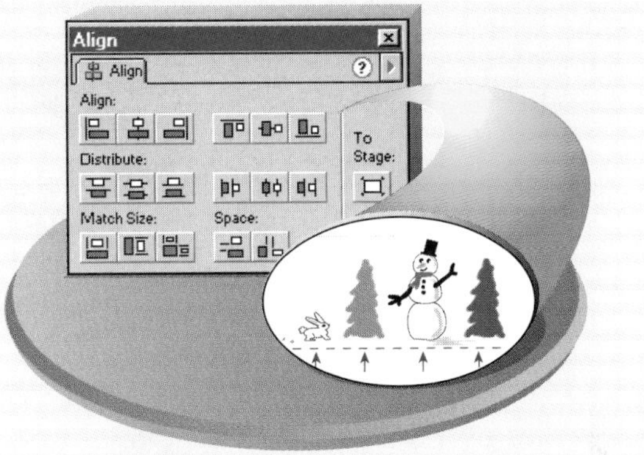

COPY AN OBJECT

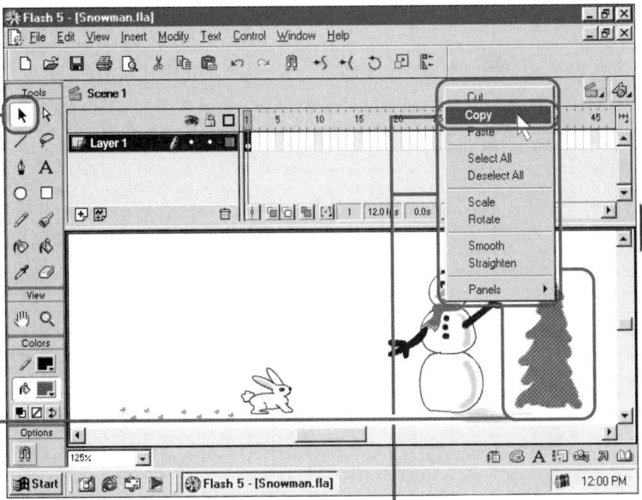

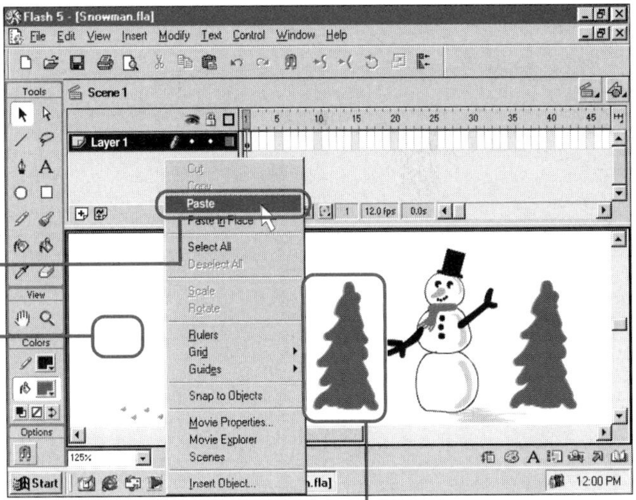

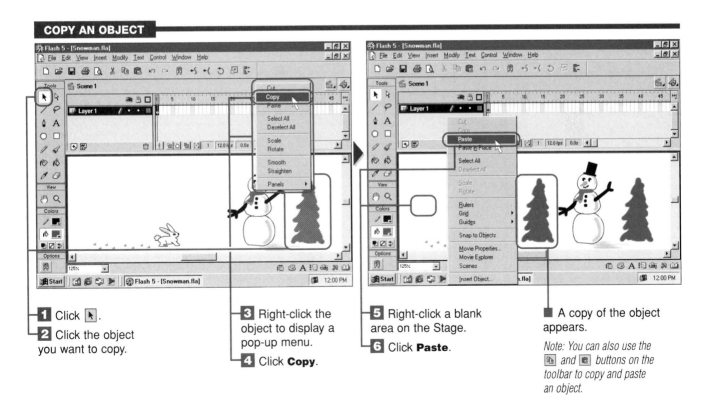

1. Click [Arrow tool].
2. Click the object you want to copy.
3. Right-click the object to display a pop-up menu.
4. Click **Copy**.
5. Right-click a blank area on the Stage.
6. Click **Paste**.

■ A copy of the object appears.

Note: You can also use the [Copy] and [Paste] buttons on the toolbar to copy and paste an object.

EDIT LINE SEGMENTS

You can change a line by adjusting its length or reshaping its curve. For example, you might want to change a line's angle, extend a curved line to make it appear longer, or just simply make the curve more curvy.

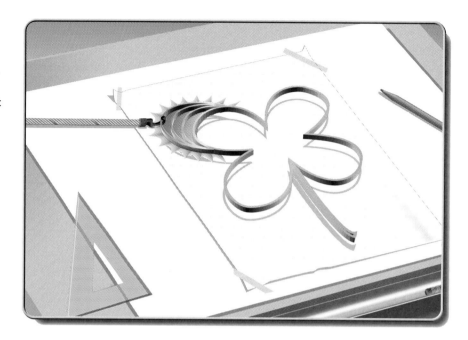

CHANGE A LINE SEGMENT LENGTH

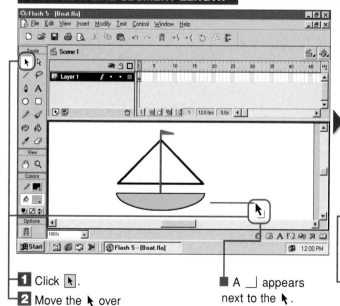

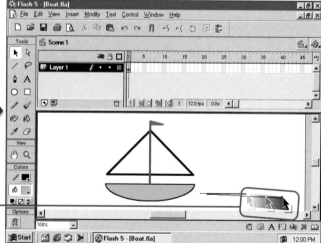

1 Click ☐.

2 Move the ➤ over an end of the line.

Note: Do not click the line to select it.

■ A ⌐ appears next to the ➤.

3 Click and drag the end of the line to shorten or lengthen the segment.

■ As you drag the corner pointer in any direction, you can change the line's angle.

4 Release the mouse button.

■ The line is resized.

How do I draw perfect vertical and horizontal lines?

It can be difficult to have a steady hand while drawing a line on the Stage. You can draw perfectly straight horizontal and vertical lines if you hold the Shift key down while dragging the Line tool across the Stage.

CHANGE A LINE SHAPE

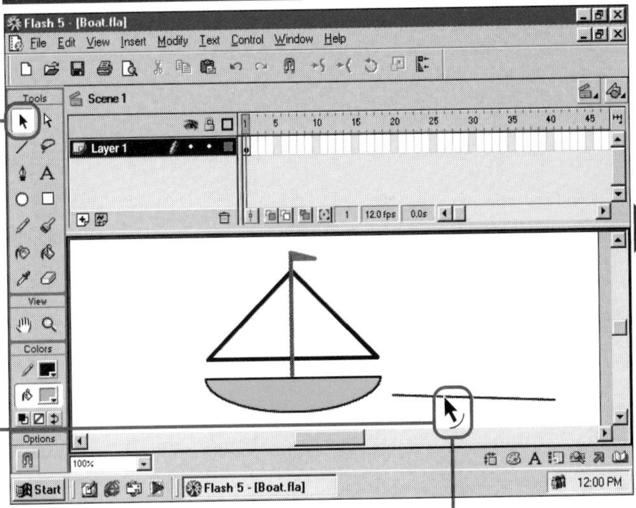

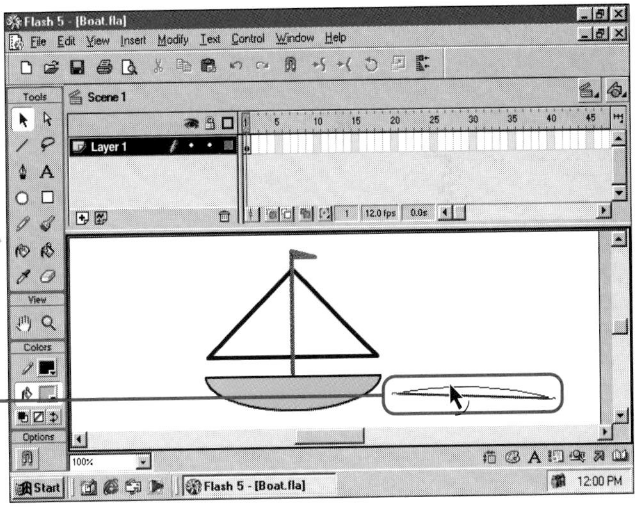

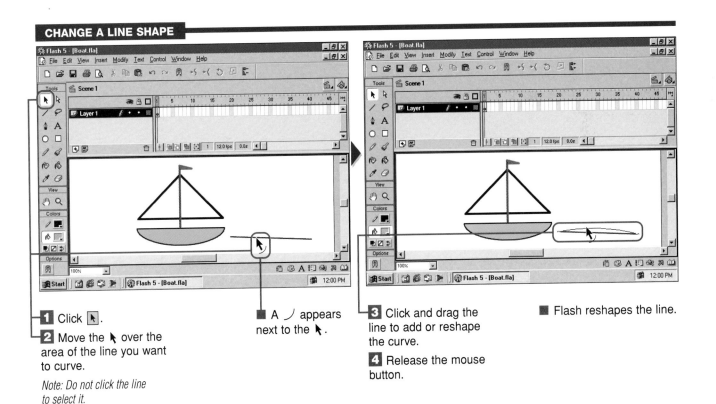

1 Click .

2 Move the over the area of the line you want to curve.

Note: Do not click the line to select it.

■ A appears next to the .

3 Click and drag the line to add or reshape the curve.

4 Release the mouse button.

■ Flash reshapes the line.

EDIT FILLS

You can edit fills just as you can edit line segments. For example, you can change a fill shape by adjusting the sides of the fill, and you can change the fill color at any time.

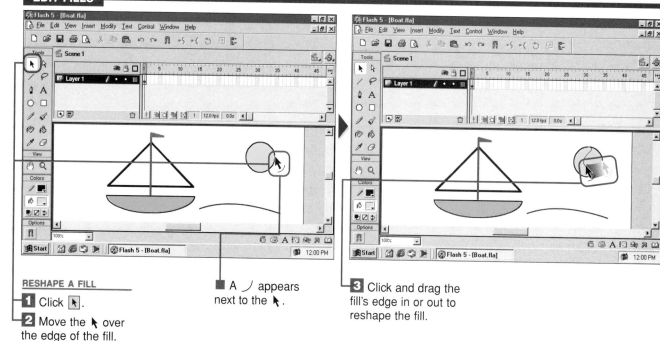

RESHAPE A FILL

1 Click ▶.

2 Move the ▶ over the edge of the fill.

Note: Do not select the fill.

■ A ⟋ appears next to the ▶.

3 Click and drag the fill's edge in or out to reshape the fill.

Can I use other ways to edit fill shapes?

You can find additional Shape commands on the Modify menu that can help you edit fills. For example, to soften a fill's edges, perform the following steps:

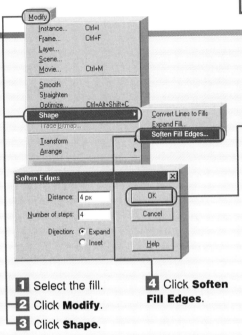

5 From the Soften Edges dialog box, adjust the settings and click **OK**.

■ Experiment with the settings to see what sort of effects you can create. See Chapter 2 to learn more about drawing shapes in Flash.

1 Select the fill.

2 Click **Modify**.

3 Click **Shape**.

4 Click **Soften Fill Edges**.

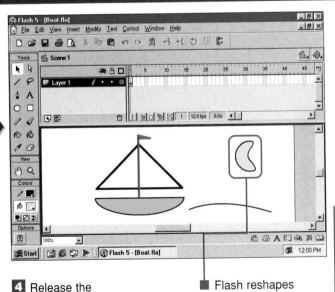

4 Release the mouse button.

■ Flash reshapes the fill.

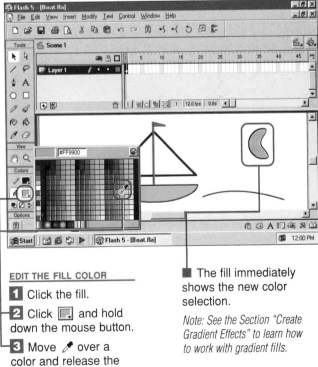

EDIT THE FILL COLOR

1 Click the fill.

2 Click 🖼 and hold down the mouse button.

3 Move 🖋 over a color and release the mouse button.

■ The fill immediately shows the new color selection.

Note: See the Section "Create Gradient Effects" to learn how to work with gradient fills.

RESIZE OBJECTS

You can scale objects in Flash to make them bigger or smaller than their original size. Scaling changes the object's dimensions without changing the basic shape.

RESIZE OBJECTS

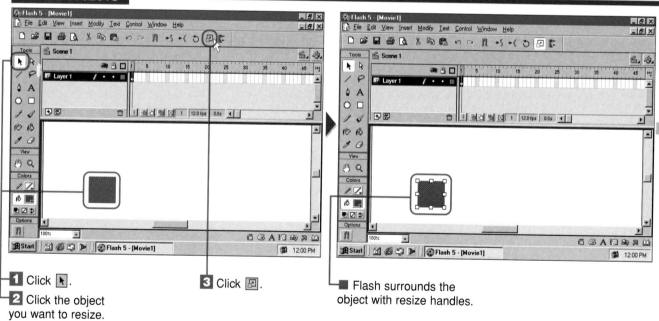

1 Click ![cursor icon].

2 Click the object you want to resize.

3 Click ![icon].

■ Flash surrounds the object with resize handles.

60

How do I set a precise size?

Click 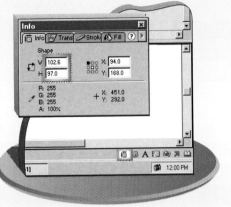. This opens the
Info panel. Here you can set
a precise size for the object
using the width (W) and
height (H) text boxes. Simply
type in the measurement you
want and then click outside
the panel to see the changes
take effect.

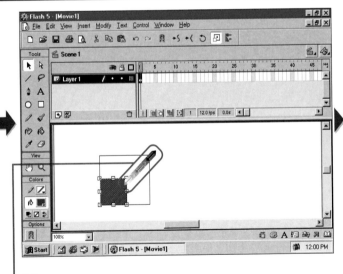

4 Click and drag a
resize handle to scale the
object.

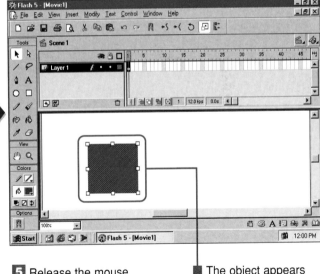

5 Release the mouse
button.

■ The object appears
at the new scale size.

ADD STROKES TO SHAPES

The Ink Bottle tool can quickly add outlines to fills or change existing outline strokes. You can control the stroke's thickness and color and even add inside and outside strokes at the same time.

ADD STROKES TO SHAPES

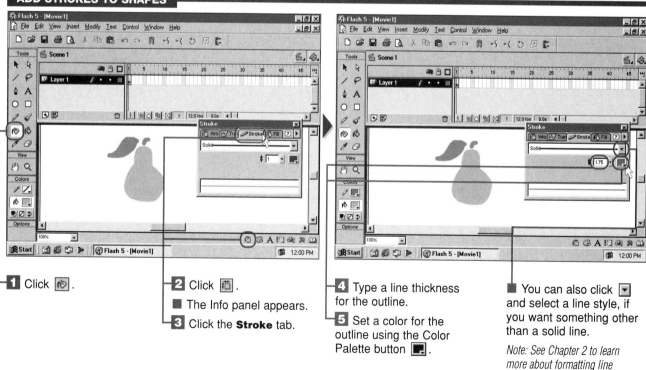

1 Click .

2 Click 🔲.

■ The Info panel appears.

3 Click the **Stroke** tab.

4 Type a line thickness for the outline.

5 Set a color for the outline using the Color Palette button 🔲.

■ You can also click 🔽 and select a line style, if you want something other than a solid line.

Note: See Chapter 2 to learn more about formatting line segments using the Stroke panel.

Can I add multiple strokes?

If your drawing has a shape inside
a shape, you can add outlines to
both at the same time. Just click
anywhere between the inside
shape and the outside shape
using the Ink Bottle tool. Do not
forget to set a line thickness, color,
or style first unless you want to
use the current stroke settings.

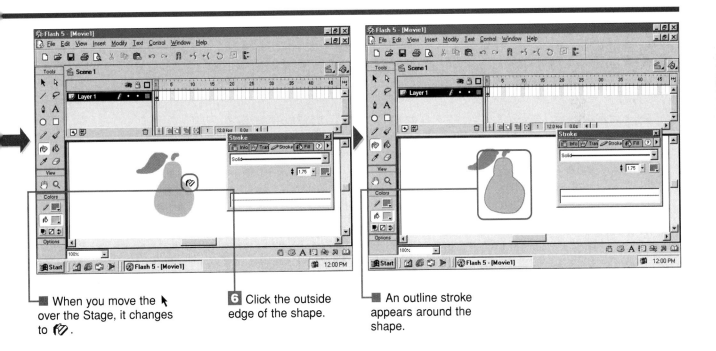

■ When you move the ▶
over the Stage, it changes
to 🖋.

6 Click the outside
edge of the shape.

■ An outline stroke
appears around the
shape.

ROTATE AND FLIP OBJECTS

You can spin an object based on its center point, or you can flip an object vertically or horizontally. Both actions enable you to quickly change an object's position in a drawing.

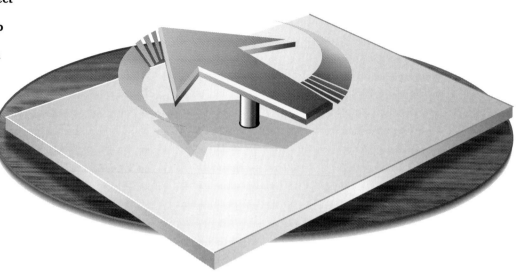

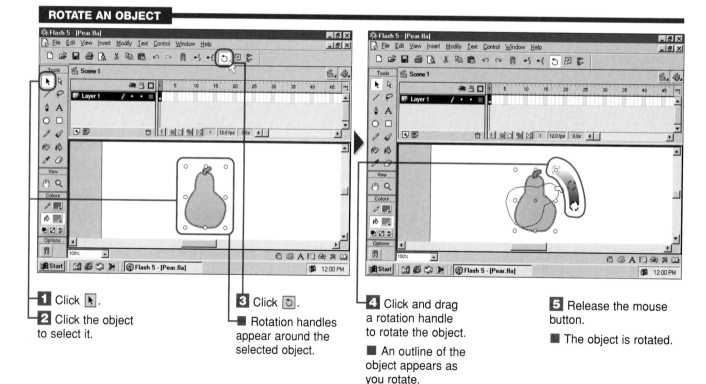

1 Click ▶.

2 Click the object to select it.

3 Click ↺.

■ Rotation handles appear around the selected object.

4 Click and drag a rotation handle to rotate the object.

■ An outline of the object appears as you rotate.

5 Release the mouse button.

■ The object is rotated.

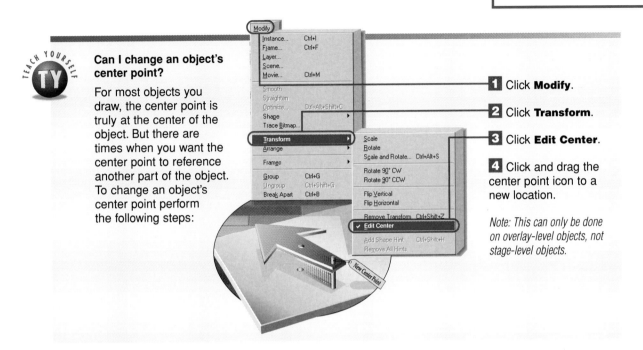

Can I change an object's center point?

For most objects you draw, the center point is truly at the center of the object. But there are times when you want the center point to reference another part of the object. To change an object's center point perform the following steps:

1 Click **Modify**.

2 Click **Transform**.

3 Click **Edit Center**.

4 Click and drag the center point icon to a new location.

Note: This can only be done on overlay-level objects, not stage-level objects.

FLIP AN OBJECT

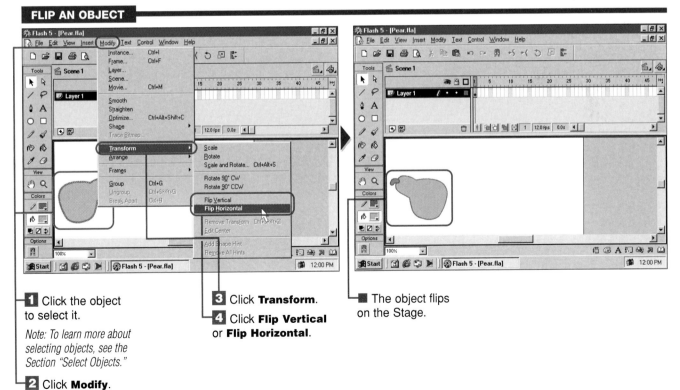

1 Click the object to select it.

Note: To learn more about selecting objects, see the Section "Select Objects."

2 Click **Modify**.

3 Click **Transform**.

4 Click **Flip Vertical** or **Flip Horizontal**.

■ The object flips on the Stage.

USING THE ERASER TOOL

You can use the Eraser tool to erase stray parts of a drawing or object, or you can use it to create new shapes within an object. The Eraser tool has several modifiers you can use to control how the tool works.

USING THE ERASER TOOL

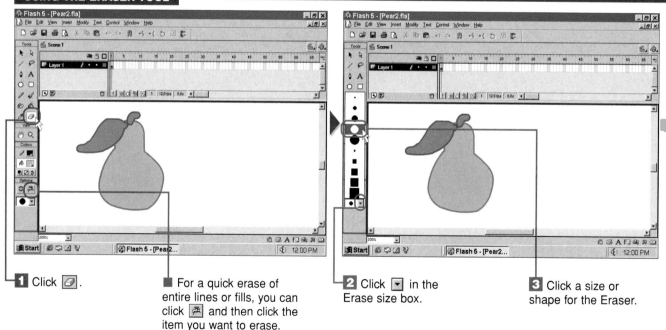

1 Click .

■ For a quick erase of entire lines or fills, you can click and then click the item you want to erase.

2 Click ▼ in the Erase size box.

3 Click a size or shape for the Eraser.

What do the Eraser modifiers do?

You can use one of five modifiers with the Eraser tool. Erase Normal lets you erase over anything on the Stage. Erase Fills erases inside fill areas but not lines. Erase Lines erases only lines. Erase Selected Fills does just that—erases only the selected fill. Erase Inside erases only inside the selected area.

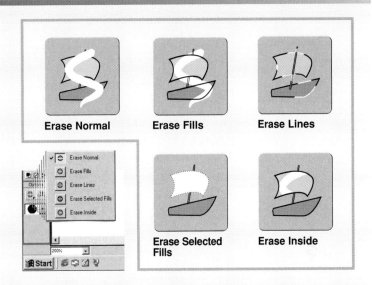

Erase Normal   **Erase Fills**   **Erase Lines**

Erase Selected Fills   **Erase Inside**

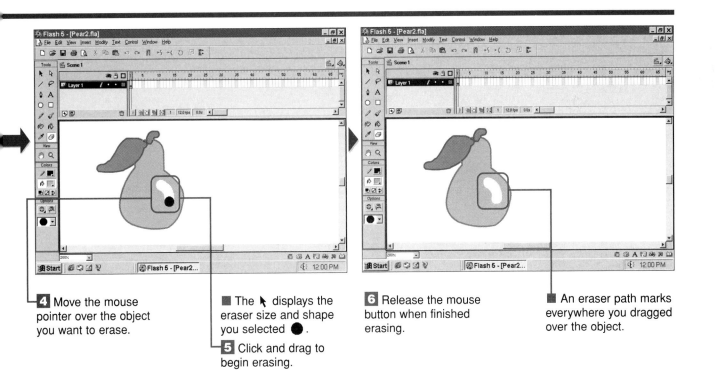

4 Move the mouse pointer over the object you want to erase.

■ The ▶ displays the eraser size and shape you selected ●.

5 Click and drag to begin erasing.

6 Release the mouse button when finished erasing.

■ An eraser path marks everywhere you dragged over the object.

CREATE GRADIENT EFFECTS

A *gradient* effect is a band of blended color or shading. Gradient effects can add depth and dimension to your Flash drawings. By default, the Fill Color palette offers several gradient effects you can use, or you can create your own.

CREATE GRADIENT EFFECTS

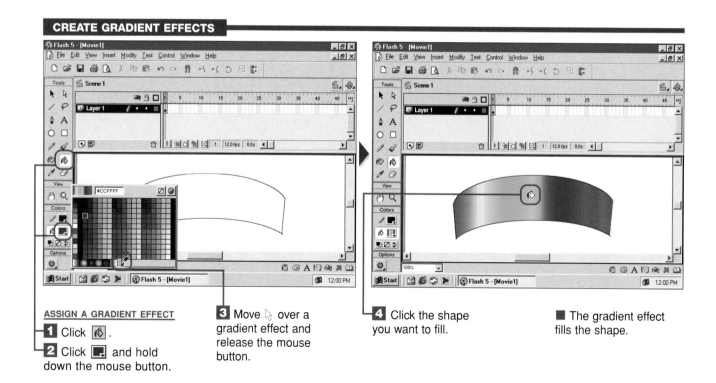

ASSIGN A GRADIENT EFFECT

1 Click 🖌.

2 Click 🟦 and hold down the mouse button.

3 Move ⌖ over a gradient effect and release the mouse button.

4 Click the shape you want to fill.

■ The gradient effect fills the shape.

68

What makes a gradient effect?

The term "gradient" refers to an effect in which two or more colors graduate in color intensity from one color to another. For example, a two-color gradient effect might show the color red blending into yellow from the left to the right. The middle area of the effect shows the subtle blending of the two colors. You can create gradient effects in Flash that blend colors from left to right. Gradient effects can also create a three-dimensional appearance. You can create a radial effect that intensifies color from the middle to the outer edges, or from the outer edges to the middle.

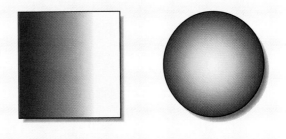

CREATE A NEW GRADIENT

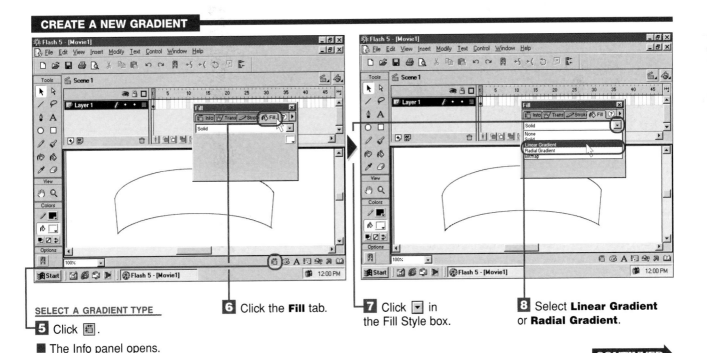

SELECT A GRADIENT TYPE

5 Click 🔲.

■ The Info panel opens.

6 Click the **Fill** tab.

7 Click ▼ in the Fill Style box.

8 Select **Linear Gradient** or **Radial Gradient**.

CONTINUED ▶

CREATE GRADIENT EFFECTS

You can change the properties of the gradient you create by adjusting different colors, color markers, or color intensity bandwidths. You are not limited to the number of colors you use in the gradient, and once you create the gradient just the way you want it, you can save it to reuse again in other Flash projects.

CREATE A NEW GRADIENT (CONTINUED)

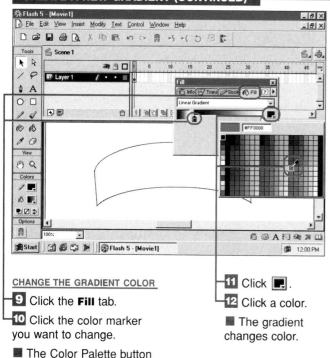

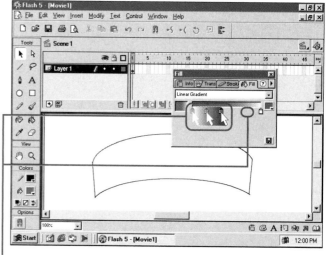

CHANGE THE GRADIENT COLOR

9 Click the **Fill** tab.

10 Click the color marker you want to change.

■ The Color Palette button appears.

11 Click ■.

12 Click a color.

■ The gradient changes color.

ADJUST THE COLOR INTENSITY

13 Drag the color marker left or right to adjust the color intensity bandwidth on the gradient.

■ To add another color marker to the effect, click below the gradient bar.

■ To remove a color marker, drag it off the panel.

■ Continue creating the gradient effect by adding color markers, assigning colors, and dragging the markers to change the intensity.

Can I make changes to an existing gradient in the palette?

Yes, perform the following steps:

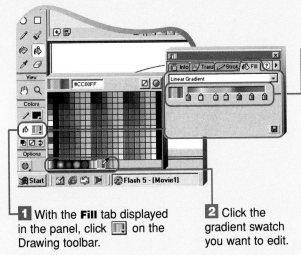

■ The gradient appears in the Fill panel, with color markers for each color used in the effect. You can now make changes to the colors or intensities.

3 Save the edits as a new gradient color swatch by following Step 14 in this Section.

1 With the **Fill** tab displayed in the panel, click ▦ on the Drawing toolbar.

2 Click the gradient swatch you want to edit.

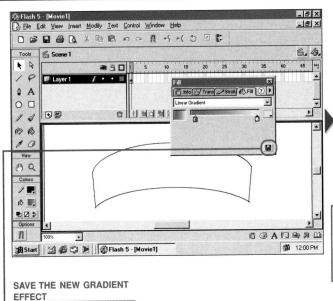

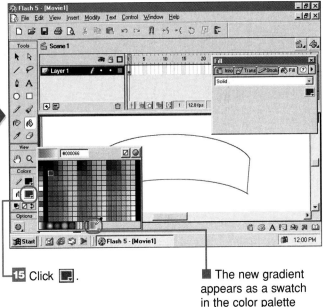

SAVE THE NEW GRADIENT EFFECT

14 To save the gradient and add it to the color palette, click 🖫 .

15 Click 🖫 .

■ The new gradient appears as a swatch in the color palette ready to use.

EDIT A COLOR SET

Flash comes with a default color set, but you can make new color sets based on the default set by removing colors you do not need for a particular project. You can then save the edited color set as a new color set for use in other Flash projects. Color sets are saved with the .clr file extension.

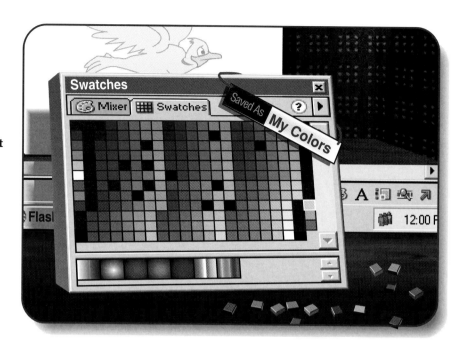

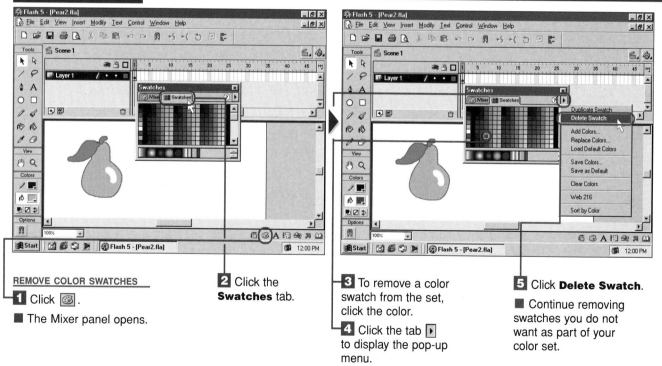

REMOVE COLOR SWATCHES

1 Click .

■ The Mixer panel opens.

2 Click the **Swatches** tab.

3 To remove a color swatch from the set, click the color.

4 Click the tab ▶ to display the pop-up menu.

5 Click **Delete Swatch**.

■ Continue removing swatches you do not want as part of your color set.

72

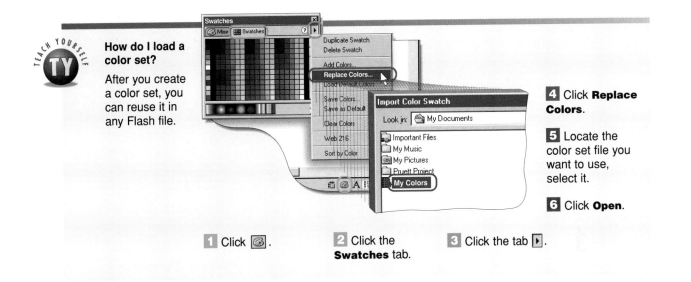

How do I load a color set?

After you create a color set, you can reuse it in any Flash file.

4 Click **Replace Colors**.

5 Locate the color set file you want to use, select it.

6 Click **Open**.

1 Click 🎨.

2 Click the **Swatches** tab.

3 Click the tab ▶.

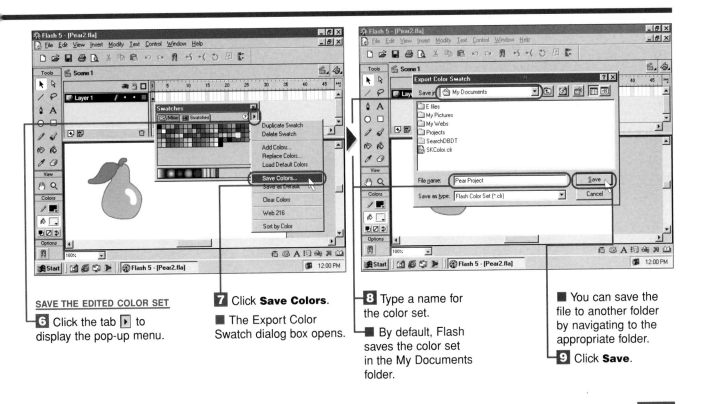

SAVE THE EDITED COLOR SET

6 Click the tab ▶ to display the pop-up menu.

7 Click **Save Colors**.

■ The Export Color Swatch dialog box opens.

8 Type a name for the color set.

■ By default, Flash saves the color set in the My Documents folder.

■ You can save the file to another folder by navigating to the appropriate folder.

9 Click **Save**.

COPY LINE ATTRIBUTES

You can use the Dropper tool to quickly copy line attributes from one line segment to another. The Dropper tool copies line attributes and enables you to copy the same formatting to other lines.

COPY LINE ATTRIBUTES

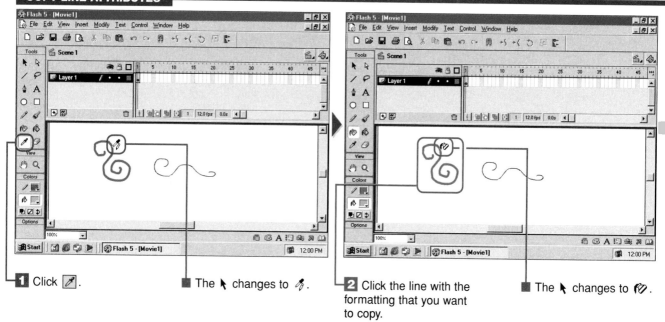

1 Click 🖉.

■ The ▶ changes to 🖉.

2 Click the line with the formatting that you want to copy.

■ The ▶ changes to 🖉.

Can I copy fill attributes, too?

You can copy fill attributes just
like you copy line attributes.
Click , move ⬆ over the
fill you want to copy, and then
click the fill. Move ⬆ over the
fill to which you want to copy
the attribute and click again.
Flash immediately changes the
second fill to match the first.

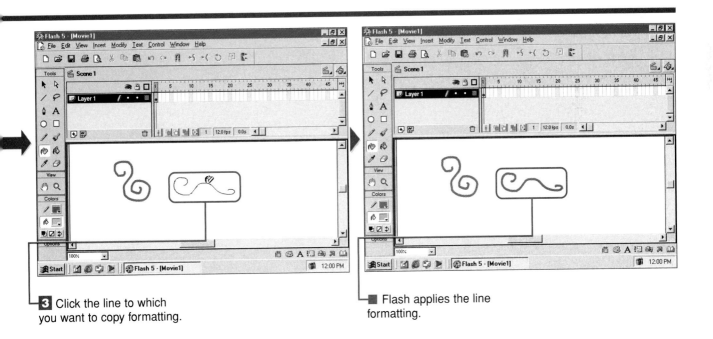

3 Click the line to which
you want to copy formatting.

■ Flash applies the line
formatting.

GROUP OBJECTS

To work on multiple items at the same time, place them in a group. A group enables you to treat the items as a single unit. Any edits you make affect any items in the group.

GROUP OBJECTS

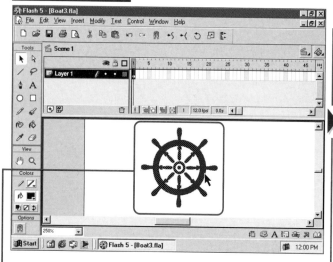

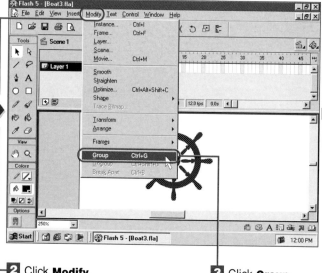

CREATE A GROUP

1 Select all the objects to be included in a group.

Note: See the Section "Select Objects" to learn more about selecting items on the Flash Stage.

Note: To select multiple items, press and hold the Shift *key down while clicking each item.*

2 Click **Modify**.

3 Click **Group**.

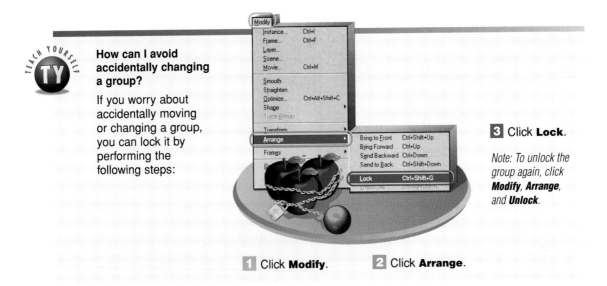

**How can I avoid
accidentally changing
a group?**

If you worry about
accidentally moving
or changing a group,
you can lock it by
performing the
following steps:

■ Click **Modify**. ■ Click **Arrange**.

3 Click **Lock**.

*Note: To unlock the
group again, click
Modify, **Arrange**,
and **Unlock**.*

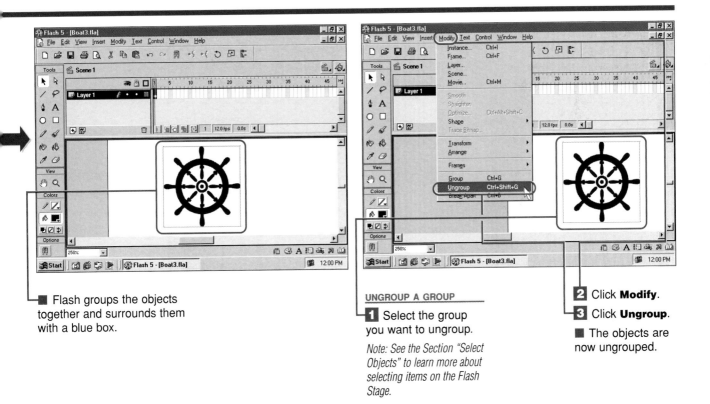

■ Flash groups the objects
together and surrounds them
with a blue box.

UNGROUP A GROUP

1 Select the group
you want to ungroup.

*Note: See the Section "Select
Objects" to learn more about
selecting items on the Flash
Stage.*

2 Click **Modify**.

3 Click **Ungroup**.

■ The objects are
now ungrouped.

STACK OBJECTS

When creating a drawing, you might need to move an object on top of another object. When placing objects over other objects, you can control exactly where an object appears in the stack. You can place an object at the very back of a stack, at the very front, or somewhere in-between.

STACK OBJECTS

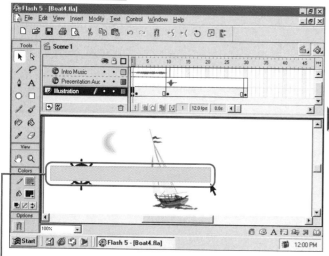

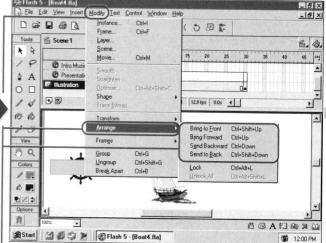

1 Select the object or group you want to reorder.

Note: See the Section "Select Objects" to learn more about selecting items on the Flash Stage.

2 Click **Modify**.

3 Click **Arrange**.

4 Select whether you want to send the object to the front or back of the stack.

■ To send an object to the very back of the stack, click **Send to Back**.

■ To bring an object to the very front of the stack, click **Bring to Front**.

How do I move an object in a stack using the keyboard?

Move the object up one layer	Press Ctrl + ↑ (Windows)
	Press ⌘ + ↑ (Mac)
Move the object directly to the top of the stack	Press Ctrl + Shift + ↑ (Windows)
	Press ⌘ + Shift + ↑ (Mac)
Move the object back a layer	Press Ctrl + ↓ (Windows)
	Press ⌘ + ↓ (Mac)
Move the object directly to the back of the stack	Press Ctrl + Shift + ↓ (Windows)
	Press ⌘ + Shift + ↓ (Mac)

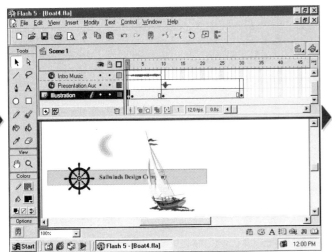

■ The object now relocates in the stacking order as directed.

■ In this example, the blue bar moved to the back of the stack.

■ In this example the text block moves in front of the sail boat.

ALIGN OBJECTS

The Align panel has tools for controlling precisely where an object sits on the Stage. You can align objects vertically and horizontally by their edges or centers. You can align objects with other objects, with the edges of the Stage, or even control the amount of space between the objects.

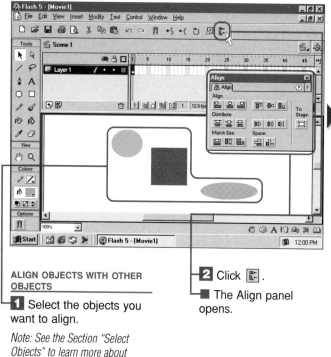

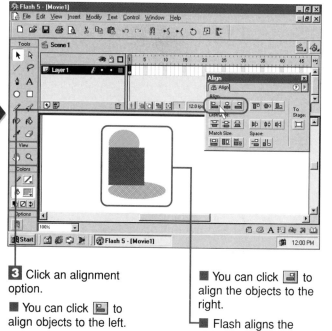

ALIGN OBJECTS WITH OTHER OBJECTS

1 Select the objects you want to align.

Note: See the Section "Select Objects" to learn more about selecting items on the Flash Stage.

2 Click 🖫.

■ The Align panel opens.

3 Click an alignment option.

■ You can click 🖪 to align objects to the left.

■ You can click 🖪 to center-align the objects.

■ You can click 🖪 to align the objects to the right.

■ Flash aligns the objects as directed.

How can I align objects vertically?

The Align panel has buttons for setting vertical alignments along with horizontal alignments. Each button in the Align panel has an image that shows how the objects will align when that button is selected. You can use the three vertical alignment buttons to align objects vertically with each other or align them vertically with the Flash Stage. To align objects with the Stage, be sure to click the 🔲 button first before clicking an alignment button.

■ Click to align objects with the bottom-most object or to the bottom edge of the Stage.

■ Click to align objects with the top-most object or the top of the Stage.

▨ Click to center objects evenly with each other, or between the top and bottom of the Stage.

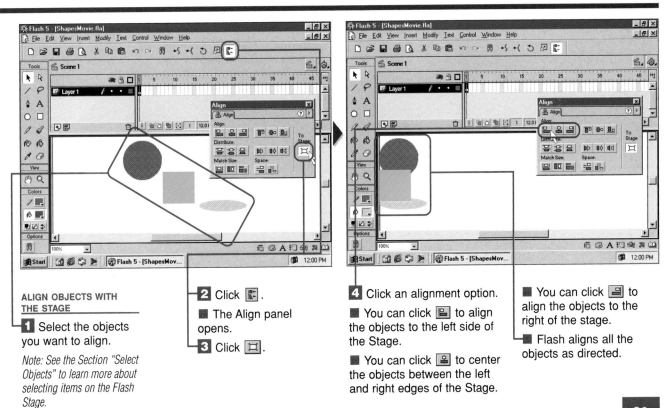

ALIGN OBJECTS WITH THE STAGE

1 Select the objects you want to align.

Note: See the Section "Select Objects" to learn more about selecting items on the Flash Stage.

2 Click 🖹 .

■ The Align panel opens.

3 Click 🔲 .

4 Click an alignment option.

■ You can click 🖹 to align the objects to the left side of the Stage.

■ You can click 🖹 to center the objects between the left and right edges of the Stage.

■ You can click 🖹 to align the objects to the right of the stage.

■ Flash aligns all the objects as directed.

CHAPTER 4

Creating Text Effects

Does your Flash project need some text? Learn how to add text elements to your drawings with the Flash text tools.

ADD TEXT WITH THE TEXT TOOL

Use the Text tool to add text to a movie or graphic. You can insert label or block text boxes on the Stage area. With a label text box, you can click where you want the text to appear and start typing. With block text, you define the box size first.

ADD TEXT WITH THE TEXT TOOL

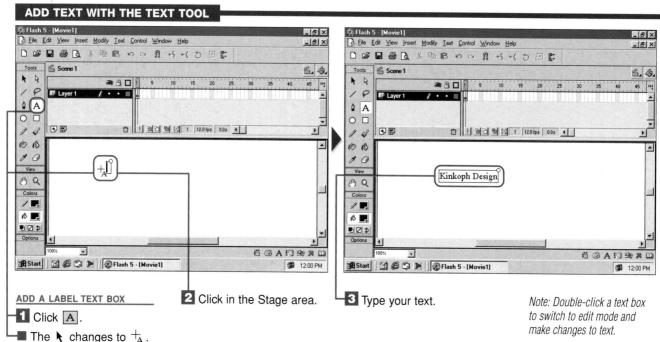

ADD A LABEL TEXT BOX

1 Click A.

■ The ▶ changes to +A.

2 Click in the Stage area.

3 Type your text.

Note: Double-click a text box to switch to edit mode and make changes to text.

**What is the difference
between labels and blocks?**

When you type text into a
label text box, text does not
wrap. The width of the text
box keeps expanding as you
type characters. With a block
text box, you specify a width,
and when the text you are
typing reaches the end of
the block, it wraps to start
a new line, increasing the
depth of the text box.

Label text box

Block text box

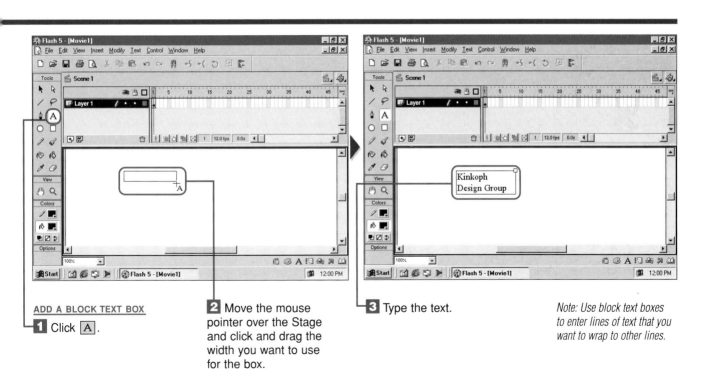

<u>ADD A BLOCK TEXT BOX</u>

1 Click A.

2 Move the mouse
pointer over the Stage
and click and drag the
width you want to use
for the box.

3 Type the text.

*Note: Use block text boxes
to enter lines of text that you
want to wrap to other lines.*

FORMAT TEXT

You can easily format text by using the Character panel. It has all the controls for formatting text located in one convenient mini-window.

APPLY BOLD AND ITALICS

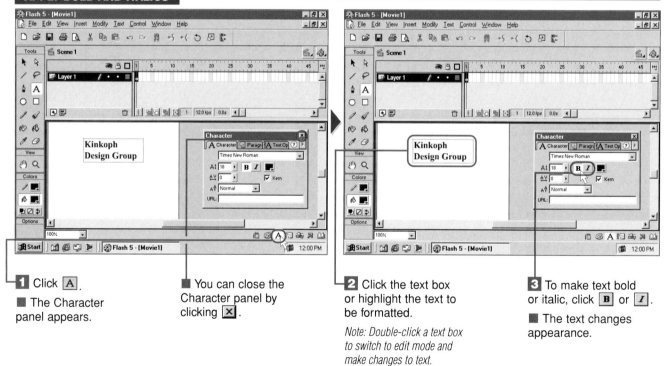

1 Click **A**.

■ The Character panel appears.

■ You can close the Character panel by clicking ⊠.

2 Click the text box or highlight the text to be formatted.

Note: Double-click a text box to switch to edit mode and make changes to text.

3 To make text bold or italic, click **B** or **I**.

■ The text changes appearance.

Do I have to use the Character panel to format text?

You can also find text formatting controls in the Text menu. For example, to change the font:

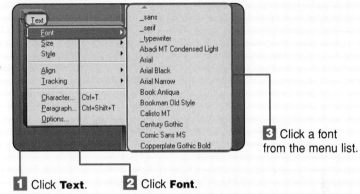

3 Click a font from the menu list.

1 Click **Text**.

2 Click **Font**.

CHANGE FONT AND SIZE

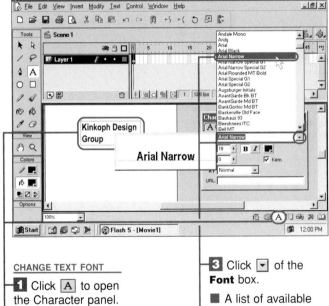

CHANGE TEXT FONT

1 Click A to open the Character panel.

2 Click the text box or select the text to be formatted.

3 Click ⬇ of the **Font** box.

■ A list of available fonts appears, along with a sample box.

4 Click a font name.

■ The text changes font type.

CHANGE THE FONT SIZE

1 Click A to open the Character panel.

2 Click the text box or select the text to be formatted.

3 Click the **Size** button.

4 Select a new size by dragging the slider (⬜).

■ You can also type the exact size in the Size box.

■ The text changes size.

ALIGN TEXT

You can control the position of text within a text box using the alignment options found in the Paragraph panel or on the Text menu.

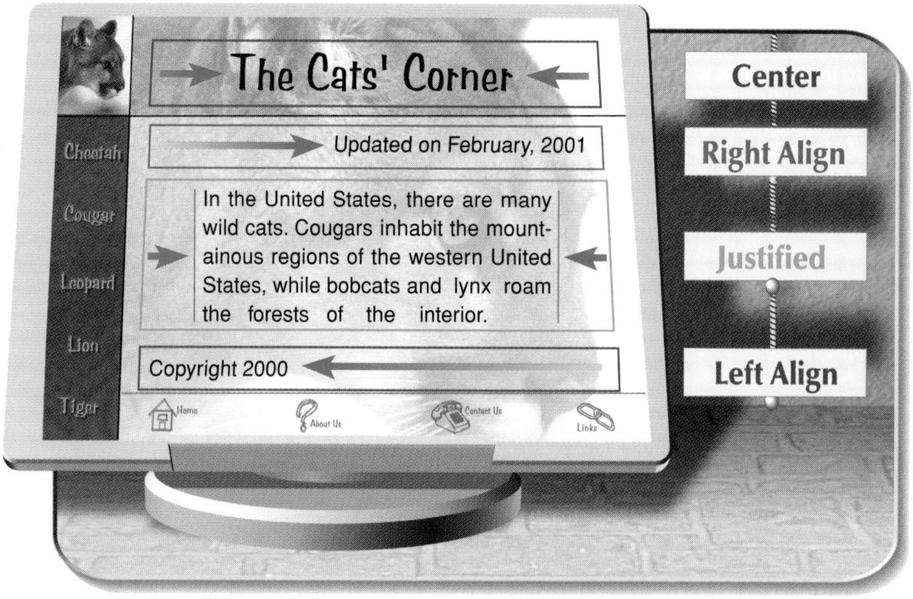

ALIGN TEXT

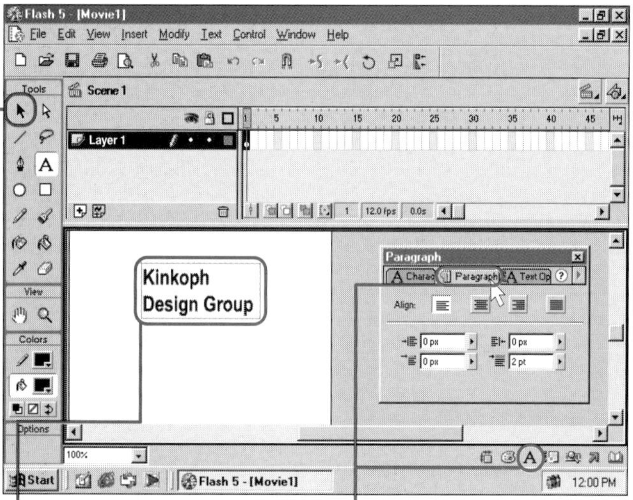

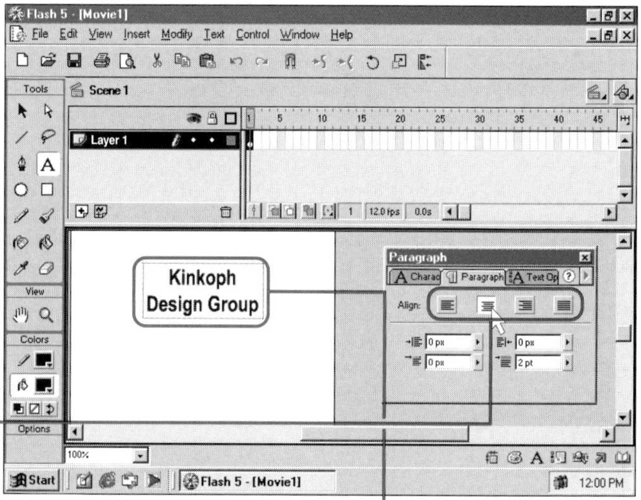

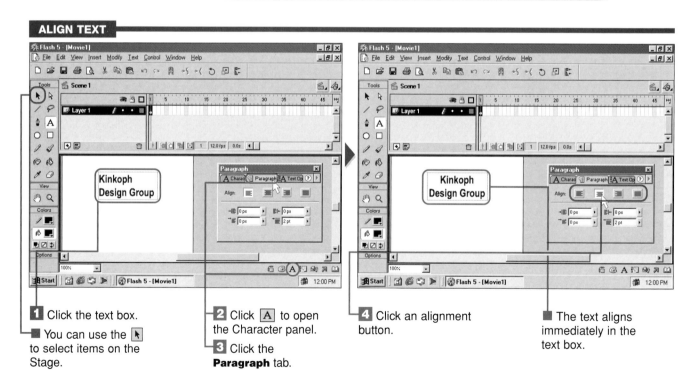

1 Click the text box.

■ You can use the to select items on the Stage.

2 Click A to open the Character panel.

3 Click the **Paragraph** tab.

4 Click an alignment button.

■ The text aligns immediately in the text box.

What is kerning?

Kerning refers to the spacing of characters. By changing the kerning setting, you can create text effects such as word characters squished together or pulled apart.

KERN TEXT

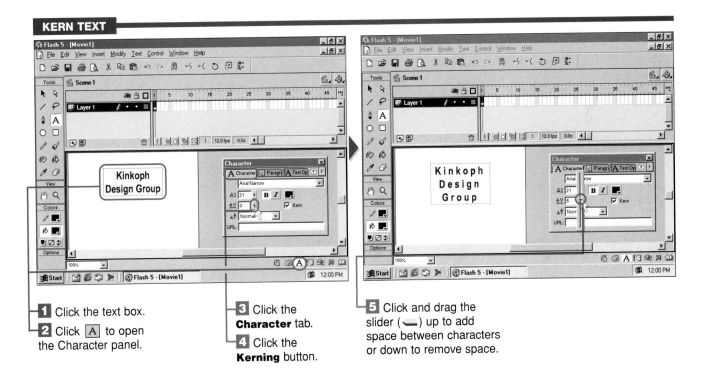

1 Click the text box.

2 Click A to open the Character panel.

3 Click the **Character** tab.

4 Click the **Kerning** button.

5 Click and drag the slider ( ) up to add space between characters or down to remove space.

SET TEXT BOX MARGINS AND INDENTS

Set margins and indents within text boxes for greater control of text positioning. You can find margin and indent commands in the Paragraph panel or on the Text menu.

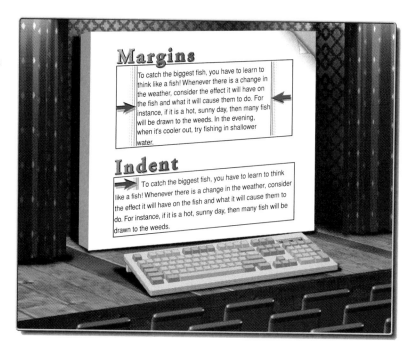

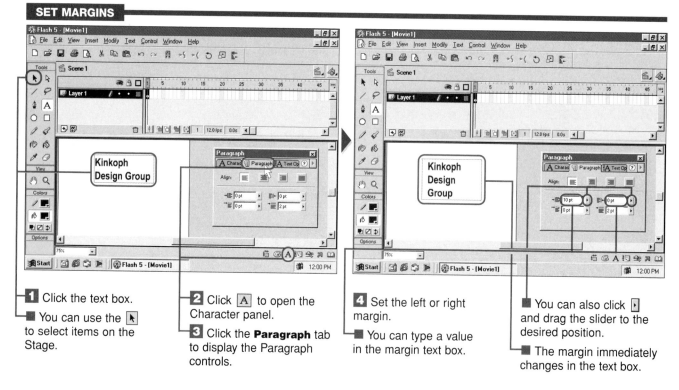

1 Click the text box.

■ You can use the ![k] to select items on the Stage.

2 Click ![A] to open the Character panel.

3 Click the **Paragraph** tab to display the Paragraph controls.

4 Set the left or right margin.

■ You can type a value in the margin text box.

■ You can also click ![▶] and drag the slider to the desired position.

■ The margin immediately changes in the text box.

How do I change the margin's unit of measurement value?

By default, Flash assumes you want to work with pixels as your unit of measurement, but you can change it to the unit of your choice, such as points or inches. Here's how:

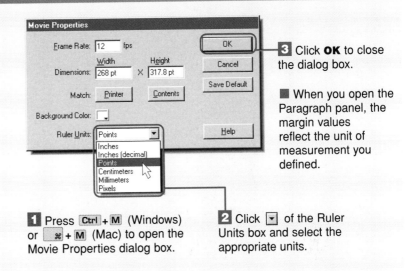

3 Click **OK** to close the dialog box.

■ When you open the Paragraph panel, the margin values reflect the unit of measurement you defined.

1 Press **Ctrl** + **M** (Windows) or **⌘** + **M** (Mac) to open the Movie Properties dialog box.

2 Click ▾ of the Ruler Units box and select the appropriate units.

SET AN INDENT

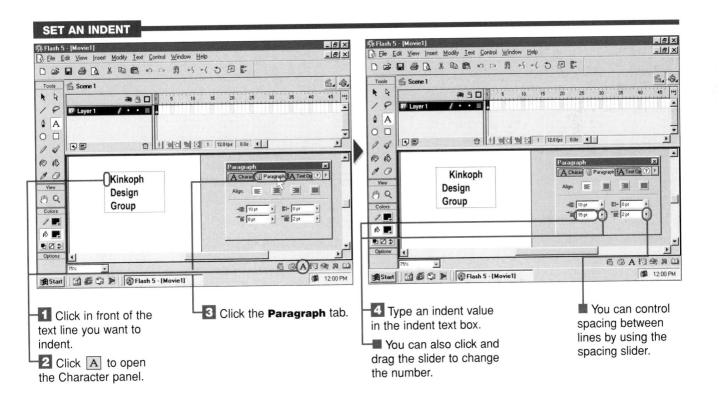

1 Click in front of the text line you want to indent.

2 Click **A** to open the Character panel.

3 Click the **Paragraph** tab.

4 Type an indent value in the indent text box.

■ You can also click and drag the slider to change the number.

■ You can control spacing between lines by using the spacing slider.

MOVE AND RESIZE TEXT BOXES

You can move text
boxes around on
the Flash Stage,
or resize them
as needed.

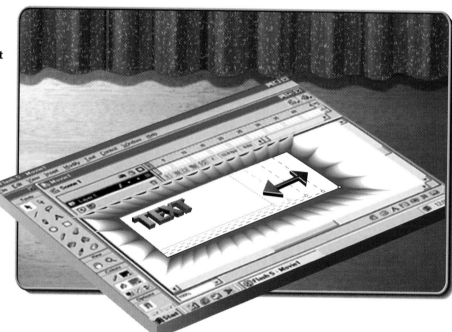

MOVE A TEXT BOX

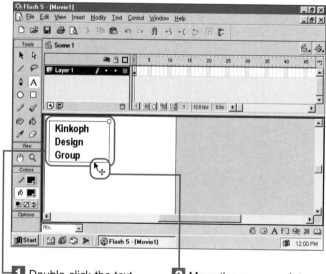

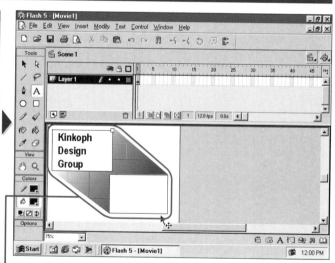

1 Double-click the text
box you want to move.

2 Move the mouse pointer
over a text box border until
↖ changes to ↖⊕.

3 Click and drag
the box to a new
location and release
the mouse button.

How do I turn text into an effect?

Effects, like gradients or fills, cannot be applied to text until it is broken apart into vector shapes. To turn text into graphic objects:

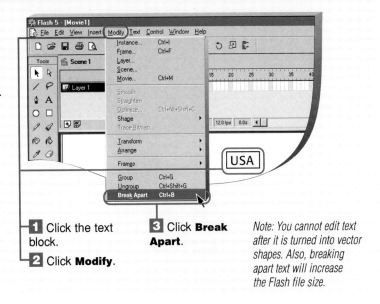

1 Click the text block.

2 Click **Modify**.

3 Click **Break Apart**.

Note: You cannot edit text after it is turned into vector shapes. Also, breaking apart text will increase the Flash file size.

RESIZE A TEXT BOX

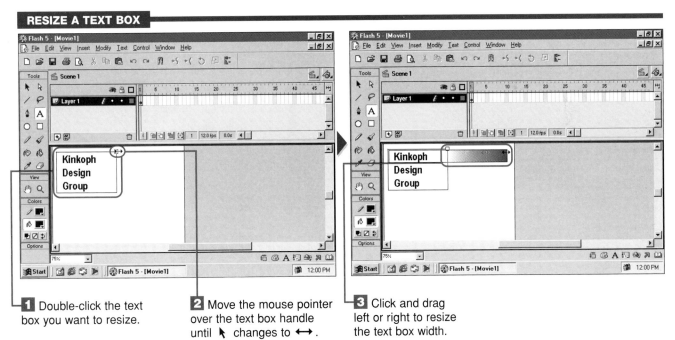

1 Double-click the text box you want to resize.

2 Move the mouse pointer over the text box handle until ▶ changes to ↔.

3 Click and drag left or right to resize the text box width.

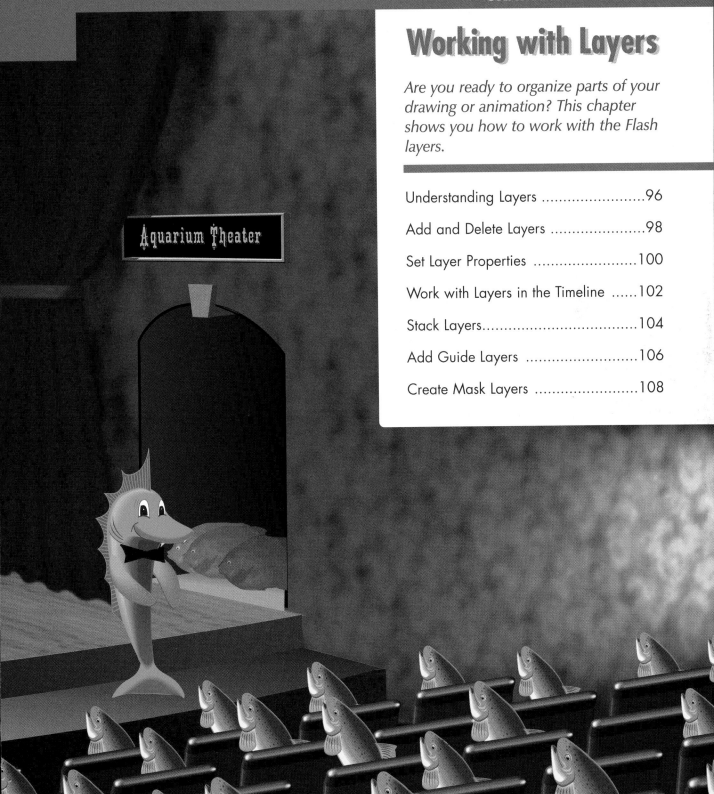

CHAPTER 5

Working with Layers

Are you ready to organize parts of your drawing or animation? This chapter shows you how to work with the Flash layers.

Aquarium Theater

UNDERSTANDING LAYERS

The key to working with graphic objects and animation is layers. Layers can help you organize elements and add depth to your Flash projects.

LAYERS CAN ORGANIZE

You can place related objects on a single layer to keep them organized. You can edit objects in one layer without affecting objects on another layer.

LAYERS ADD DEPTH

Layers are stacked in Flash. Items you place on the top layer appear in front of items placed on a bottom layer. You might place a background on the bottom layer, and add other objects to subsequent layers to create a feeling of depth.

LAYERS ASSIST WITH ANIMATING

The more complex your movies, the more you utilize layers. Layers are great for working with multiple animations.

LAYERS ON THE TIMELINE

Layers appear as horizontal blocks on the Timeline. You can quickly add and delete layers as you work, and rename them so you can keep them organized. You can lock layers to keep them safe from accidental changes.

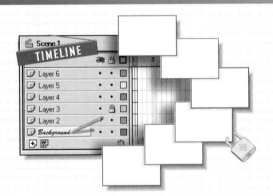

TYPES OF LAYERS

There are several different kinds of layers in Flash. A plain layer holds various elements such as graphics, sounds, and movie clips. Guide layers can help you with the layout and positioning of objects on other layers. Mask layers enable you to hide elements in underlying layers from view.

ADD AND DELETE LAYERS

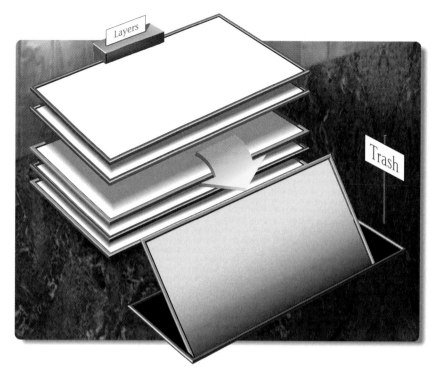

When you create a new movie or scene, Flash starts you out with a single layer and a Timeline. You can add layers to the Timeline, or delete layers you no longer need. Additional layers do not affect the file size, so you can add and delete as many layers as your project requires.

ADD A LAYER

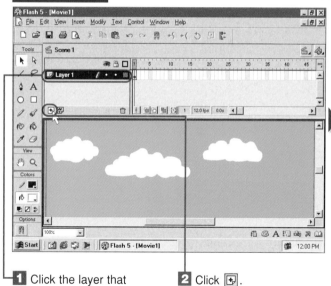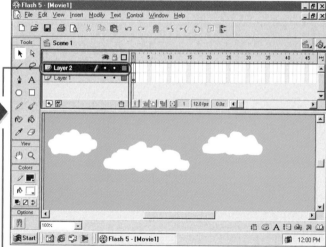

1 Click the layer that will appear below the new layer.

2 Click 🗗.

■ A new layer immediately appears.

■ Flash adds the same amount of frames to the new layer to match the layer with the longest frame sequence.

Note: See Chapter 8 to learn more about frames.

Can I delete several layers at once?

You can delete more than one layer at a time. Click the first layer to remove, then press Ctrl (Windows) or ⌘ (Mac) while clicking other layers to remove. Click 🗑 to remove them all at once.

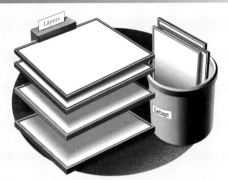

DELETE A LAYER

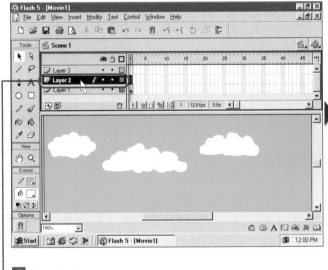

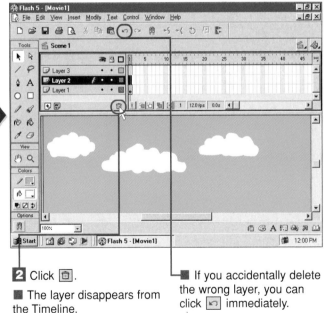

1 Click the layer you want to delete.

2 Click 🗑.

■ The layer disappears from the Timeline.

■ If you accidentally delete the wrong layer, you can click ↺ immediately.

SET LAYER PROPERTIES

You can define the aspects of any given layer through the Layer Properties dialog, a one-stop shop for controlling a layer's name, function, and appearance.

To create a layer, see the Section "Add and Delete Layers."

SET LAYER PROPERTIES

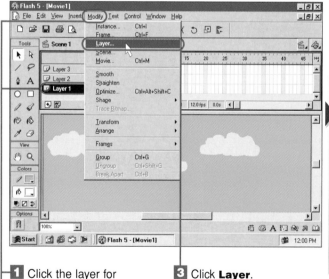

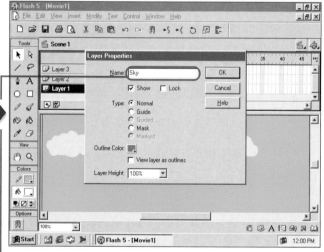

1 Click the layer for which you want to set controls.

2 Click **Modify**.

3 Click **Layer**.

■ The Layer Properties dialog box opens.

4 Type a distinctive name for the layer in the Name text box.

What are layer types?

By default, all layers you add to the Timeline are *normal*, which means all the objects on the layer appear in the movie. Objects you place on guide layers do not appear in the movie. A regular *guide* layer can be used for reference points and alignment. A *guided* layer is a layer linked to a regular guide layer. A *mask* layer hides any layers linked to it. To change the layer type, click a type in the Layer Properties dialog box (○ changes to ⊙).

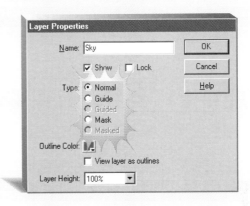

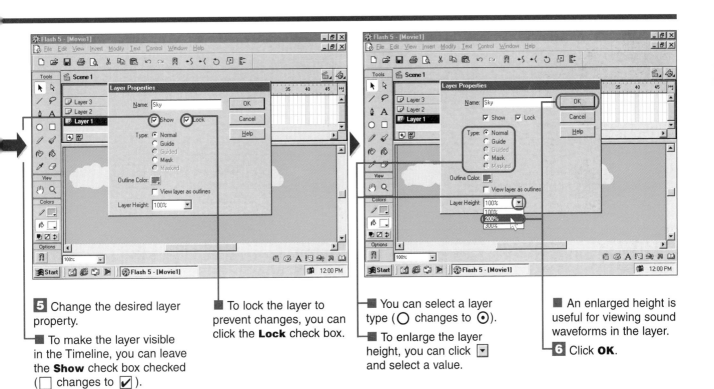

5 Change the desired layer property.

■ To make the layer visible in the Timeline, you can leave the **Show** check box checked (☐ changes to ☑).

■ To lock the layer to prevent changes, you can click the **Lock** check box.

■ You can select a layer type (○ changes to ⊙).

■ To enlarge the layer height, you can click ▾ and select a value.

■ An enlarged height is useful for viewing sound waveforms in the layer.

6 Click **OK**.

WORK WITH LAYERS IN THE TIMELINE

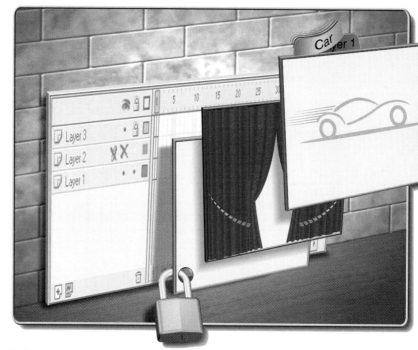

Flash makes it easy to control layers in the Timeline. You can quickly rename a layer, hide a layer, or lock a layer to prevent changes.

To learn more about the Flash Timeline, see Chapter 1.

WORK WITH LAYERS IN THE TIMELINE

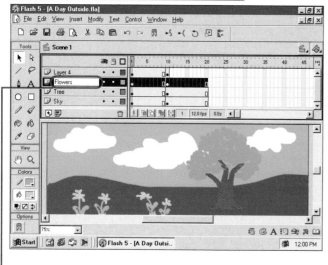

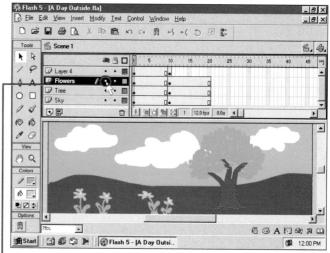

RENAME A LAYER

1 Double-click the layer name.

2 Type a new name.

3 Press Enter.

■ The layer's name changes.

HIDE A LAYER

1 Click ● beneath the eye icon column.

How can I tell which objects are on which layer?

You can choose to view layer contents as outlines, making it easy to distinguish the objects from other layers. Click ■ under the square icon column (■ changes to □). All objects on the layer are now outlined in the same color as the square you clicked.

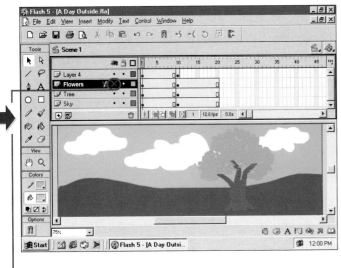

■ An ✕ marks the layer bullet and all the objects on the layer are invisible.

Note: To make the layer objects visible again, you can click ✕ under the eye icon column (✕ changes to ●).

LOCK A LAYER

1 Under the padlock icon column, click the layer's bullet (• changes to 🔒).

■ The layer is now locked and you cannot edit the contents.

2 To unlock a layer, click the layer's padlock icon (🔒 changes to •).

STACK LAYERS

To rearrange how objects appear in the movie, you can stack Flash layers in a manner similar to how you stack objects in a drawing. For example, if you have a layer containing background elements, you can move it to the back of the layer stack.

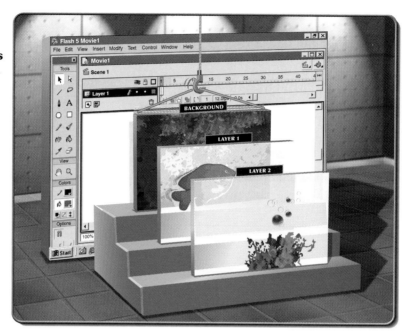

To create a layer, see the Section "Add and Delete Layers."

CHANGE THE STACKING ORDER

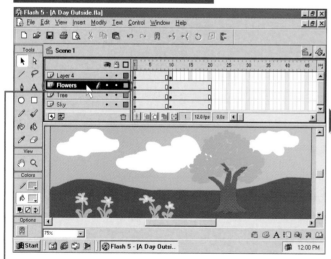

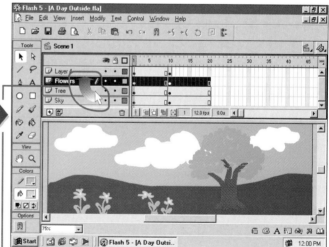

1 Click the layer you want to move.

2 Drag the layer up or down to its new location in the stack.

■ An insertion point appears, showing where the dragged layer will rest.

Can I copy a layer?

First create a new layer (see
the Section "Add and Delete
Layers"), then click the layer
you want to copy. Click
on the toolbar. Click the
new layer, then click
on the toolbar. Flash copies
the contents of the first layer
and places them on the
second layer, slightly offset.

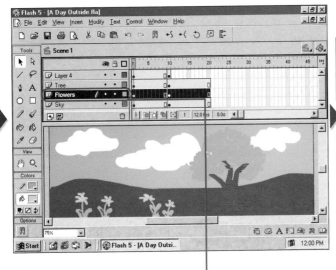

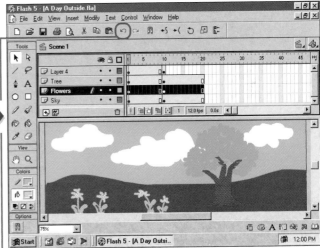

3 Release the
mouse button.

■ The layer assumes
its new position.

■ To move the layer
back to its original
position, click .

ADD GUIDE LAYERS

Guide layers help you position objects. There are two types of guide layers in Flash: *plain* and *motion*. A plain guide layer can help you position objects on the Stage, but it does not appear in your final movie.

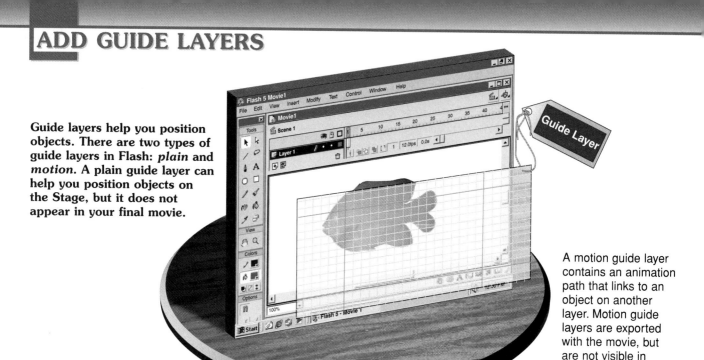

A motion guide layer contains an animation path that links to an object on another layer. Motion guide layers are exported with the movie, but are not visible in the movie.

ADD A PLAIN GUIDE LAYER

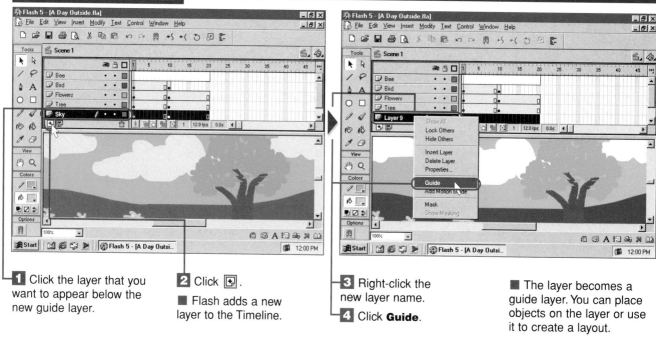

1 Click the layer that you want to appear below the new guide layer.

2 Click .

■ Flash adds a new layer to the Timeline.

3 Right-click the new layer name.

4 Click **Guide**.

■ The layer becomes a guide layer. You can place objects on the layer or use it to create a layout.

How does a motion guide layer work?

Motion guide layers are linked to layers containing objects you want to animate along a given path. The motion guide layer contains the path and can be linked to one or more layers. The motion guide layer always appears directly above the layer (or layers) to which it is linked. To learn more about animating in Flash, see Chapter 9.

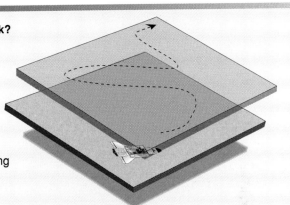

ADD A MOTION GUIDE LAYER

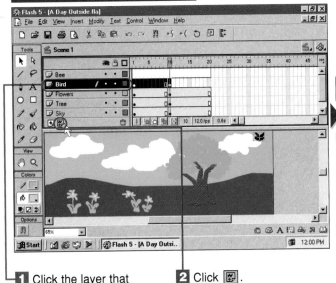

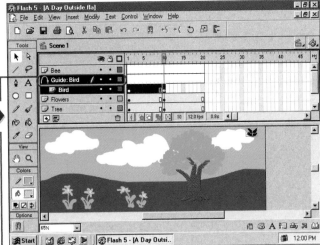

1 Click the layer that you want to link to a motion guide layer.

2 Click 🔲.

■ Flash adds the motion guide layer to the Timeline and links it to the layer you selected.

CREATE MASK LAYERS

You can use mask layers to hide various elements on underlying layers. Much like a stencil you tape to a wall, only certain portions of the underlying layer appear through the mask design, while other parts of the layer are hidden, or "masked." Masked layers are linked to layers and are exported in the final movie file.

ADD A MASK LAYER

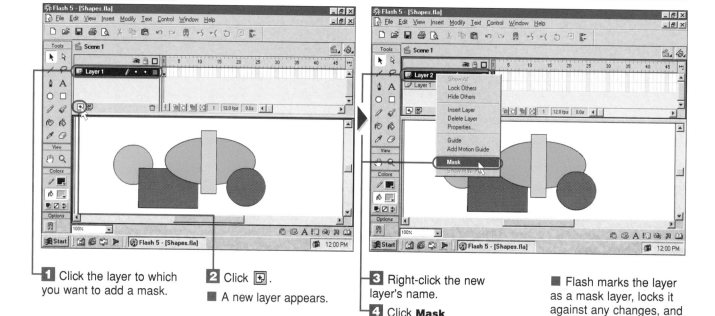

1 Click the layer to which you want to add a mask.

2 Click ⊞.

■ A new layer appears.

3 Right-click the new layer's name.

4 Click **Mask**.

■ Flash marks the layer as a mask layer, locks it against any changes, and links it to the layer below.

How do mask layers work?

You can add a shape with a fill, such as a circle or rectangle, on the mask layer. The masking shape hides anything that lies outside the shape area in the layers below.

CREATE A MASK

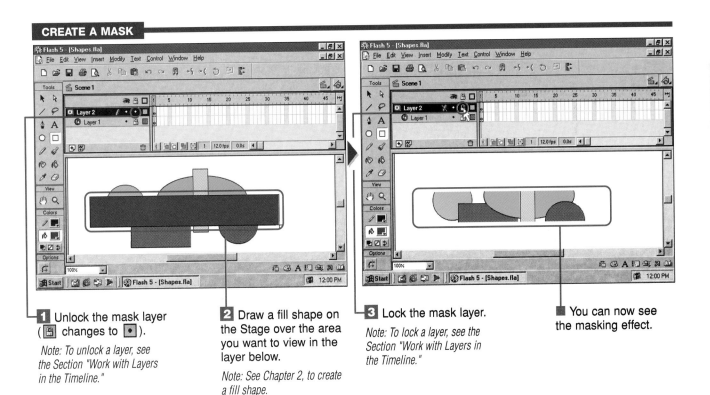

1 Unlock the mask layer
(🔒 changes to 🔘).

Note: To unlock a layer, see the Section "Work with Layers in the Timeline."

2 Draw a fill shape on the Stage over the area you want to view in the layer below.

Note: See Chapter 2, to create a fill shape.

3 Lock the mask layer.

Note: To lock a layer, see the Section "Work with Layers in the Timeline."

■ You can now see the masking effect.

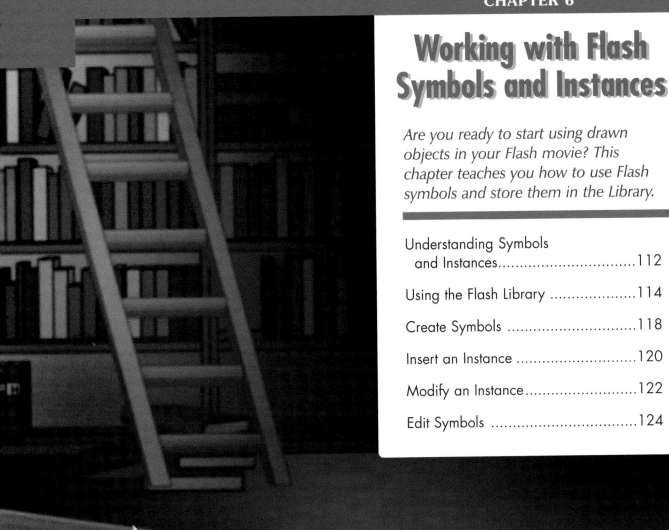

CHAPTER 6

Working with Flash Symbols and Instances

Are you ready to start using drawn objects in your Flash movie? This chapter teaches you how to use Flash symbols and store them in the Library.

UNDERSTANDING SYMBOLS AND INSTANCES

A symbol is a
reusable element
you can store in
the Flash Library.
After you have
placed a symbol
in the Library,
you can use
it repeatedly
throughout
your movie.

FLASH SYMBOLS

A *symbol* is any graphical element you save in the
Flash Library. A symbol can be a graphic object, a
movie clip, a graphic created in another program,
or a button. Symbols can also be sound clips.

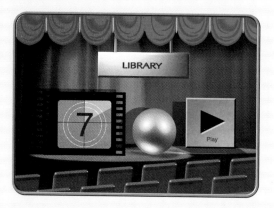

FLASH INSTANCES

Anytime you insert a copy of the symbol into your
project, you are inserting an *instance*. The instance
references the original so the file size is not greatly
affected by how many times you reuse a symbol.

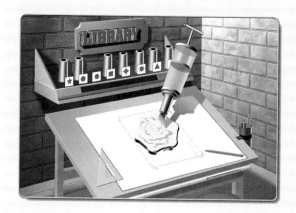

GRAPHIC SYMBOLS

Graphic objects, such as those you create in Flash with the drawing tools, can be reused for creating animation in the Flash Timeline.

MOVIE CLIPS

Movie clip symbols are simply mini-movies that reside inside the main Flash movie file. Movie clips utilize timelines that are independent of the main movie's timeline.

BUTTON SYMBOLS

Interactive buttons can also be saved as symbols and reused with different actions associated with the same button.

USING THE FLASH LIBRARY

A Flash project can contain hundreds of graphics, sounds, interactive buttons, and movie clips. The Flash Library can help you organize these elements. For example, you can store related symbols in the same folder, create new folders, or delete folders and symbols you no longer need.

OPEN THE LIBRARY WINDOW

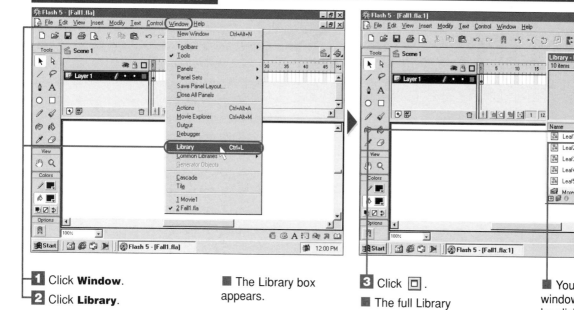

1 Click **Window**.

2 Click **Library**.

■ The Library box appears.

3 Click ▢.

■ The full Library window displays.

■ You can return the window to Narrow state by clicking ▢.

Can I use symbols from another movie's Library?

You can easily insert symbols into your current project from another file's library.

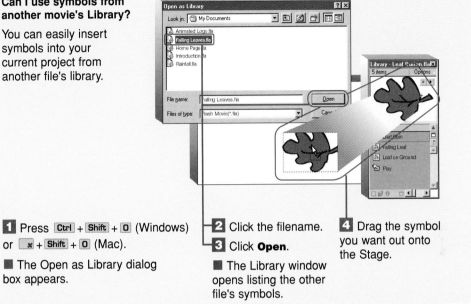

1 Press Ctrl + Shift + O (Windows) or ⌘ + Shift + O (Mac).

■ The Open as Library dialog box appears.

2 Click the filename.

3 Click **Open**.

■ The Library window opens listing the other file's symbols.

4 Drag the symbol you want out onto the Stage.

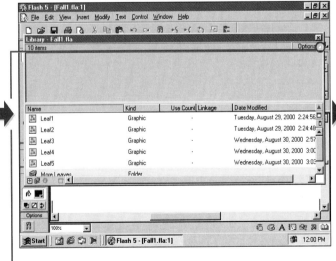

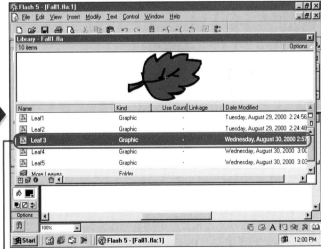

■ You can click ☐ next to the Options box to display a pop-up menu of commands related to Library tasks and items.

■ You can preview an item in the Library by clicking the item.

CONTINUED ▶

USING THE FLASH LIBRARY

Symbols are stored in folders. You can use folders in the Library window to help you organize symbols. You can add and delete folders, and move symbols from one folder to another.

ORGANIZE SYMBOLS WITH FOLDERS

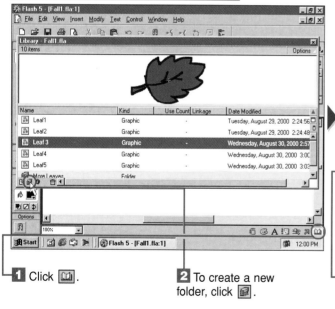

1 Click .

2 To create a new folder, click 📁.

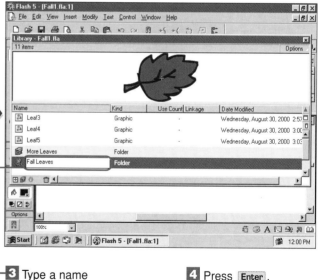

3 Type a name for the folder.

4 Press Enter.

How do I delete symbols from the Library?

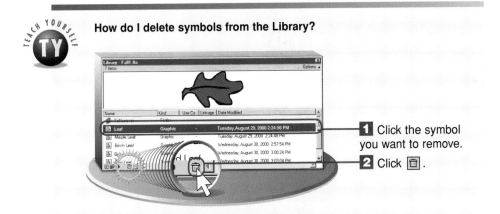

1 Click the symbol you want to remove.

2 Click 🗑 .

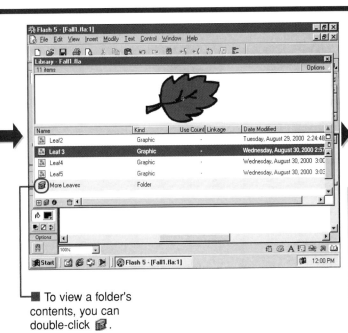

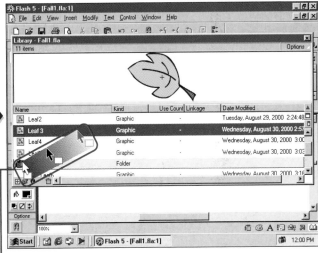

■ To view a folder's contents, you can double-click 📁 .

■ To move a symbol into another folder, you can drag the symbol over the folder icon. When you release the mouse button, the symbol moves into the folder.

CREATE SYMBOLS

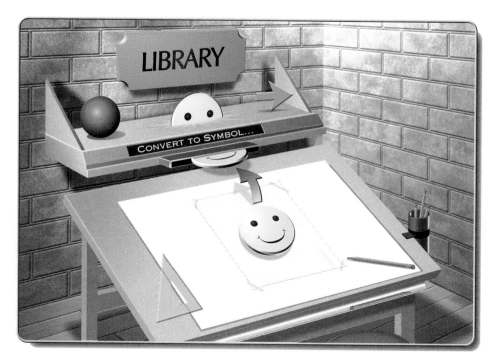

You can easily turn any object you draw on the Flash Stage into a symbol you can reuse throughout your project.

CREATE SYMBOLS

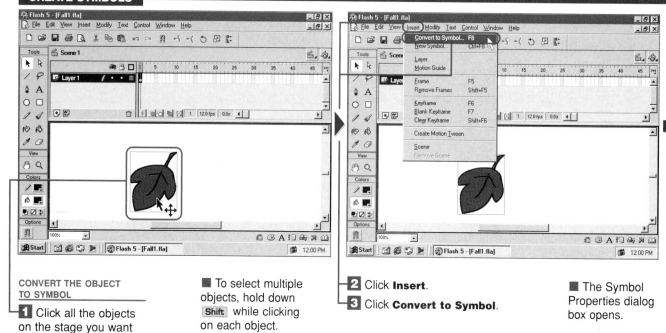

CONVERT THE OBJECT TO SYMBOL

1 Click all the objects on the stage you want to convert into a symbol.

■ To select multiple objects, hold down Shift while clicking on each object.

2 Click **Insert**.

3 Click **Convert to Symbol**.

■ The Symbol Properties dialog box opens.

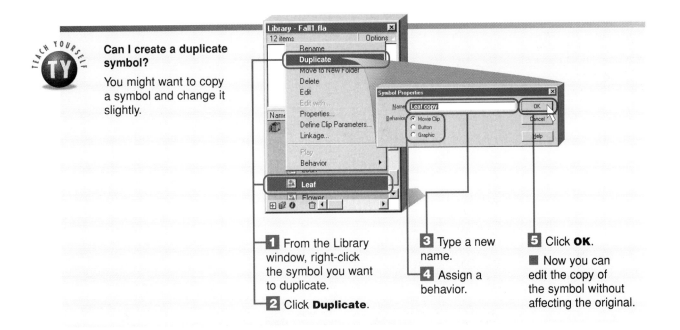

Can I create a duplicate symbol?

You might want to copy a symbol and change it slightly.

1 From the Library window, right-click the symbol you want to duplicate.

2 Click **Duplicate**.

3 Type a new name.

4 Assign a behavior.

5 Click **OK**.

■ Now you can edit the copy of the symbol without affecting the original.

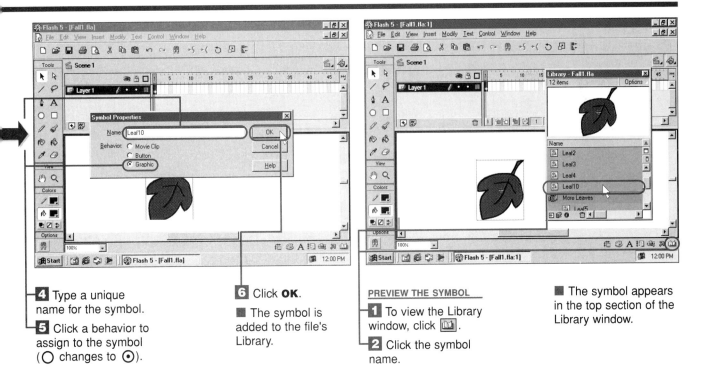

4 Type a unique name for the symbol.

5 Click a behavior to assign to the symbol (○ changes to ⊙).

6 Click **OK**.

■ The symbol is added to the file's Library.

PREVIEW THE SYMBOL

1 To view the Library window, click [⌐].

2 Click the symbol name.

■ The symbol appears in the top section of the Library window.

INSERT AN INSTANCE

To reuse a symbol in your Flash project, you can place an *instance* of it on the Stage. An instance is a copy of the original symbol. The copy references the original instead of duplicating it all over again, which decreases the movie's file size.

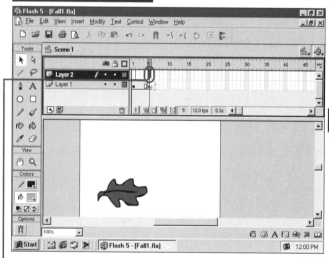

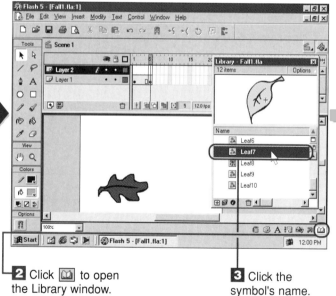

1 Open the frame and layer where you want to insert the instance.

Note: To learn more about frames, see Chapter 8. To learn more about layers, turn to Chapter 5.

2 Click 🔲 to open the Library window.

3 Click the symbol's name.

Can I replace one instance with another?

To replace an existing symbol in your project with another from the library:

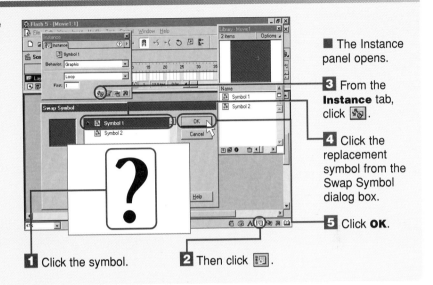

■ The Instance panel opens.

3 From the **Instance** tab, click 🔳.

4 Click the replacement symbol from the Swap Symbol dialog box.

5 Click **OK**.

1 Click the symbol.

2 Then click 🔳.

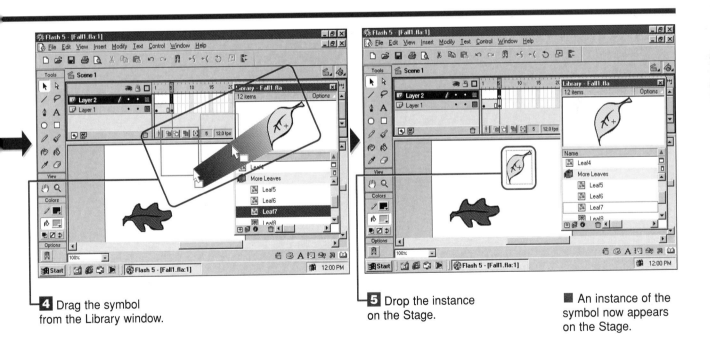

4 Drag the symbol from the Library window.

5 Drop the instance on the Stage.

■ An instance of the symbol now appears on the Stage.

MODIFY AN INSTANCE

After you place a symbol instance on the Stage, you can change the way it appears without changing the original symbol. For example, you can change its color or make it appear transparent.

MODIFY COLOR EFFECTS

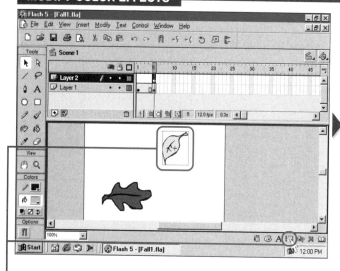

1 Click the instance you want to modify.

2 Click 🔲.

■ The Instance panel opens.

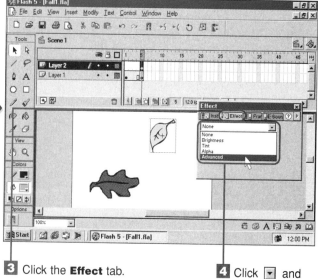

3 Click the **Effect** tab.

4 Click ▼ and select **Advanced**.

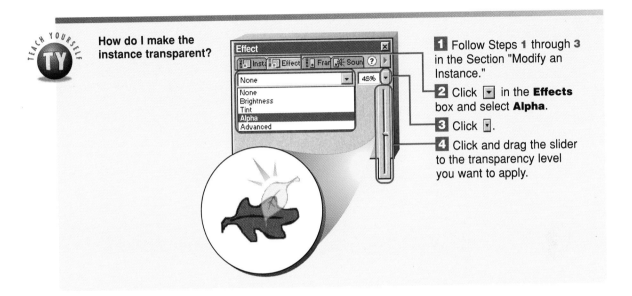

How do I make the
instance transparent?

1 Follow Steps **1** through **3**
in the Section "Modify an
Instance."

2 Click ▼ in the **Effects**
box and select **Alpha**.

3 Click ▼.

4 Click and drag the slider
to the transparency level
you want to apply.

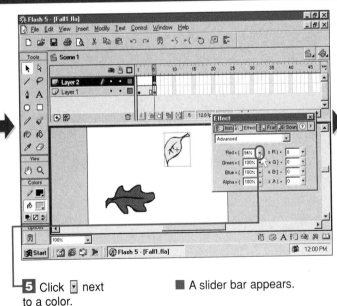

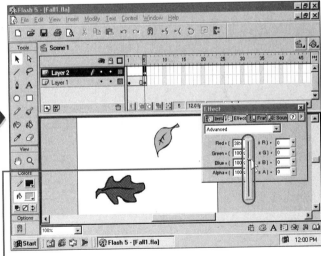

5 Click ▼ next
to a color.

■ A slider bar appears.

6 Drag the slider to
a new color setting.

■ The selected object
changes color as you
drag the slider.

■ You might want to
experiment with the various
color settings to achieve
the color effect you want.

123

EDIT SYMBOLS

You can make changes to the original symbol and Flash will automatically update all instances of it in your movie.

See the Sections "Create Symbols" and "Insert an Instance" to learn more about creating and using Flash symbols.

SWITCH TO SYMBOL-EDIT MODE

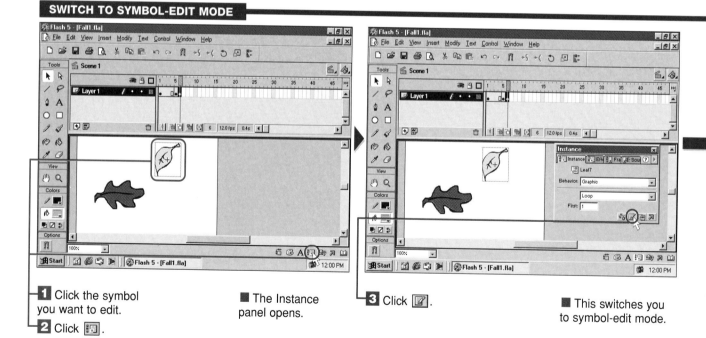

1 Click the symbol you want to edit.

2 Click [image].

■ The Instance panel opens.

3 Click [image].

■ This switches you to symbol-edit mode.

Can I test how my edits affect the movie?

As you edit a symbol, you might want to see the results of your edits before exiting symbol-edit mode. Click **Control, Test Movie** to run the movie and check the symbol's appearance.

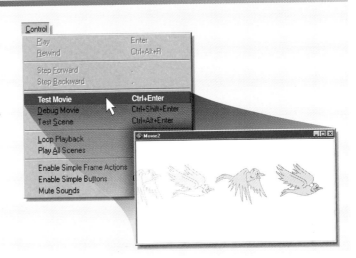

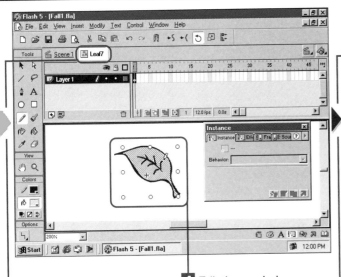

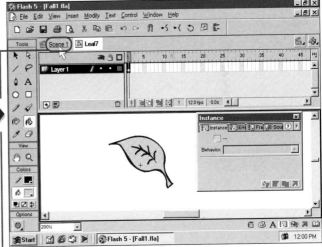

■ If the symbol name is highlighted at the top of the Timeline, you know you are in symbol-edit mode.

4 Edit the symbol as you desire. For example, you can use the Flash drawing tools to make changes to the object, such as changing the fill color, or adjusting a line segment.

Note: See Chapter 3 to learn more about editing objects.

5 After editing the symbol, click the **Scene** button.

■ You are no longer in symbol-edit mode.

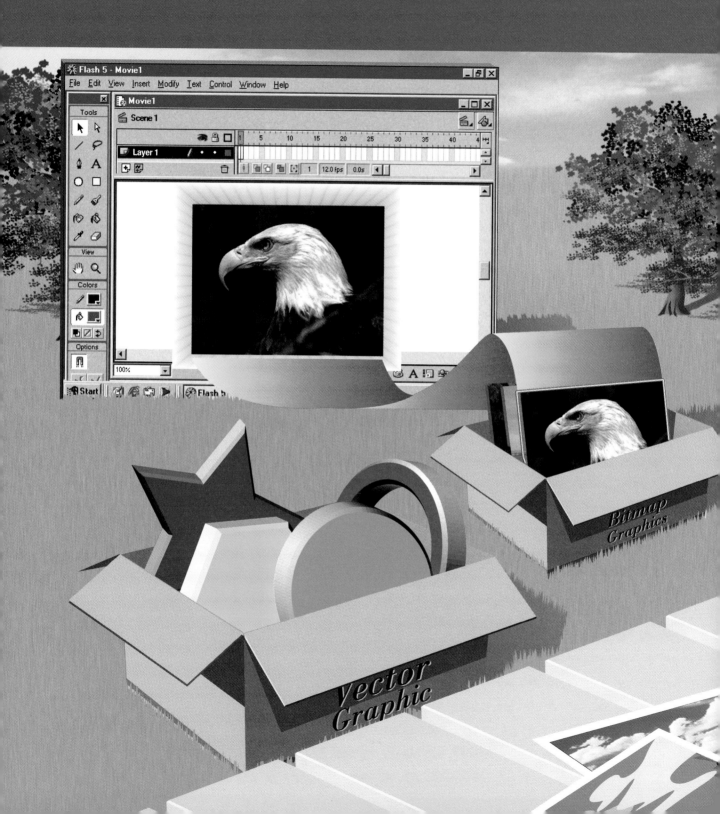

CHAPTER 7

Working with Imported Graphics

Do you want to use artwork from a non-Flash program? Follow the steps in these tasks to import art from other programs to work with in Flash.

UNDERSTANDING VECTOR AND BITMAP IMAGES

You can create your own vector graphics in Flash, or import graphics from other sources for use in your movies. Before you do, it is important to understand the basic differences between vector and bitmap graphics.

Bitmap

Vector

BITMAP GRAPHICS

Until recently, bitmap graphics (also called *raster* graphics) were the traditional way to illustrate Web pages. While bitmap images offer a great deal of detail, their file sizes are often large, requiring lots of bandwidth when transferred across a network or the Internet (see Appendix A: bandwidth).

BITMAP GRAPHICS CONSIST OF PIXELS

Bitmap graphics are made up of square dots, called *pixels*. The dots are arranged in a grid pattern, and each dot includes information about its color and position. Most bitmap images use thousands of pixels.

VECTOR GRAPHICS

Vector graphics use mathematical equations, or *vectors*, to define an image's shape, color, position, and size. The use of equations instead of pixels make the image file size the same, regardless of whether the image is large or small.

VECTOR GRAPHICS DOWNLOAD FASTER

Vector graphics are easily scaled, unlike bitmap graphics. Because of their smaller file size, vector graphics download much more quickly onto Web pages.

IMPORTING BITMAPS

You can import bitmap graphics into Flash for use in your movies. Flash supports BMP, GIF, JPEG, PICT, and PNG bitmap file types.

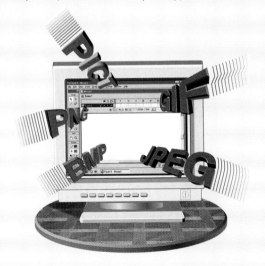

CONVERTING BITMAP GRAPHICS

After you import a bitmap graphic, you can convert it into a vector graphic, or utilize other Flash tools to optimize the graphic's file size.

IMPORT GRAPHICS

You can import
graphics, including
vector or bitmap
graphics, from
other sources
to use in Flash.

See the Section
"Understanding
Vector and Bitmap
Images" to learn
more about vector
and bitmap graphic
types.

IMPORT GRAPHICS

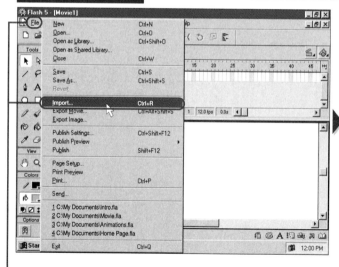

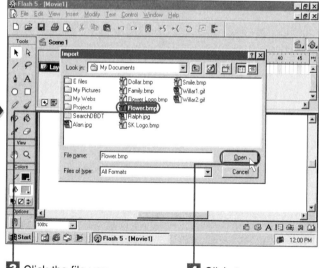

IMPORT A GRAPHIC FILE

1 Click **File**.

2 Click **Import**.

■ The Import dialog box
opens.

3 Click the file you
want to import.

*Note: You might need to
specify a file type to locate
the file you want.*

4 Click **Open**.

■ Flash places the
graphic on the Stage
as a grouped object.

Can I reuse the bitmap graphic?

When you import a bitmap graphic, it is immediately added to the Flash library for use in other frames in your movie. To view the Library, click 📖.

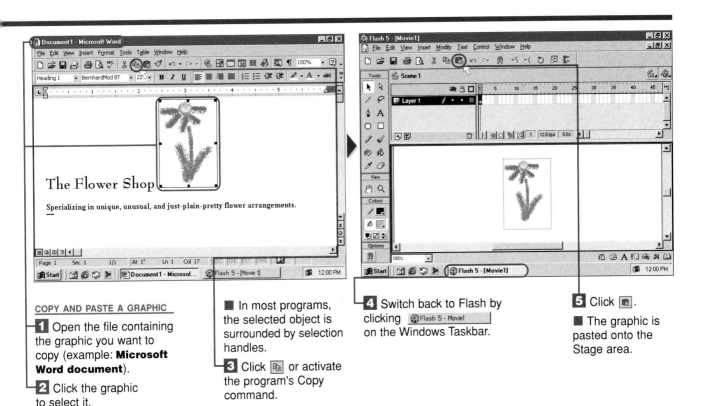

COPY AND PASTE A GRAPHIC

1 Open the file containing the graphic you want to copy (example: **Microsoft Word document**).

2 Click the graphic to select it.

■ In most programs, the selected object is surrounded by selection handles.

3 Click 📋 or activate the program's Copy command.

4 Switch back to Flash by clicking 🎬 Flash 5 - Movie1 on the Windows Taskbar.

5 Click 📋.

■ The graphic is pasted onto the Stage area.

MAKE BITMAPS INTO VECTOR GRAPHICS

Turning a bitmap graphic
into a vector graphic can
minimize the file size and
enable you to utilize the
Flash tools to manipulate
the graphic. Use the
Trace Bitmap command to
convert a bitmap graphic.

TRACE A BITMAP GRAPHIC

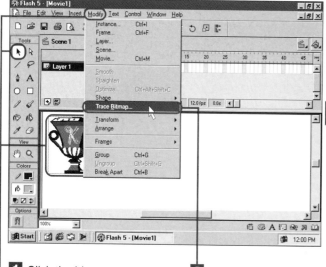

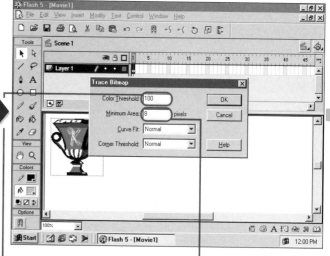

1 Click the bitmap graphic.

■ You can use the ▶ to
select items on the Stage.

2 Click **Modify**.

3 Click **Trace Bitmap**.

■ The Trace Bitmap
dialog box opens.

4 Type a value that
determines the amount
of color variance between
neighboring pixels.

■ A smaller value results
in many vector shapes;
a larger value results in
fewer vectors.

5 Type a minimum
pixel size for any
vector shape.

What if my graphic looks funny?

When applying the Trace Bitmap controls, you might need to experiment with the settings to get the results you want. Start with the default settings. If those do not work, click [↺] and try again, making a few adjustments.

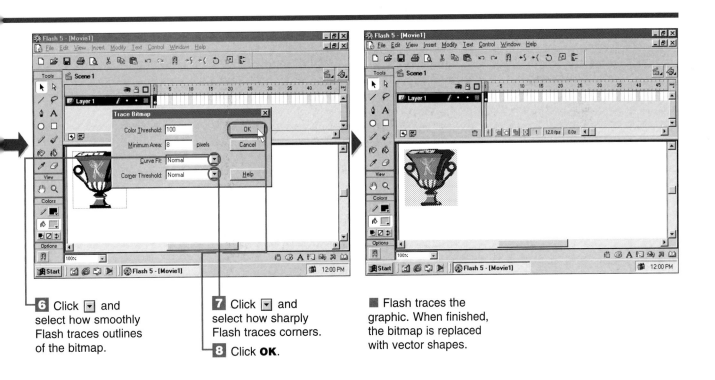

■6 Click ▾ and select how smoothly Flash traces outlines of the bitmap.

■7 Click ▾ and select how sharply Flash traces corners.

■8 Click **OK**.

■ Flash traces the graphic. When finished, the bitmap is replaced with vector shapes.

TURN BITMAPS INTO FILLS

You can turn a bitmap image into a fill for use with Flash drawing tools that use fills, such as the Oval, Rectangle, or Brush.

TURN BITMAPS INTO FILLS

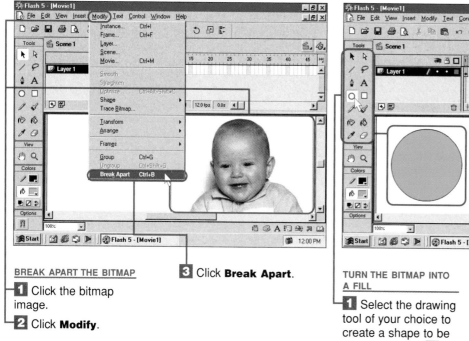

BREAK APART THE BITMAP

1 Click the bitmap image.

2 Click **Modify**.

3 Click **Break Apart**.

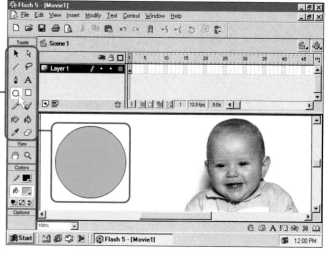

TURN THE BITMAP INTO A FILL

1 Select the drawing tool of your choice to create a shape to be filled (example: ☐).

Note: You might want to place the new shape on another layer. (See Chapter 5.)

What types of edits can I perform on the bitmap fill?

You can edit a bitmap fill just as you can any other fill. For example, you can rotate the fill shape, or scale it to another size. To rotate the bitmap fill, click the fill, then click 🔄. The fill is surrounded by rotation handles. Drag a handle to rotate the image.

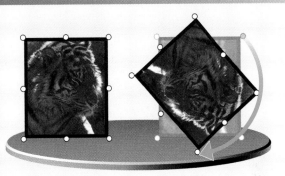

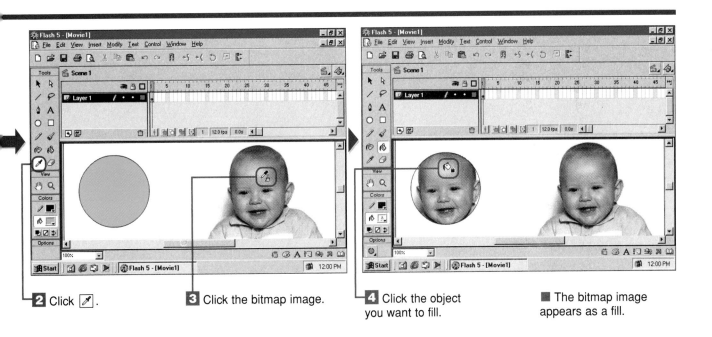

2 Click 🖋.

3 Click the bitmap image.

4 Click the object you want to fill.

■ The bitmap image appears as a fill.

CHAPTER 8

Animation Techniques

Are you ready to start animating? This chapter shows you how to use frames and create simple animations.

INTRODUCING ANIMATION

One of the most exciting aspects of Flash is its animation features. You can animate objects, synchronize the animation with sounds, add backgrounds, animate buttons, and much more. After you complete a Flash project, you can place it on a Web page or distribute for others to view.

See Chapter 13 to find out more about distributing your Flash movies. For more helpful definitions, see the Appendix "Web Graphic and Animation Terms."

HOW DO I USE ANIMATIONS?

You can use Flash animations to present a lively message or to simply entertain. Animations you create in Flash can make a Web site come to life. For example, you can create a cartoon to play in your site's banner, or animate buttons for the user to click. With the Flash animation tools, you have complete control over your movies.

HOW DO ANIMATIONS WORK?

Animation effects use frames to hold scenes or objects. The scene or object changes slightly from frame to frame to create the illusion of movement. When you play the animation back, each frame appears for less than a moment before the next frame replaces it.

ANIMATION HISTORY

Back in the early days of animating, cartoonists and other animators painted objects and scenes on transparent cels. The cels were stacked to create an image. A movie camera then took a snapshot of that image to create a single frame. The animators reused some of the cels for the next frame, such as backgrounds, and changed other cels to create an object's movement across the foreground.

ANIMATION IN FLASH

Flash uses similar principles to create animations today. Instead of transparent cels, you add content to frames and layers, then stack the layers to create depth. Anytime you want the content to change, you can add keyframes to the Timeline and vary the position or appearance of the content. When the animation, or movie, is played back, the content appears to move.

FRAME-BY-FRAME ANIMATION

Frame-by-frame animation is just as its name implies, creating the effect of movement by subtly changing the content's appearance from frame to frame. This type of animation method gives you a great deal of control over how the content changes across the Flash Timeline. However, this type of animation increases file size.

See Chapter 1 to learn the basics of the Flash Timeline.

TWEENED ANIMATION

The other method of animating in Flash is called *tweened animation*. With tweened animation, you tell Flash to calculate the in-between frames from one keyframe to the content change in the next keyframe. Flash then draws the in-between phases of change to get from the first keyframe to the next.

This in-between framing is where the term "tweened" comes from. Tweened animation is faster, easier to edit, and consumes less file size.

LUNDERSTANDING FRAMES

Frames are the backbone of your animation effects. When you start a new Flash file, it opens with a single layer and hundreds of placeholder frames in the Timeline. Before you start animating objects, you need to understand how frames work.

For more helpful definitions, see the Appendix "Web Graphic and Animation Terms."

FRAMES CONTROL TIME AND MOVEMENT

The number of frames you use in your Flash movie combined with the speed at which they play determine the length of the movie.

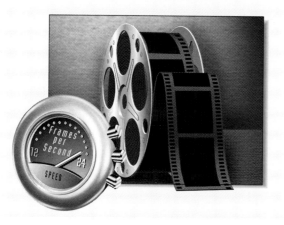

FRAME TYPES

You can work with several different types of frames in the Flash Timeline: placeholder frames, keyframes, static frames, and tweened frames.

PLACEHOLDER FRAMES

A placeholder frame is merely an empty frame. It has no content. When your movie reaches an empty frame, it stops playing. With the exception of the first frame in a new layer, the remaining frames are all placeholders until you assign another frame type.

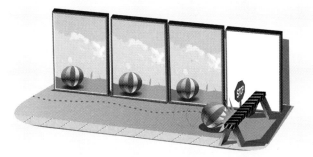

STATIC FRAMES

Static or regular frames display the same content as the previous frame in the Timeline. Static frames must be preceded by a keyframe. Static frames are used to hold content that you want to remain visible until you add another keyframe in the layer.

KEYFRAMES

A keyframe defines a change in animation, such as an object moving or taking on a new appearance. By default, Flash inserts a blank keyframe for you in the first frame of every new layer you add to the Timeline. When you add a keyframe, it duplicates the content from the previous keyframe. This technique makes it easy to tweak the contents slightly to create the illusion of movement between frames.

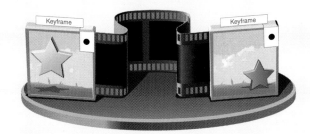

TWEENED FRAMES

One way to create animation in a movie is to allow Flash to calculate the number of frames between two keyframes to create movement. Called *tweening*, Flash determines the in-between positions of the animated object from one keyframe to the next and spaces out the changes in the tweened frames between the two keyframes.

See Chapter 9 to find out more about tweening effects.

SET MOVIE DIMENSIONS AND SPEED

Before you begin an animation project, take time to set up the size of your movie and the speed at which you want it to play. A movie's dimensions refer to its vertical and horizontal size on the Flash Stage. The movie's play speed determines the number of frames per second, or fps, that the animation occurs. Planning out your project in advance saves you time and headaches later.

For more helpful definitions, see the Appendix "Web Graphic and Animation Terms."

SET MOVIE DIMENSIONS AND SPEED

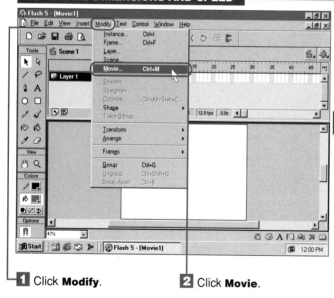

1 Click **Modify**.

2 Click **Movie**.

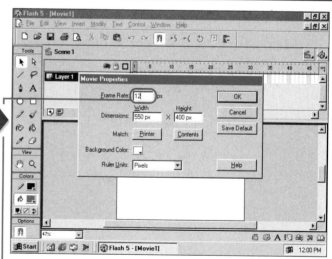

■ The Movie Properties dialog box opens.

3 Type the number of frames per second you want the movie to play in the **Frame Rate** text box.

Note: If you use a higher fps setting, slower computers might not be able to play back your movie properly.

What is a good frame rate for my movie?

The default frame rate of 12 fps works well for most projects. The maximum rate you should set is 24 fps, unless you are exporting your movie as a QuickTime or Windows AVI video file (which can handle higher rates without consuming computer processor power). If you set a higher frame rate, slower computers struggle to play at such speeds. Most simply cannot, and a very high fps rate slows all but a supercomputer down.

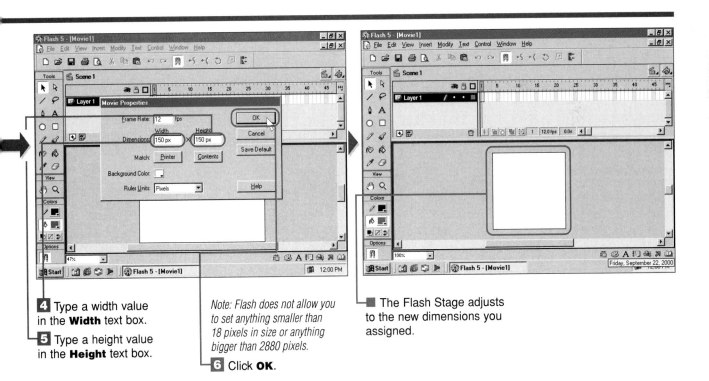

4 Type a width value in the **Width** text box.

5 Type a height value in the **Height** text box.

Note: Flash does not allow you to set anything smaller than 18 pixels in size or anything bigger than 2880 pixels.

6 Click **OK**.

■ The Flash Stage adjusts to the new dimensions you assigned.

ADD FRAMES

When you add a new layer or start a new file, Flash starts you out with one keyframe in the Timeline and lots of placeholder frames. To add content to your movie, you must add frames to the Timeline. You can add keyframes to define changes in the animation's appearance, or add regular frames to repeat keyframe content.

See Chapter 9 to learn more about working with tweened frames.

ADD FRAMES

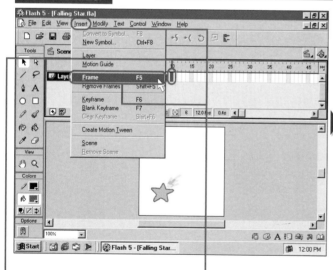

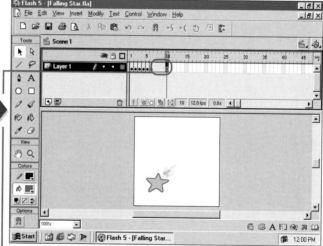

ADD A REGULAR FRAME

1 Click an empty frame on the Timeline where you want to insert a new frame.

Note: See the Section "Understanding Frames" to find out more about Flash frame types.

2 Click **Insert**.

3 Click **Frame**.

■ Flash inserts regular frames between the last regular frame or keyframe up to the frame you clicked in Step **1**.

■ If you added a regular frame in the midst of existing regular frames, all the frames to the right of the insertion move over to make room for the new frame.

How can I tell which frames are which in the Timeline?

You can identify Flash frames by the following characteristics:

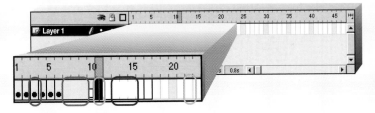

■ Empty frames appear white.

■ In-between frames without content appear as a block of white.

■ Keyframes with content appear with a solid bullet in the Timeline.

■ In-between frames that contain content appear tinted or grayed on the Timeline.

■ When you insert a blank keyframe, which has no content added yet, Flash places a hollow box in the preceding frame.

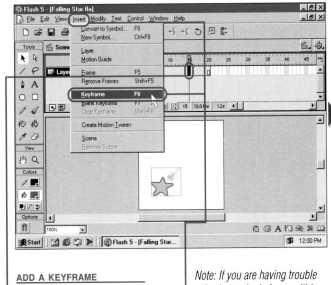

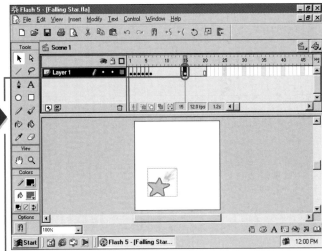

ADD A KEYFRAME

1 Click an empty frame or a regular frame on the Timeline where you want to place a new keyframe.

Note: If you are having trouble selecting a single frame within a group of frames, press **Ctrl** *(Windows) or* **⌘** *(Mac) while clicking the frame.*

2 Click **Insert**.

3 Click **Keyframe**.

■ If the frame you selected in Step **1** was a regular frame, Flash converts it to a keyframe.

■ If the frame was an empty frame, Flash inserts regular frames in between the last regular frame or keyframe up to the frame you clicked in Step **1**.

CONTINUED

ADD FRAMES

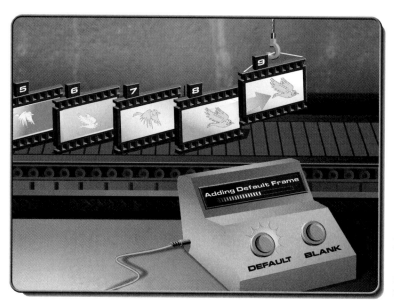

You can choose between adding a blank keyframe or adding a default keyframe. If you add a default keyframe, Flash copies the contents of the previous keyframe and you can quickly edit the content on the Stage to create a change in your animation sequence. If you add a blank keyframe, the frame is completely empty and ready for brand-new content to be placed on the Stage.

See the Section "Understanding Frames" to find out more about Flash frame types.

ADD FRAMES (CONTINUED)

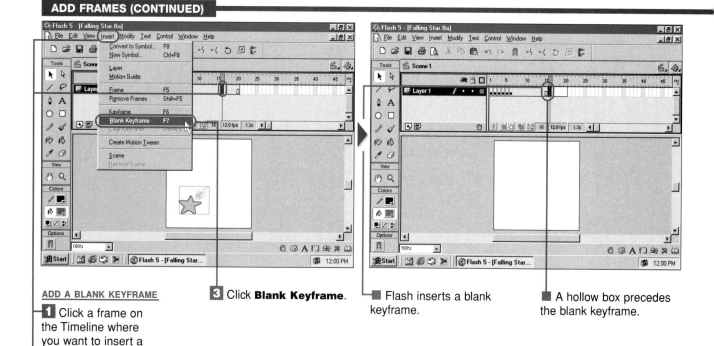

ADD A BLANK KEYFRAME

1 Click a frame on the Timeline where you want to insert a blank keyframe.

2 Click **Insert**.

3 Click **Blank Keyframe**.

■ Flash inserts a blank keyframe.

■ A hollow box precedes the blank keyframe.

Can I change the size of the Timeline frames?

You can change the size of the frames in the Timeline using the Timeline menu. By default, the frames appear in Normal size. You can change them to Tiny or Small to fit more frames in the Timeline view, or try Medium or Large to make the frames easier to see.

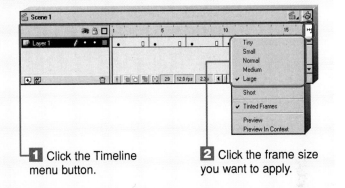

1 Click the Timeline menu button.

2 Click the frame size you want to apply.

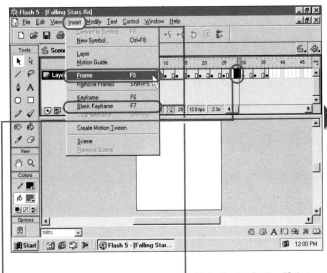

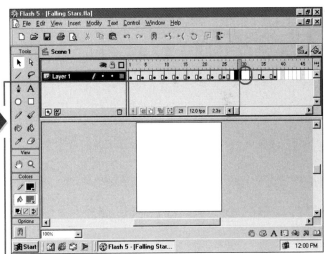

ADD MULTIPLE FRAMES

1 Select two or more frames by clicking them.

■ To select multiple frames, click the first frame in the range, press the Shift key and click the last frame in the range.

Note: See the Section "Select Frames" to find out more about selecting frames.

2 Click **Insert**.

3 Click **Frame** to insert regular frames, or click **Blank Keyframe** to make the new frames all keyframes.

■ Flash inserts the same number of new frames and lengthens the movie.

DELETE FRAMES

You can remove frames you no longer need. If you want to remove a frame, or several frames, completely from the Timeline, use the Remove Frames command. To turn a keyframe into a regular frame, you can remove the frame's keyframe status and demote it to a regular frame. If you change a keyframe's status, all in-between frames are altered as well.

See the Section "Understanding Frames" to find out more about Flash frame types.

DELETE FRAMES

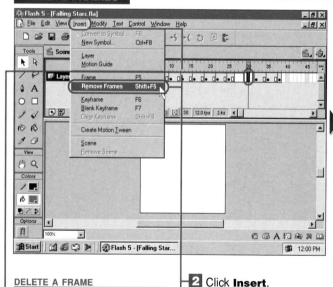

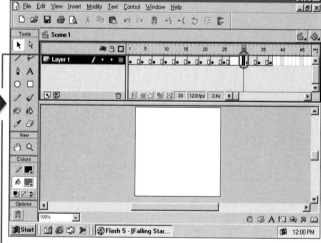

DELETE A FRAME

1 Click the frame, or range of frames, you want to delete.

■ To delete a range of frames, select the range first. See the Section "Select Frames" to find out more about selecting frames.

2 Click **Insert**.

3 Click **Remove Frames**.

■ Flash removes the frame and any existing frames to the right move over to fill the void.

Can I delete a keyframe?

To remove a keyframe completely
from the Timeline, you must select
both the keyframe and all the in-
between frames associated with it;
otherwise, the **Remove Frames**
command does not work properly
to remove the keyframe.

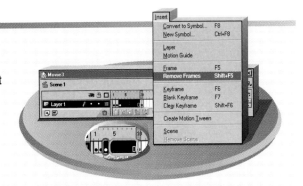

■ **Keyframe**　　　■ **In-between frames**

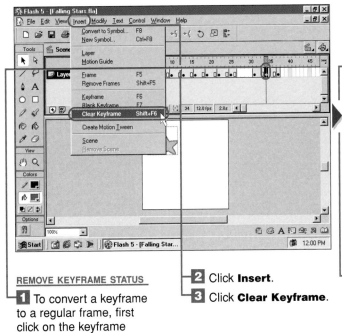

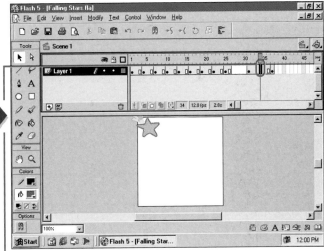

REMOVE KEYFRAME STATUS

1 To convert a keyframe
to a regular frame, first
click on the keyframe
you want to change.

2 Click **Insert**.

3 Click **Clear Keyframe**.

■ Flash converts the
frame to a regular frame,
and changes the frame
to match the previous
keyframe's contents.

*Note: You cannot change the
status of the first keyframe in
a layer.*

CREATE FRAME-BY-FRAME ANIMATION

You can create the illusion of movement in a Flash movie by changing the placement or appearance of the Stage content from keyframe to keyframe in the Flash Timeline. This type of animation is called, appropriately, *frame-by-frame animation.*

See the Section "Introducing Animation" to find out more about animating techniques in Flash.

CREATE FRAME-BY-FRAME ANIMATION

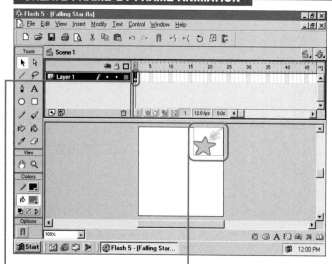

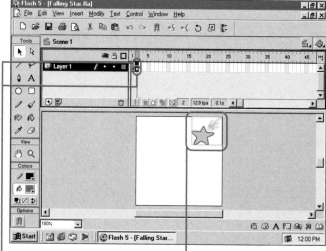

ADD CONTENT TO THE FIRST KEYFRAME

1 Click the first keyframe in the layer you want to animate.

Note: See the Section "Understanding Frames" to find out more about Flash frame types.

2 Place the object you want to animate on the Flash Stage. For example, you can drag a symbol from the Flash Library onto the Stage, or use the drawing tools to create a new object.

Note: See Chapter 6 to find out more about using symbols. See Chapter 2 to find out how to use the Flash drawing tools.

ADD THE SECOND KEYFRAME

3 Click the next frame in the Timeline.

4 Add a keyframe.

Note: See the Section "Add Frames" to find out how to add a keyframe to the Timeline.

■ Flash inserts a keyframe that duplicates the previous frame's contents.

150

Can I add in-between frames to the animation?

To slow down the animation sequence, especially if the changes between keyframes are happening too fast to see very well, just add regular frames between keyframes in your frame-by-frame animation.

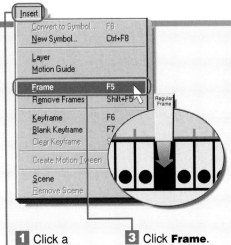

1 Click a keyframe.

2 Click **Insert**.

3 Click **Frame**.

■ Flash adds a regular frame behind the keyframe.

You can keep adding more regular frames to achieve the effect you want. When you play back the movie, the animation appears to slow down a bit in its movement.

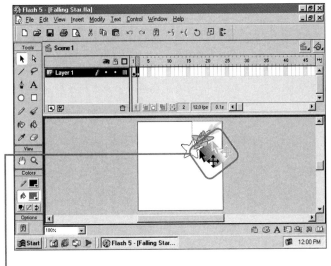

MOVE THE OBJECT SLIGHTLY

5 Change the object slightly to animate. For example, move the object a bit on the Stage, or change the object's appearance (such as a different color or size).

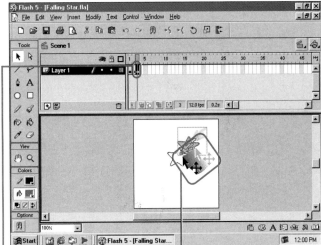

ADD THE THIRD KEYFRAME

6 Click the next frame in the layer and add a keyframe.

■ Flash duplicates the previous keyframe's contents.

7 Change the object slightly again. For example, move the object a bit more on the Stage, or change the object's appearance (such as a different color or size).

CONTINUED

CREATE FRAME-BY-FRAME ANIMATION

You can learn the principles of frame-by-frame animation by creating a simple animation sequence, such as making an object move across the Flash Stage. The illustrations in this section show how to create the illusion of a falling star by moving the star ever so slightly down the Stage in each keyframe. By the last keyframe, the star has reached the bottom. When the animation is played back, the star appears to drop from the top-right corner to the bottom-left corner.

CREATE FRAME-BY-FRAME ANIMATION (CONTINUED)

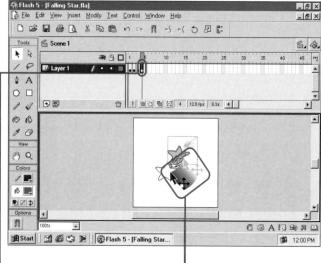

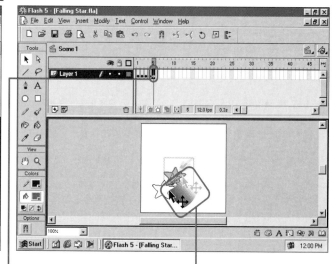

ADD THE FOURTH KEYFRAME

8 Click the next frame in the layer and add a keyframe.

■ Flash duplicates the previous keyframe's contents.

9 Change the object again. For example, move the object a bit more on the Stage, or change the object's appearance (such as a different color or size).

ADD A FIFTH KEYFRAME

10 Click the next frame in the layer and add a keyframe.

■ Flash duplicates the previous keyframe's contents.

11 Change the object again. For example, move the object a bit more on the Stage, or change the object's appearance (such as a different color or size).

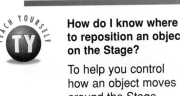

How do I know where to reposition an object on the Stage?

To help you control how an object moves around the Stage, turn on the Flash gridlines by performing the following steps:

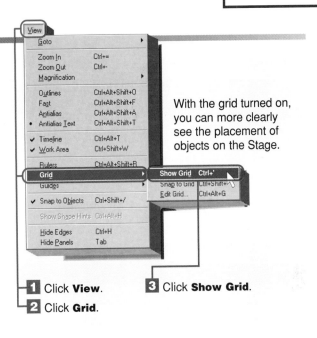

With the grid turned on, you can more clearly see the placement of objects on the Stage.

1 Click **View**.

2 Click **Grid**.

3 Click **Show Grid**.

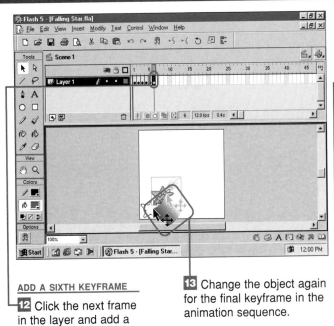

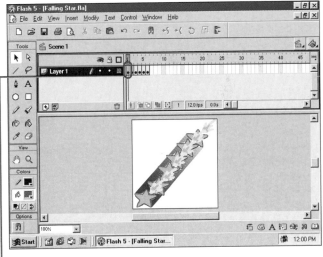

ADD A SIXTH KEYFRAME

12 Click the next frame in the layer and add a final keyframe.

■ Flash duplicates the previous keyframe's contents.

13 Change the object again for the final keyframe in the animation sequence.

PLAY BACK THE MOVIE

14 Click the first keyframe in the layer and press Enter.

■ Flash plays the entire animation sequence.

ONION-SKINNING AN ANIMATION

You can use Flash's onion-skinning feature to quickly assess the positioning of objects in surrounding frames. Onion-skinning offers two modes of display: dimmed content or outlined content. The objects in the frames surrounding the current frame are displayed as dimmed or outlined objects, but the current frame's contents are fully displayed. This feature allows you to see multiple frames and how their movements relate to the current frame.

See the Section "Understanding Frames" to find out more about Flash frame types.

ONION-SKINNING AN ANIMATION

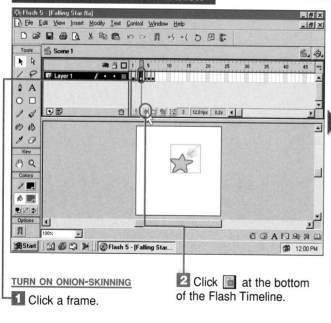

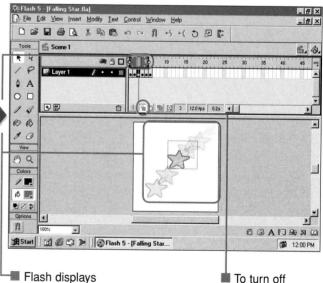

TURN ON ONION-SKINNING

1 Click a frame.

2 Click 🖼 at the bottom of the Flash Timeline.

■ Flash displays dimmed images from the surrounding frames and places onion-skin markers at the top of the Timeline.

■ To turn off onion-skinning, you can click 🖼 again.

154

Can I edit the onion-skinned frames?

You cannot edit the onion-skin frames unless you click 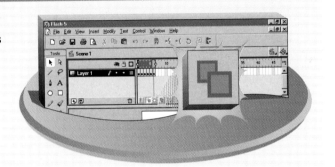. When you make the other frames editable, you can select and move the onion-skinned objects to fine-tune the animation sequence.

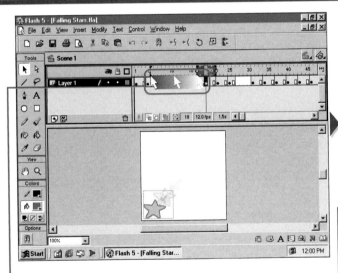

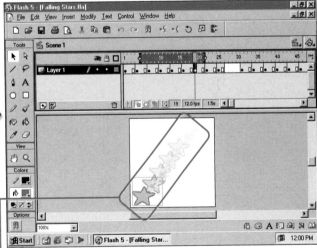

■ Flash adds or subtracts the additional frames from the view.

MOVE THE ONION-SKIN MARKERS

1 To view more or less frames with onion-skinning, you can click and drag an onion-skin marker left or right.

CONTINUED ▶

ONION-SKINNING AN ANIMATION

The onion-skinning features can help you better gauge the changes needed to create your animations. You can control which frames appear in onion-skin mode using the onion-skin markers that appear on the Timeline. You can also opt to control the markers using the Modify Onion Markers pop-up menu.

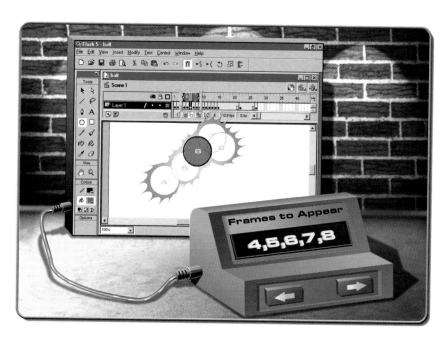

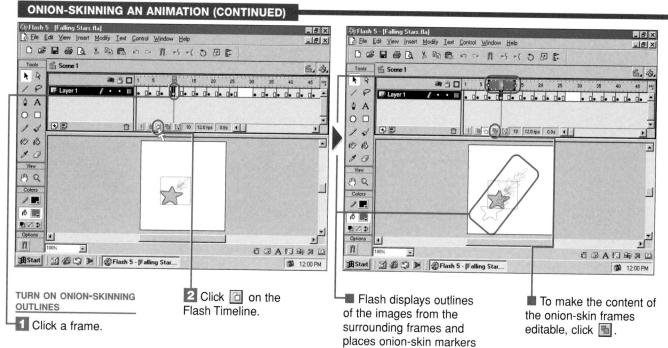

TURN ON ONION-SKINNING OUTLINES

1 Click a frame.

2 Click on the Flash Timeline.

■ Flash displays outlines of the images from the surrounding frames and places onion-skin markers at the top of the Timeline.

■ To make the content of the onion-skin frames editable, click .

What are my options for modifying the onion-skin markers?

When you click , the pop-up menu displays several choices for controlling markers on the Timeline.

■ Click **Always Show Markers** to leave the markers on even when onion-skinning is turned off.

■ Click **Anchor Onion** to lock the markers in place, even as you view frames at the other end of the Timeline.

■ Click **Onion 2** or **Onion 5** to display the corresponding number of frames before and after the current frame.

■ Click **Onion All** to onion-skin all the frames.

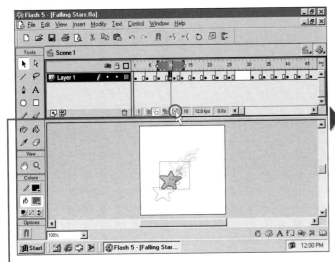

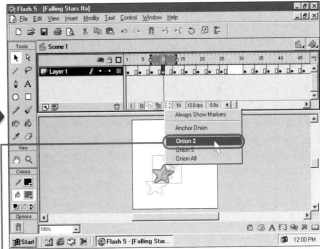

CHANGE THE MARKER DISPLAY

1 To change how the onion-skin markers appear on the Timeline, click.

■ The Modify menu appears with options for changing the marker display.

2 Click the marker setting you want to apply.

PREVIEW A FLASH ANIMATION

You can click on an animation sequence one frame at a time to see each frame's contents, but a faster way to check the sequence is to play the movie. One way to play a movie is to use the Test Movie command and preview the animation in the Flash Player window.

PREVIEW A FLASH ANIMATION

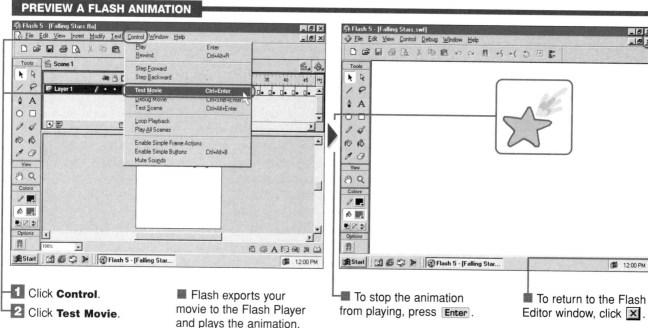

1 Click **Control**.

2 Click **Test Movie**.

■ Flash exports your movie to the Flash Player and plays the animation.

■ To stop the animation from playing, press [Enter].

■ To return to the Flash Editor window, click [X].

A Flash movie's frame rate is constant throughout the movie, but you can slow or speed up an animation by adding or subtracting frames in your movie. For example, if part of your animation seems to happen too quickly, you can insert regular frames to slow the sequence down a bit. By adding in-between frames rather than keyframes, you do not increase the movie's file size.

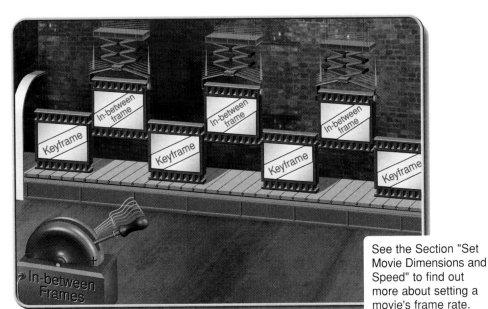

See the Section "Set Movie Dimensions and Speed" to find out more about setting a movie's frame rate.

ADJUST THE ANIMATION SPEED

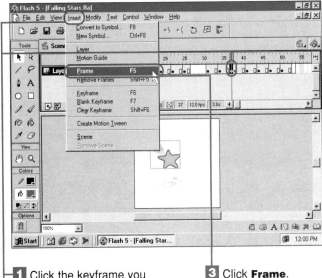

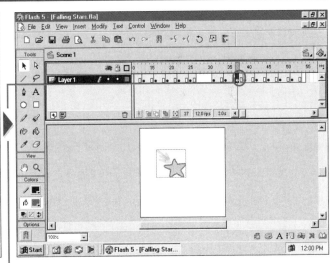

1 Click the keyframe you want to add frames to.

2 Click **Insert**.

3 Click **Frame**.

■ Flash adds a frame after the keyframe.

4 Because adding just one regular frame is not always enough, repeat Steps **2** and **3** to add a few more frames to the sequence.

■ To test the animation, click the first frame in the Timeline and press Enter.

SELECT FRAMES

When you work with frames in the Flash Timeline, you must select the frame or frames you want to edit. You can use a couple of selection techniques.

See the Sections "Add Frames" and "Delete Frames" to find out more about adding and deleting frames from the Timeline.

SELECT FRAMES

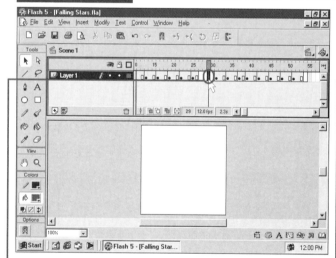

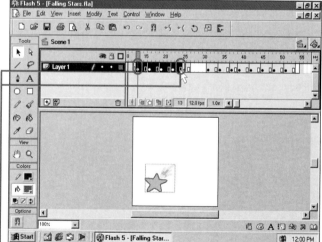

SELECT A SINGLE FRAME

■1 Click the frame to select it.

■ Flash highlights the frame in the Timeline.

■ If you have difficulty selecting a regular frame between two keyframes, press and hold **Ctrl** (Windows) or **⌘** (Mac), then click the frame you want to select.

Note: See the Section "Understanding Frames" to find out more about frame types.

SELECT MULTIPLE FRAMES

■1 Click the first frame in the range of frames you want to select.

■2 Press and hold **Shift** and click the last frame in the range.

■ Flash selects all the frames in-between.

■ To select multiple frames between two keyframes, click anywhere between the two keyframes.

You can use the Frame panel to help organize frames with labels, assign actions, or even add sound clips.

See the Section "Understanding Frames" to find out more about using frames in Flash.

MODIFY FRAME PROPERTIES

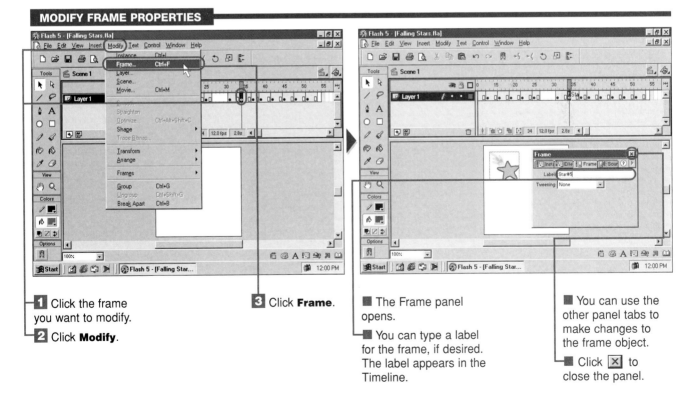

1 Click the frame you want to modify.

2 Click **Modify**.

3 Click **Frame**.

■ The Frame panel opens.

■ You can type a label for the frame, if desired. The label appears in the Timeline.

■ You can use the other panel tabs to make changes to the frame object.

■ Click ✕ to close the panel.

MOVE AND COPY FRAMES

One way you can edit your Flash movie is to move or copy frames in the animation sequence. For example, you might want to move a keyframe up or back in the Timeline, or copy multiple regular frames to place between two keyframes. You cannot copy frames like you copy other objects in Flash; you must use the Copy Frames and Paste Frames commands found in the Edit menu.

See the Sections "Add Frames" and "Delete Frames" to find out more about adding and deleting frames from the Timeline.

MOVE AND COPY FRAMES

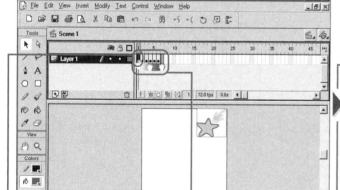

MOVE A FRAME

1 Click the frame to select it.

■ Flash highlights the frame in the Timeline.

2 Click and drag the frame to a new location in the Timeline (▶ changes to 🖑).

3 Drop the frame in place.

■ The frame moves.

I pasted a copy in the wrong place, what do I do?

Anytime you make a mistake in Flash, click 🔄 to undo your last action. This command only works if you click the button immediately after performing the action. If you perform another action before clicking 🔄, Flash undoes the most recent action and the previous action is lost.

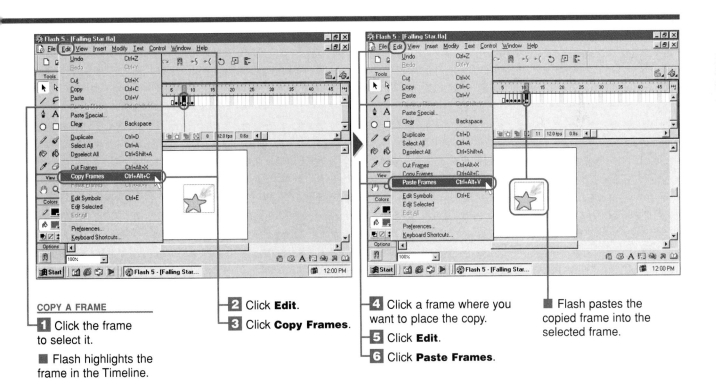

COPY A FRAME

1 Click the frame to select it.

■ Flash highlights the frame in the Timeline.

2 Click **Edit**.

3 Click **Copy Frames**.

4 Click a frame where you want to place the copy.

5 Click **Edit**.

6 Click **Paste Frames**.

■ Flash pastes the copied frame into the selected frame.

CREATE SCENES

To help you organize really long movies, you can break up your movie into scenes. Scenes are actually chunks of the animation frames turned into their own independent Timelines.

For example, one scene might include frames 1-50, another scene might include frames 51-75. Scenes are still part of the overall movie, but handily organized into sections that you can label and rearrange as needed. You can even use Flash actions to jump to different scenes. By default, Flash starts you out with a scene, labeled Scene 1. You can rename the scene and add others.

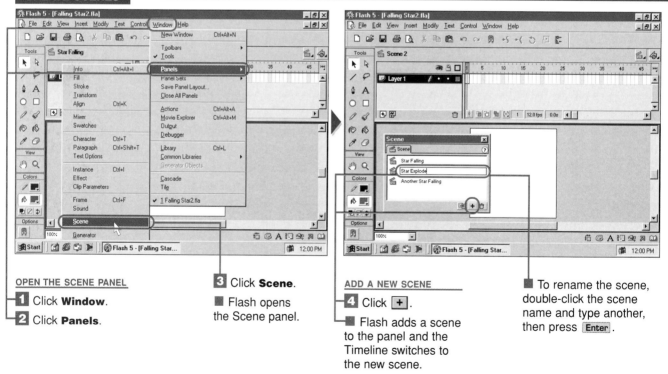

OPEN THE SCENE PANEL

1 Click **Window**.

2 Click **Panels**.

3 Click **Scene**.

■ Flash opens the Scene panel.

ADD A NEW SCENE

4 Click ⊞.

■ Flash adds a scene to the panel and the Timeline switches to the new scene.

■ To rename the scene, double-click the scene name and type another, then press Enter.

How do I rearrange the scene order?

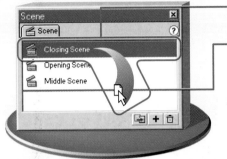

2 Click on the scene
you want to move.

3 Click and drag the
scene to a new
location in the list.

4 Release the mouse
button and the scenes
are reordered.

1 Open the Scene panel
to display a list of all the
available scenes (Steps 1
through 3 in this section).

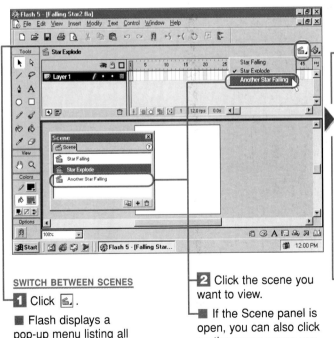

SWITCH BETWEEN SCENES

1 Click 🖼.

■ Flash displays a
pop-up menu listing all
the available scenes.

2 Click the scene you
want to view.

■ If the Scene panel is
open, you can also click
on the scene name you
want to view.

■ The Flash Timeline
switches to the scene
you selected.

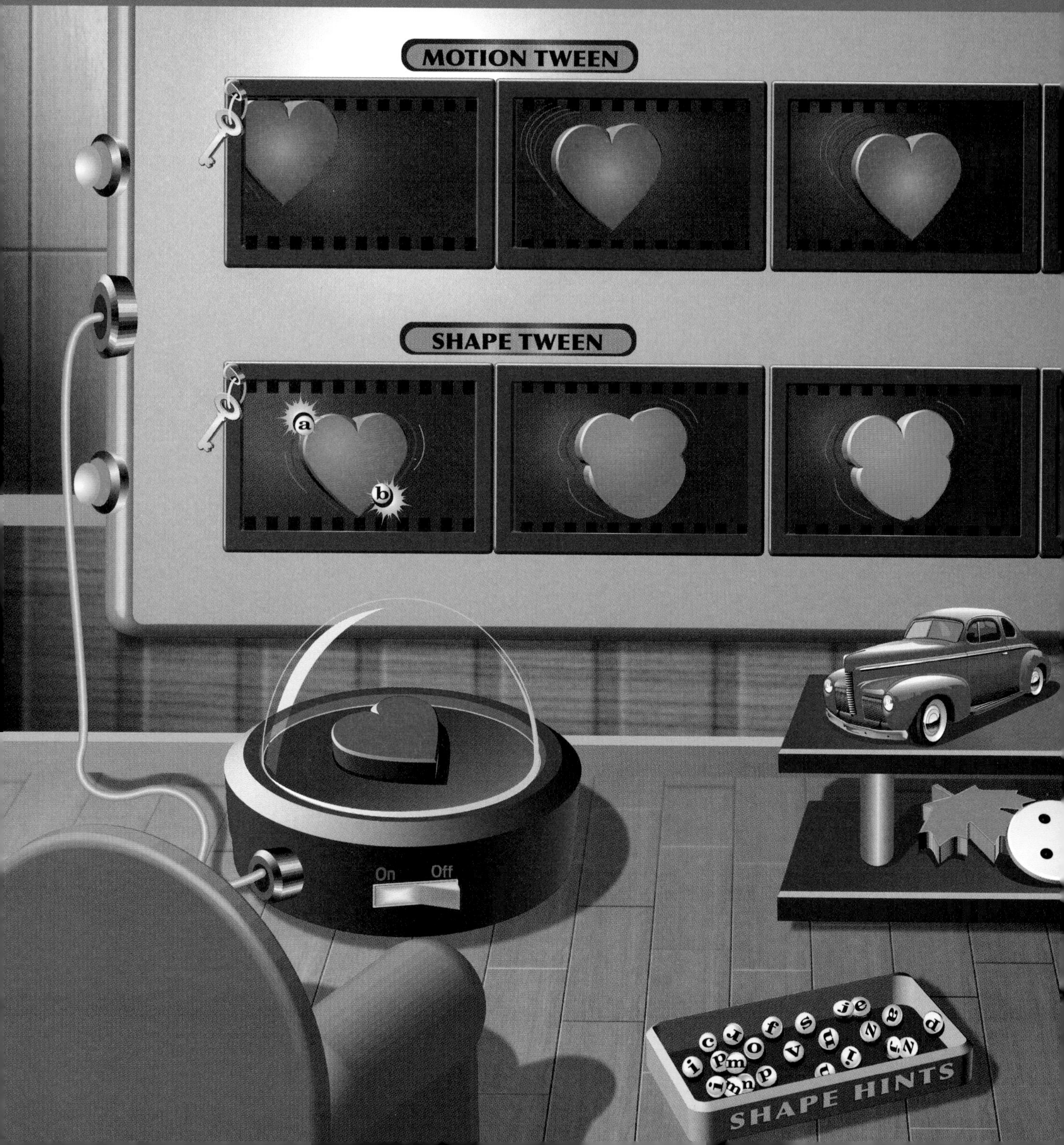

MOTION TWEEN

SHAPE TWEEN

On   Off

SHAPE HINTS

CHAPTER 9

Animating with Tweening Effects

Are you ready to utilize Flash's built-in animating techniques? This chapter shows you how to create animation effects using motion and shape tweening.

CREATE A MOTION TWEEN

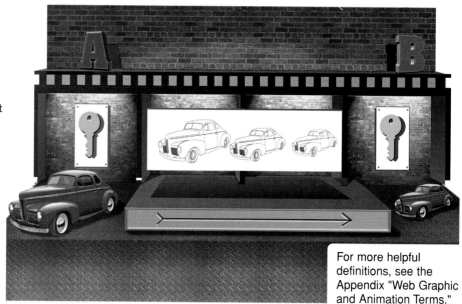

Flash can help you animate moving symbols when you apply a *motion* tween. A motion tween is when you define two points of movement in the Timeline with two keyframes, then let Flash calculate all the in-between frames necessary to get from point A to point B. Motion-tweened animations take up much less file space than frame-by-frame animations. You can only motion tween symbols or grouped objects and you can only tween one symbol per layer.

For more helpful definitions, see the Appendix "Web Graphic and Animation Terms."

CREATE A MOTION TWEEN

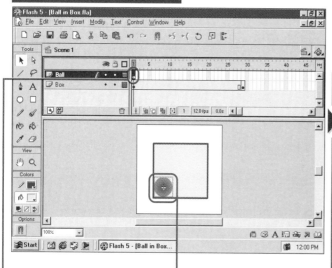

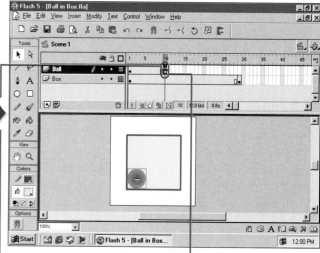

SELECT KEYFRAMES AND SYMBOL

1 Insert a keyframe where you want to start the motion tween.

Note: See Chapter 8 to find out more about adding frames to the Timeline.

2 Place the symbol you want to animate on the Stage.

■ The symbol's position should be the starting point of the animation effect, such as a corner or side of the movie area.

Note: See Chapter 6 to find out more about working with symbols.

3 Click the last frame you want to include in the motion tween.

4 Insert a keyframe.

Note: See Chapter 8 to find out how to add keyframes.

What is the difference between a motion tween and a frame-by-frame animation?

When you create a frame-by-frame animation, you manually input the changes made to each frame in the sequence. When you use a motion tween, you specify the first frame and the last frame and tell Flash to calculate all the in-between frames. By having Flash calculate the in-between frames, the resulting file size is much smaller than the same sequence created manually frame-by-frame.

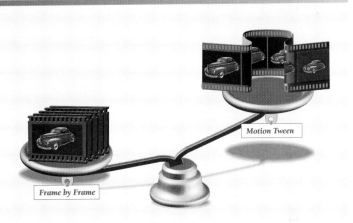

Motion Tween

Frame by Frame

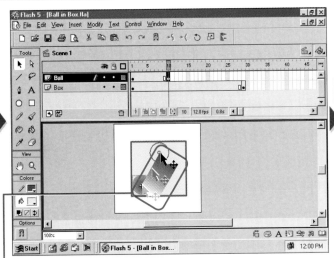

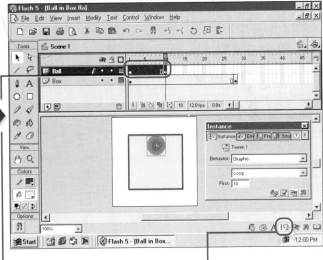

5 Move the symbol to the position on which you want the motion tween to end (for example, the other side of the Stage).

Note: See Chapter 3 to find out how to move objects on the Flash Stage.

6 Click between the two keyframes that make up your motion tween to select the frames.

Note: See Chapter 8 to find out how to select frames.

7 Click 📷 .

■ Flash opens the Instance panel.

CONTINUED

CREATE A MOTION TWEEN

You can assign as many motion tween segments as you like throughout your movie, or you can make your animation one long motion tween.

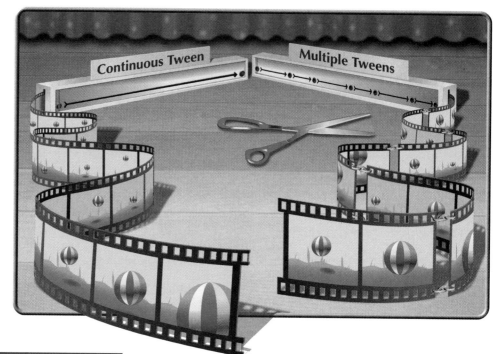

Continuous Tween

Multiple Tweens

CREATE A MOTION TWEEN (CONTINUED)

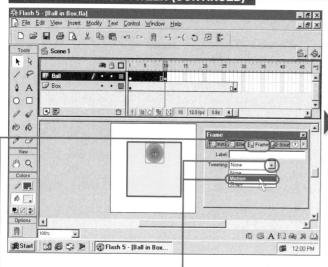

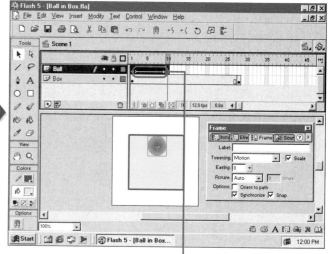

CREATE TWEEN EFFECT

■8 Click the **Frame** tab.

■ Flash displays the Frame tab and its related options.

■9 Click ▼ in the **Tweening** box.

■10 Click **Motion**.

■ Flash calculates the in-between changes the symbol must undergo to move from the first keyframe to the next keyframe.

■ Flash adds a motion tween arrow ▭ from the first keyframe in the tween effect to the last keyframe in the tween effect.

170

Can I create a motion tween as I go?

You can start a motion tween without defining the end keyframe in the sequence. To do so, perform the following steps:

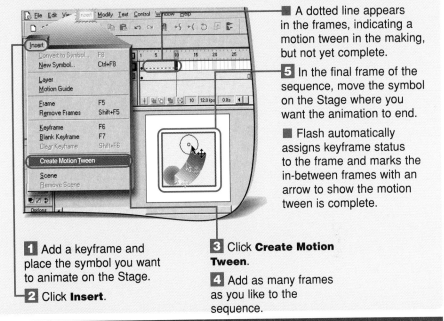

■ A dotted line appears in the frames, indicating a motion tween in the making, but not yet complete.

5 In the final frame of the sequence, move the symbol on the Stage where you want the animation to end.

■ Flash automatically assigns keyframe status to the frame and marks the in-between frames with an arrow to show the motion tween is complete.

1 Add a keyframe and place the symbol you want to animate on the Stage.

2 Click **Insert**.

3 Click **Create Motion Tween**.

4 Add as many frames as you like to the sequence.

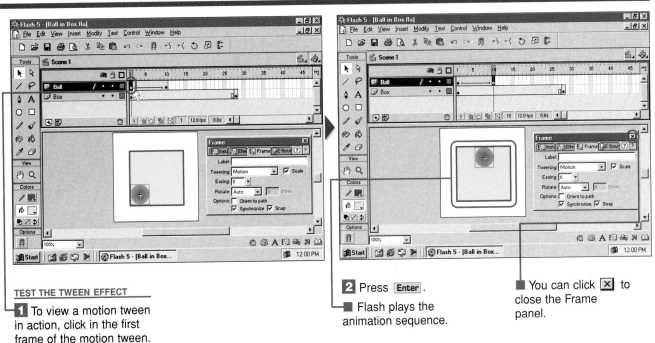

TEST THE TWEEN EFFECT

1 To view a motion tween in action, click in the first frame of the motion tween.

2 Press `Enter`.

■ Flash plays the animation sequence.

■ You can click ☒ to close the Frame panel.

STOP A MOTION TWEEN

If your movie uses a motion tween, the tween is in effect until you tell it to stop. If you add additional frames to the end of the movie, Flash tries to create more motion tween effects, unless you turn off the motion tween property.

For more helpful definitions, see the Appendix "Web Graphic and Animation Terms."

STOP A MOTION TWEEN

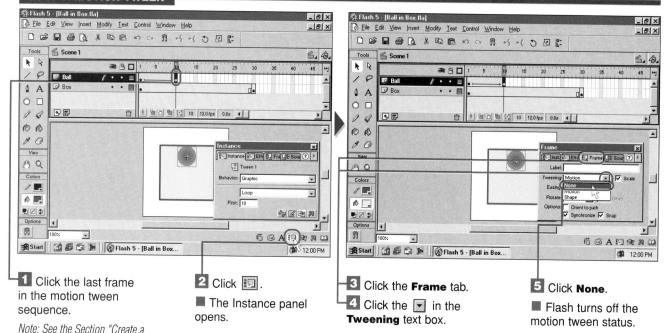

1 Click the last frame in the motion tween sequence.

Note: See the Section "Create a Motion Tween" to find out how to add a tween effect to your movie.

2 Click 🔲.

■ The Instance panel opens.

3 Click the **Frame** tab.

4 Click the ▼ in the **Tweening** text box.

5 Click **None**.

■ Flash turns off the motion tween status.

ADD A KEYFRAME
TO A MOTION TWEEN

You can make changes
to a motion tween by
adding keyframes to
the animation sequence.
For example, you might
want to change the
direction the object
is moving in a motion
tween animation. If
you add a keyframe to
change the direction,
Flash reconfigures the
in-between frames to
reflect changes in the
new keyframe.

See the Section
"Create a Motion
Tween" to find out
how to animate
with the motion
tween feature.

ADD A KEYFRAME TO A MOTION TWEEN

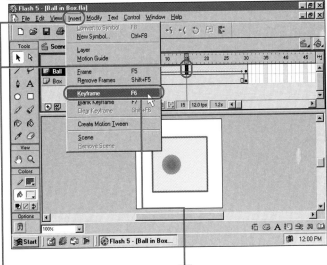

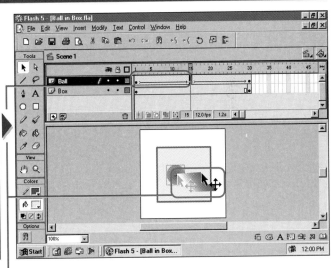

1 Click in the Timeline
where you want to
insert a new keyframe.

2 Click **Insert**.

3 Click **Keyframe**.

■ Flash duplicates the
previous keyframe in the
animation.

*Note: See Chapter 8 to find out
how to work with Flash frames.*

4 Change the symbol
you are animating by
moving it on the Stage or
changing its appearance.

■ Flash recalculates
the in-between frames to
generate the animation.

*Note: Flash cannot change the
symbol in keyframes following
the newly inserted keyframe. You
must manually make changes to
subsequent keyframes.*

ANIMATE BY ROTATING A SYMBOL

You can turn a regular symbol from your Flash Library into an animated object that rotates. This method requires a series of keyframes in which you control how much rotation occurs in each keyframe. By assigning the sequence motion tween status, Flash calculates the in-between frames to create the rotation effect.

See the Section "Create a Motion Tween" to find out more about the motion tween effect.

ANIMATE BY ROTATING A SYMBOL

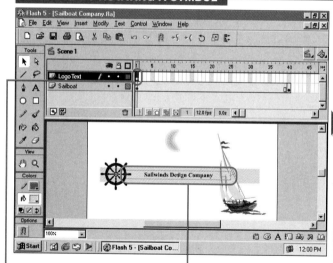

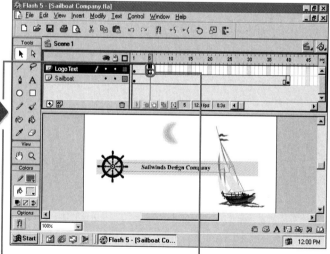

1 Insert a keyframe where you want to start the motion tween in your movie's Timeline.

Note: See Chapter 8 to find out more about adding frames to the Timeline.

2 Place the symbol you want to animate on the Stage.

Note: Placing animations on a separate layer from your movie's background is a good idea. See Chapter 5 to find out more about working with layers.

3 Click the next frame you want to include in the motion tween.

■ For example, you might start the rotation 5 frames later.

4 Insert a keyframe.

Can I rotate an object I draw on the Flash Stage?

The Flash motion tween effect does not work with items you draw on the Stage. It does work with objects that you turn into symbols or that you group together. You can also motion tween text blocks. To find out more about using Flash symbols, see Chapter 6. To find out how to group objects, turn to Chapter 3.

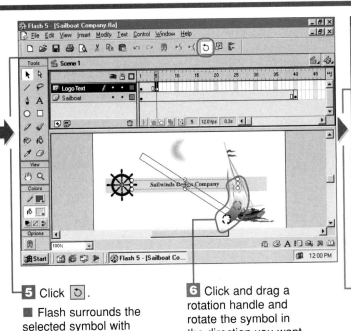

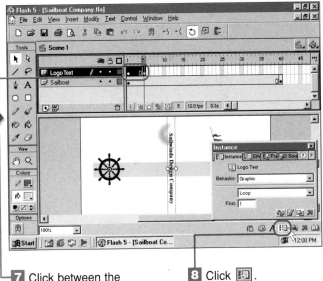

5 Click ⟳ .

■ Flash surrounds the selected symbol with rotation handles.

6 Click and drag a rotation handle and rotate the symbol in the direction you want to go.

7 Click between the two keyframes that make up your motion tween to select the frames.

Note: See Chapter 8 to find out how to select frames.

8 Click ⬚ .

■ Flash opens the Instance panel.

CONTINUED ▶

You can create keyframes at key points of the animation Timeline to rotate your symbol. For example, you might change the rotation's progress by stretching it out over 4 keyframes, rotating the symbol 90 degrees each time. Then add regular frames between the keyframes to lengthen the animation time.

ANIMATE BY ROTATING A SYMBOL (CONTINUED)

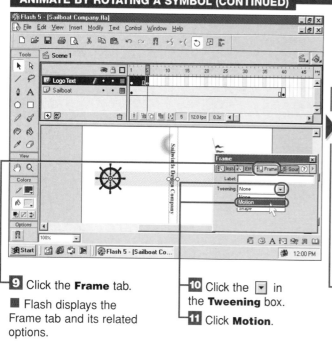

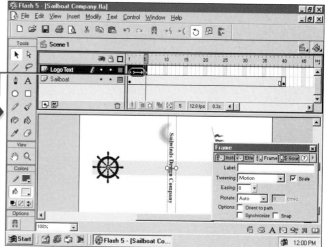

9 Click the **Frame** tab.

■ Flash displays the Frame tab and its related options.

10 Click the ▼ in the **Tweening** box.

11 Click **Motion**.

■ Flash calculates the in-between changes the symbol must undergo between keyframes and Flash adds a motion tween arrow ⟺ to the frames.

**Can I tell Flash to rotate
the symbol for me?**

Flash can help you with
the rotation process if
you prefer not to do it
manually. Follow these
steps:

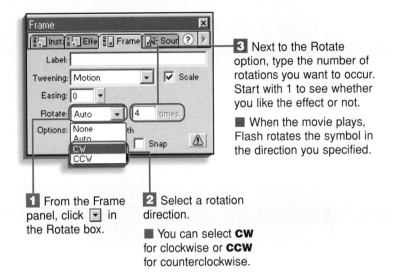

3 Next to the Rotate
option, type the number of
rotations you want to occur.
Start with 1 to see whether
you like the effect or not.

■ When the movie plays,
Flash rotates the symbol in
the direction you specified.

1 From the Frame
panel, click ▼ in
the Rotate box.

2 Select a rotation
direction.

■ You can select **CW**
for clockwise or **CCW**
for counterclockwise.

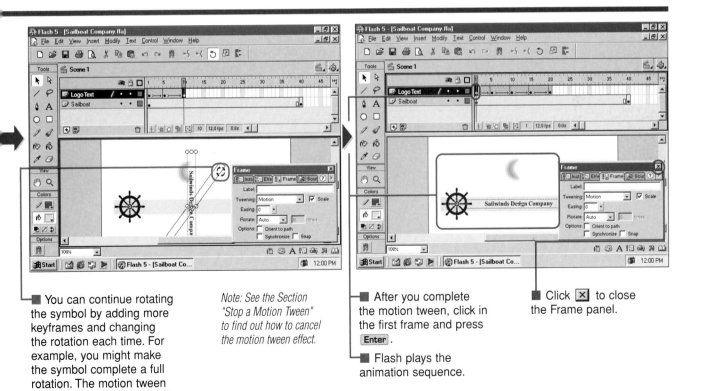

■ You can continue rotating
the symbol by adding more
keyframes and changing
the rotation each time. For
example, you might make
the symbol complete a full
rotation. The motion tween
is in effect until you cancel it.

*Note: See the Section
"Stop a Motion Tween"
to find out how to cancel
the motion tween effect.*

■ After you complete
the motion tween, click in
the first frame and press
Enter .

■ Flash plays the
animation sequence.

■ Click ⊠ to close
the Frame panel.

ANIMATE BY SPINNING A SYMBOL

You can create an animation effect that makes a symbol appear to spin. Using two identical keyframes, you can tell Flash to rotate the symbol in the in-between frames to create a spinning effect. Because a spin is a 360 degree rotation, you do not have to alter the keyframe content.

See the Section "Create a Motion Tween" to find out more about the motion tween effect.

ANIMATE BY SPINNING A SYMBOL

CREATE THE TWEEN EFFECT

1 Insert a keyframe where you want to start the motion tween in your movie's Timeline.

Note: See Chapter 8 to learn more about adding frames to the Timeline.

2 Place the symbol you want to animate on the Stage.

Note: Placing animations on a separate layer from your movie's background is a good idea. See Chapter 5 to learn more about working with layers.

3 Click the end frame in which you want to conclude the motion tween.

■ For example, you might complete the spin effect 20 frames later.

4 Insert a keyframe.

Note: See Chapter 8 to learn more about adding frames to the Timeline.

Does it matter which direction the symbol spins?

You can set a rotation direction in the Frame panel, or you can tell Flash to set a direction for you. If you let Flash pick a direction, it chooses the rotation that involves the least amount of change from frame to frame. This method creates a smoother animation sequence. To instruct Flash to handle the rotation, leave the Auto option selected.

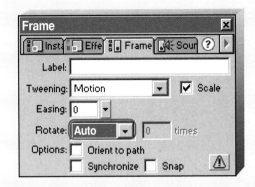

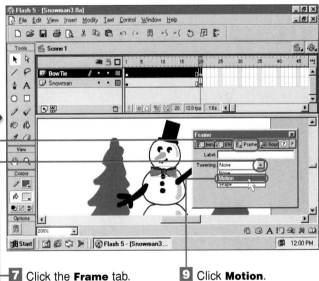

5 Click between the two keyframes that make up your motion tween to select the frames.

Note: See Chapter 8 to learn how to select frames.

6 Click 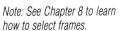.

■ Flash opens the Instance panel.

7 Click the **Frame** tab.

■ Flash displays the Frame tab and its related options.

8 Click ▼ in the **Tweening** box.

9 Click **Motion**.

■ Flash adds a motion tween arrow ➡ to the selected frames.

CONTINUED

You can use the Rotation controls to spin items such as corporate logos or text blocks. By assigning a motion tween effect, Flash takes care of the hard work of differing each frame in the sequence for you. You can specify how many times the symbol rotates in-between the two keyframes, and exactly which direction it goes.

ANIMATE BY SPINNING A SYMBOL (CONTINUED)

SELECT A SPIN ROTATION

10 Click the ▼ in the **Rotate** box.

11 Click a rotation direction for the spin.

■ Choose **CW** to spin the symbol clockwise.

■ Choose **CCW** to spin the symbol counterclockwise.

12 Next to the Rotate option, type the number of times you want the rotation to occur.

■ Flash calculates the in-between changes the symbol must undergo to move from the first keyframe to the next keyframe.

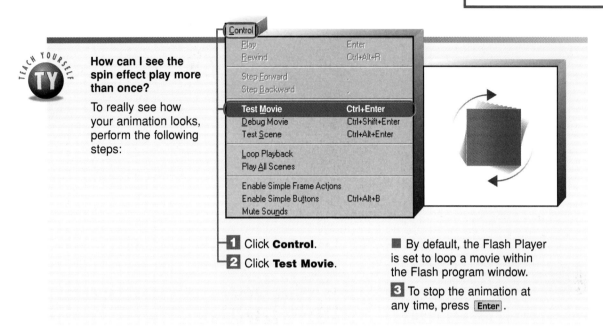

How can I see the spin effect play more than once?

To really see how your animation looks, perform the following steps:

1 Click **Control**.

2 Click **Test Movie**.

■ By default, the Flash Player is set to loop a movie within the Flash program window.

3 To stop the animation at any time, press Enter.

VIEW THE SPIN

1 To view a motion tween in action, click in the first frame of the motion tween.

2 Press Enter.

■ Flash plays the animation sequence.

■ You can click ✕ to close the Frame panel.

ANIMATE BY CHANGING SYMBOL SIZE

You can use the motion tween technique to create an animation that changes size. For example, you can make a symbol seem to grow or shrink in size. You define two keyframes, one of which includes the symbol scaled to a new size. With the motion tween effect applied, Flash fills in all the in-between frames to create the illusion of growth or shrinkage.

See the Section "Create a Motion Tween" to find out more about the motion tween effect.

ANIMATE BY CHANGING SYMBOL SIZE

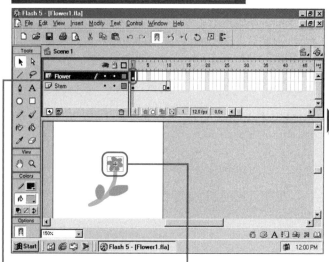

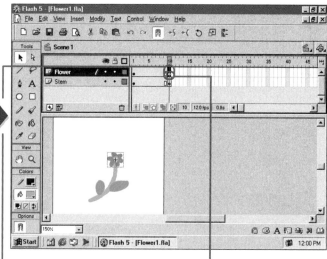

CREATE THE TWEEN EFFECT

1 Insert a keyframe where you want to start the motion tween in your movie's Timeline.

Note: See Chapter 8 to learn more about adding frames.

2 Place the symbol you want to animate on the Stage.

Note: Placing animations on a separate layer from your movie's background is a good idea. See Chapter 5 to learn more about layers.

3 Click the end frame in which you want to conclude the motion tween.

■ In this example, the flower seems to grow in the course of 10 or 20 frames.

4 Insert a keyframe.

Note: See Chapter 8 to learn more about adding frames to the Timeline.

How can I tell what size changes Flash makes in my motion tween?

You can use the onion skin tool to see the changes in the frames that surround the current frame. To turn on the feature, click at the bottom of the Timeline. Once on, you can drag the onion skin markers left or right to include other frames in the view. See Chapter 8 to learn more about how to use this feature when animating.

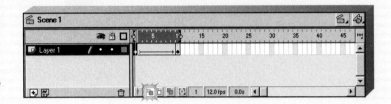

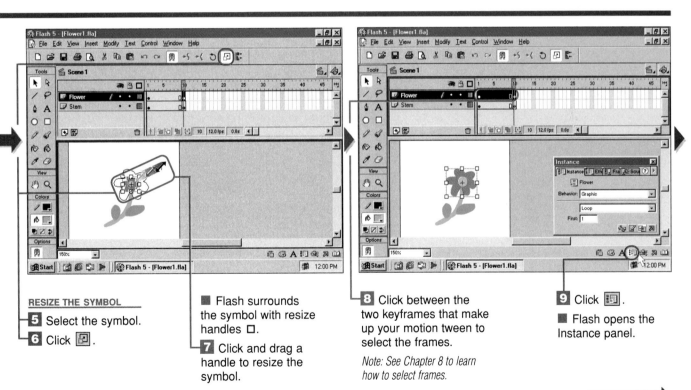

RESIZE THE SYMBOL

■5 Select the symbol.

■6 Click.

■ Flash surrounds the symbol with resize handles □.

■7 Click and drag a handle to resize the symbol.

■8 Click between the two keyframes that make up your motion tween to select the frames.

Note: See Chapter 8 to learn how to select frames.

■9 Click.

■ Flash opens the Instance panel.

CONTINUED

ANIMATE BY CHANGING SYMBOL SIZE

You can use the Scale option in the Frame panel to make symbols seem to grow or shrink. The speed at which this occurs depends on how many frames you insert between the two defining keyframes. You can experiment with the number of regular frames to create just the right animation speed.

See Chapter 8 to learn more about adding frames to the Timeline.

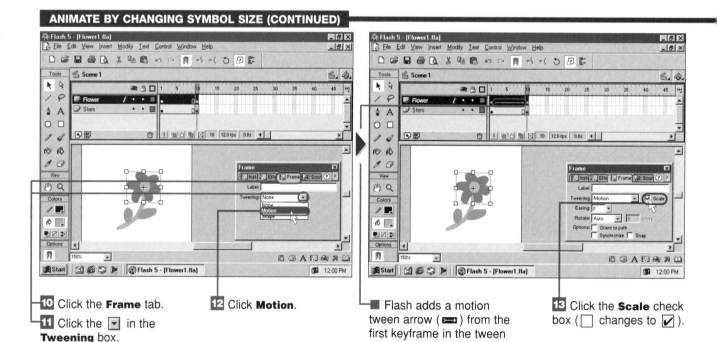

■ 10 Click the **Frame** tab.

■ 11 Click the ▾ in the **Tweening** box.

■ 12 Click **Motion**.

■ Flash adds a motion tween arrow (▬▶) from the first keyframe in the tween effect to the last keyframe in the tween effect.

■ 13 Click the **Scale** check box (☐ changes to ☑).

**My symbol does not grow or
shrink very much. Why not?**

For a maximum tween effect,
you need to make the final symbol
in the tween sequence much
smaller or larger than the symbol
shown in the first keyframe. You
should also allow plenty of regular
keyframes in-between the two
anchor keyframes. See Chapter 8
to learn more about adding frames
to the Timeline.

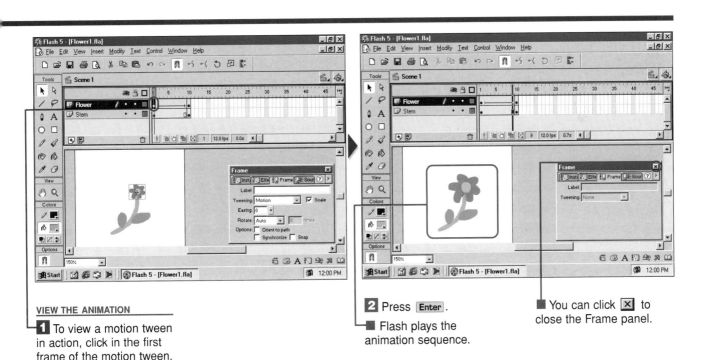

VIEW THE ANIMATION

1 To view a motion tween
in action, click in the first
frame of the motion tween.

2 Press Enter.

■ Flash plays the
animation sequence.

■ You can click ☒ to
close the Frame panel.

ANIMATE SYMBOLS ALONG A PATH

You can make a symbol follow a path in your Flash movie. Using the Flash motion tween technique and a motion guide layer, you define points A and B in the sequence, draw a line that tells Flash exactly where you want the symbol to move, and Flash calculates all the in-between frames for you. The motion guide layer is not visible when you export the movie.

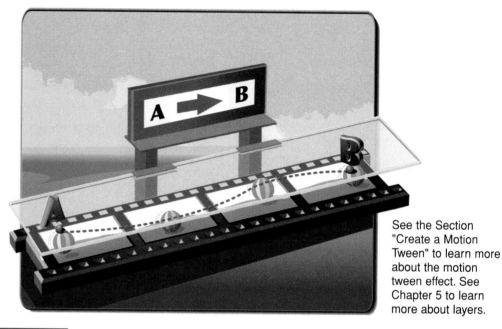

See the Section "Create a Motion Tween" to learn more about the motion tween effect. See Chapter 5 to learn more about layers.

ANIMATE SYMBOLS ALONG A PATH

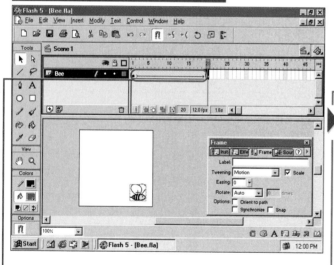

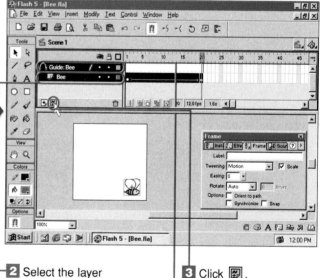

CREATE AND SELECT A TWEEN LAYER

1 Create a motion tween animation.

Note: See the Section "Create a Motion Tween" to learn how to make a motion tween animation sequence.

2 Select the layer containing the motion tween.

Note: See Chapter 5 to learn more about working with layers.

3 Click 📰.

■ Flash adds a motion guide layer directly above the layer containing the motion tween.

Does it matter what line color or thickness I use to draw the motion path?

You can use any line color or attributes you like for the motion path. You can also use the Paint Brush tool to draw the motion path. To make the line easy to see, consider using a thicker line style in a bright color. Be sure to set the line attributes before you start drawing the motion path. Click 🖿, click the **Stroke** tab, and adjust the settings to your liking. See Chapter 2 to learn more about changing line attributes.

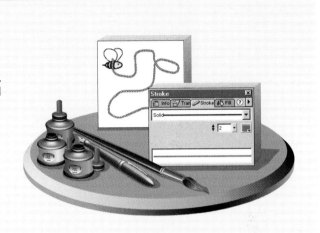

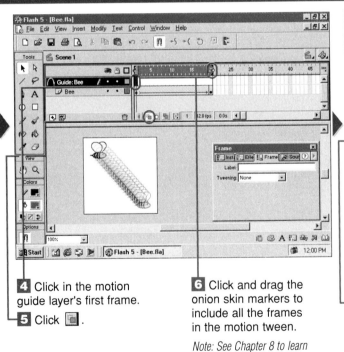

4 Click in the motion guide layer's first frame.

5 Click 🖿.

6 Click and drag the onion skin markers to include all the frames in the motion tween.

Note: See Chapter 8 to learn more about the onion-skinning feature.

DRAW THE MOTION PATH

7 Click ✏.

Note: See Chapter 2 to learn how to draw with the Pencil tool.

8 Draw a path from the center of the first motion tween symbol to the center of the last motion tween symbol.

Note: If you do not draw your path from center to center, the symbol cannot follow the motion path.

CONTINUED

ANIMATE SYMBOLS ALONG A PATH

You can make your motion tween follow any type of path, whether it is extremely curvy, or it loops back on itself, or even if it falls out of the movie area's boundaries.

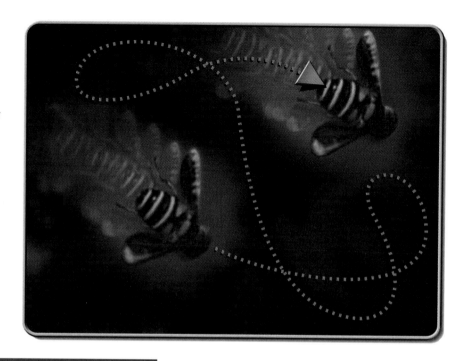

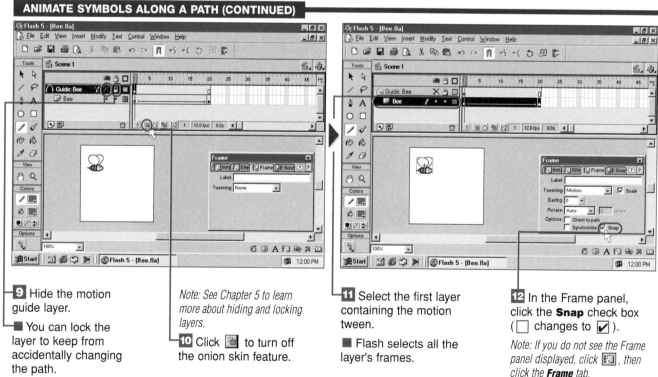

9 Hide the motion guide layer.

■ You can lock the layer to keep from accidentally changing the path.

Note: See Chapter 5 to learn more about hiding and locking layers.

10 Click 🖿 to turn off the onion skin feature.

11 Select the first layer containing the motion tween.

■ Flash selects all the layer's frames.

12 In the Frame panel, click the **Snap** check box (☐ changes to ☑).

*Note: If you do not see the Frame panel displayed, click 🖼, then click the **Frame** tab.*

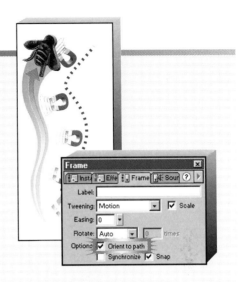

What does the Orient to path option do?

To make your symbol orient itself to the motion path you have drawn, click the **Orient to path** check box. The Orient to path option orients the symbol to the path, regardless of which direction it goes. Sometimes, the effect makes the symbol's movement seem unnatural. To remedy the situation, you can insert extra keyframes in the animation sequence and rotate the symbol to where you want it on the path. Flash recalculates the in-between frames for you. To learn more about rotating objects, see Chapter 3. To learn how to rotate animated symbols, see the Section "Animate by Rotating a Symbol."

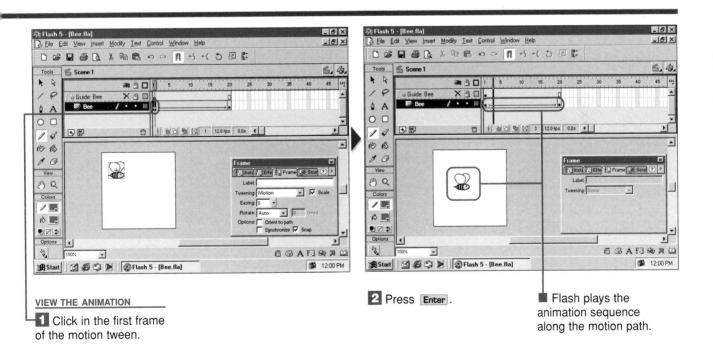

VIEW THE ANIMATION

1 Click in the first frame of the motion tween.

2 Press Enter.

■ Flash plays the animation sequence along the motion path.

SET TWEEN SPEED

You can control a tweened animation's speed by using the Flash Ease control. Found in the Frame panel, the Ease control enables you to speed up or slow down the tween effect.

See the Section "Create a Motion Tween" to learn more about the motion tween effect.

SET TWEEN SPEED

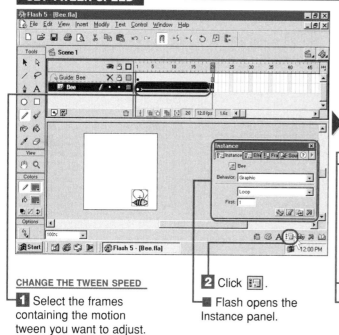

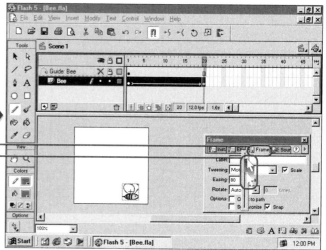

CHANGE THE TWEEN SPEED

1 Select the frames containing the motion tween you want to adjust.

Note: See Chapter 8 to learn more about selecting frames.

2 Click 🔲.

◼ Flash opens the Instance panel.

3 Click the **Frame** tab.

4 Click and drag the Easing slider to a new setting.

◼ Drag the slider up to accelerate the tween speed.

◼ Drag the slider down to decelerate the tween speed.

◼ A zero value indicates a constant rate of speed.

Does tween speed affect fps?

Tweening distributes the animation evenly between the two keyframes. When you adjust the Ease control to a setting other than the default 0, it merely accelerates or decelerates the beginning or end of the tween. It does not affect the movie's frames per second rate.

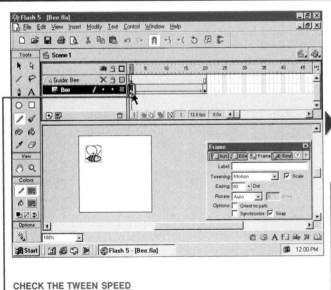

CHECK THE TWEEN SPEED

1 To check the motion tween speed, click in the first frame of the motion tween.

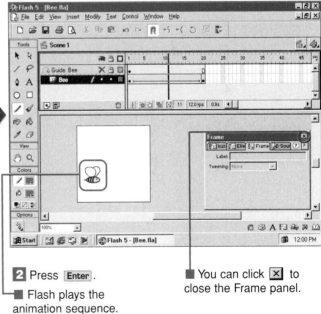

2 Press Enter.

■ Flash plays the animation sequence.

■ You can click ✕ to close the Frame panel.

CREATE A SHAPE TWEEN

You can create a shape tween to morph objects you draw on the Stage. For example, you might morph a circle shape into an oval. Shape tweening does not require the use of symbols or groups. You can animate any object you draw with the Drawing tools with the shape tween effect.

See the Section "Create a Motion Tween" to learn more about the motion tween effect.

CREATE A SHAPE TWEEN

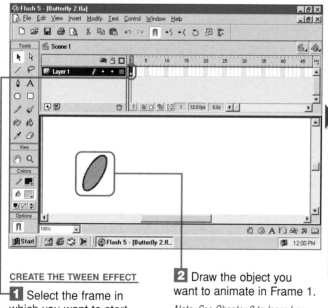

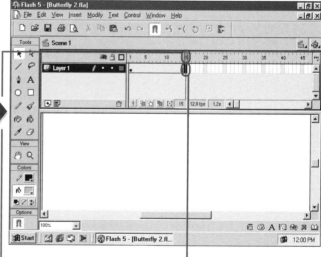

CREATE THE TWEEN EFFECT

1 Select the frame in which you want to start a shape tween.

2 Draw the object you want to animate in Frame 1.

Note: See Chapter 2 to learn how to use the Flash Drawing tools.

3 Click the frame in which you want to end the shape tween effect.

4 Insert a blank keyframe.

Note: See Chapter 8 to learn how to use Flash frames.

How is a shape tween different from a motion tween?

With a motion tween, you can only animate symbols, grouped objects, or text blocks. With a shape tween, you can animate any object you draw on the Stage. You do not have to save it as a symbol first, or group it in order for Flash to create in-between frames. You cannot shape tween a symbol or group. While a motion tween is good for moving objects from one point to another, a shape tween is the tool to use when you want to morph the object into another object entirely.

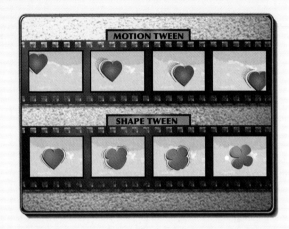

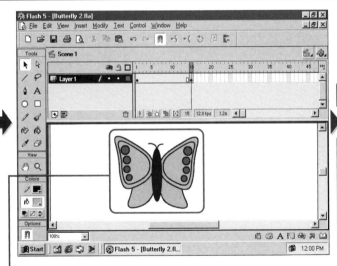

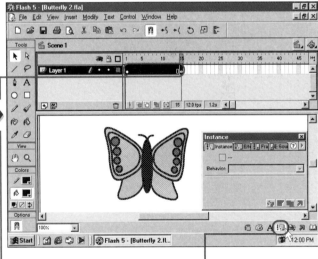

5 Draw the shape into which you want your image to morph, such as a variation of the first frame's shape, or an entirely different shape.

6 Click between the two keyframes that make up your motion tween to select the frames that comprise the shape tween.

Note: See Chapter 8 to learn how to select frames.

7 Click 🖼 .

■ Flash opens the Instance panel.

CONTINUED

CREATE A SHAPE TWEEN

You can use shape tweens to morph between all kinds of objects you draw, including text that you turn into an object. You can use as many shape tweens as you like in an animation, and you can start one right after the other in the Timeline.

CREATE A SHAPE TWEEN (CONTINUED)

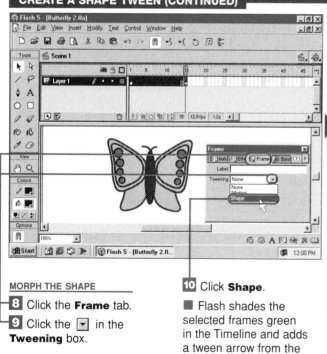

MORPH THE SHAPE

■8 Click the **Frame** tab.

■9 Click the ▼ in the **Tweening** box.

■10 Click **Shape**.

■ Flash shades the selected frames green in the Timeline and adds a tween arrow from the first keyframe to the last.

■11 Click the ▼ in the **Blend** box.

■12 Select a blend type.

■ You can use the **Distributive** blend to smooth out lines in the in-between frames.

■ You can use the **Angular** blend to keep the sharp corners and straight lines that occur during the morph effect.

Can I use a symbol from my movie's Library?

You cannot shape tween symbols, but you can take a symbol and break it apart into objects which the shape tween effect can morph. To turn a symbol into an object, perform the following steps:

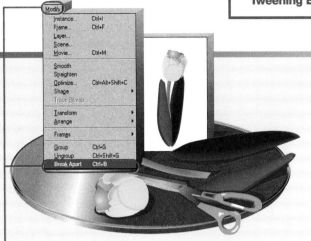

1 Place the symbol on the Stage (see Chapter 6).

2 Click **Modify**.

3 Click **Break Apart**.

■ Depending on how many groups of objects comprise the symbol, you might need to select the command several times to reach the last level of ungrouped objects.

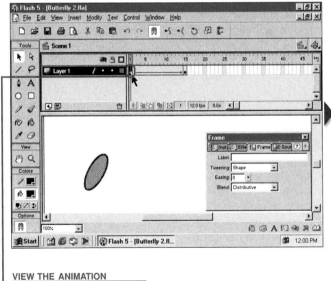

VIEW THE ANIMATION

1 To view a shape tween in action, click in the first frame of the shape tween.

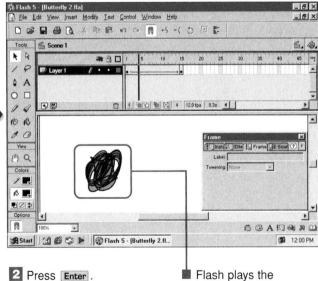

2 Press Enter.

■ Flash plays the animation sequence.

USING SHAPE HINTS

You can help Flash determine how to morph shapes during a shape tween by adding shape hints. A shape hint is a marker that identifies areas on the original shape that match up with areas on the final shape and mark crucial points of change. Shape hints are labeled *a* through *z*, which means you can use up to 26 shape hints in a shape tween.

USE SHAPE HINTS

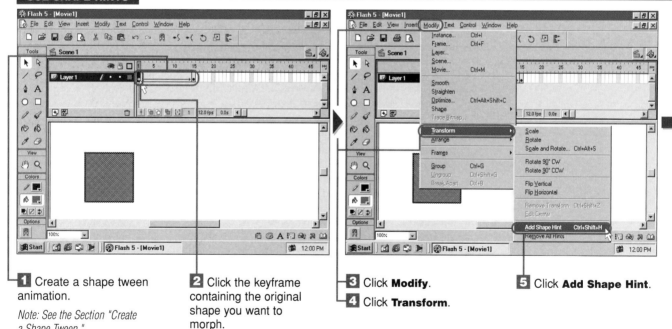

1 Create a shape tween animation.

Note: See the Section "Create a Shape Tween."

2 Click the keyframe containing the original shape you want to morph.

3 Click **Modify**.

4 Click **Transform**.

5 Click **Add Shape Hint**.

What can I do if my shape hints vary their positions between the first keyframe and the last?

Seeing exactly where you are placing shape hints around an object is not always easy. To help you, first make sure you have magnified your view so you can see where the hints are placed. Use the **View** drop-down list at the bottom of the Stage area to set a magnification. Next, turn on the onion skin feature and move the onion skin markers to show all the frames within the shape tween. Click the icon to turn on the outlining feature. See Chapter 8 to learn more about onion skinning.

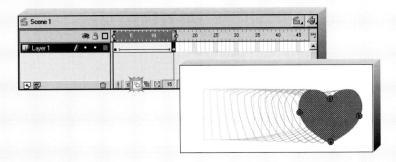

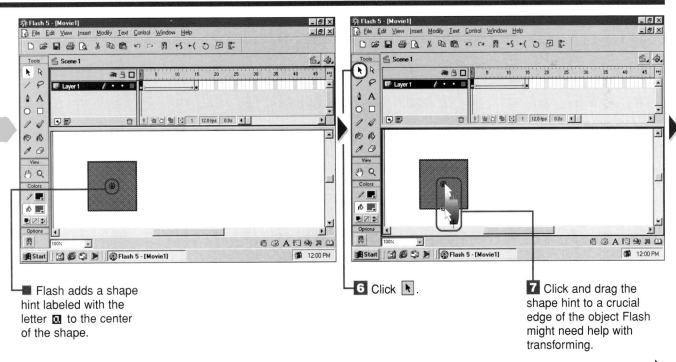

■ Flash adds a shape hint labeled with the letter **a** to the center of the shape.

6 Click the arrow tool.

7 Click and drag the shape hint to a crucial edge of the object Flash might need help with transforming.

CONTINUED

The more shape hints you add to the shape tween, the smoother the morphing transformation will be. Use the onion skin feature to help you see how the shape changes across the animation sequence.

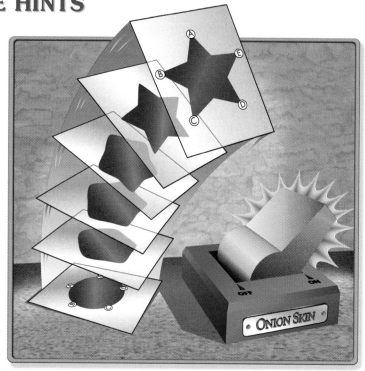

See Chapter 8 to learn more about the onion skin feature.

USE SHAPE HINTS (CONTINUED)

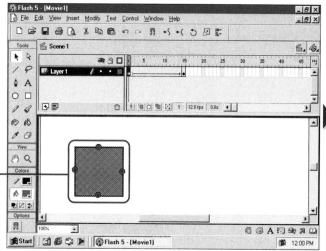

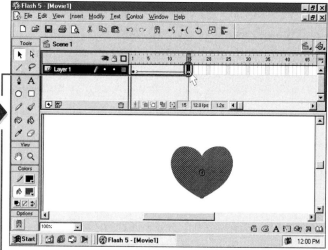

8 Repeat steps **3** through **7** to continue adding shape hints to other areas on the shape that can assist Flash with morphing the final shape design.

Note: You must arrange shape hints around the shape's edge in alphabetical order going clockwise or counterclockwise.

9 Click the last keyframe in the shape tween.

■ In this example, shape hints have been added to the final shape and stacked in the middle of the shape.

How do I remove a shape hint?

To delete a shape hint, click and drag the shape hint completely off the Stage area. To rid the keyframe of all the shape hints:

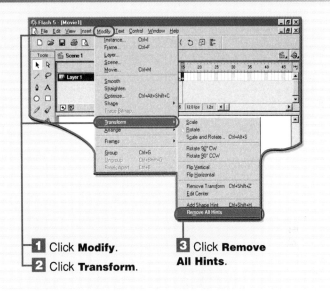

1 Click **Modify**.

2 Click **Transform**.

3 Click **Remove All Hints**.

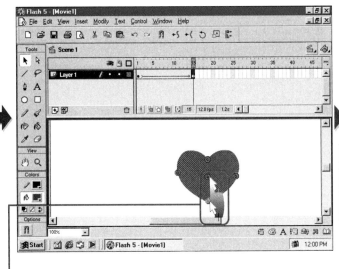

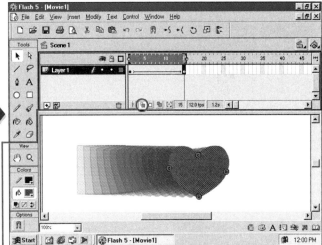

10 Click and drag each shape hint to the correct position around the final shape.

■ You can adjust the shape hints in the final frame, as needed.

■ Click 🔲 to turn on the onion skin feature to see how the in-between frames morph the shape as directed by the shape hints.

■ Play the movie to see the animation on the Stage.

Note: See the Section "Create a Shape Tween" to learn how to view the animation on the Stage.

USING REVERSE FRAMES

You can save some animating time by reusing frames in your movie. For example, if you create a motion tween that makes a symbol grow in size, you can reverse the frame sequence to create the opposite effect in the second half of the animation.

USING REVERSE FRAMES

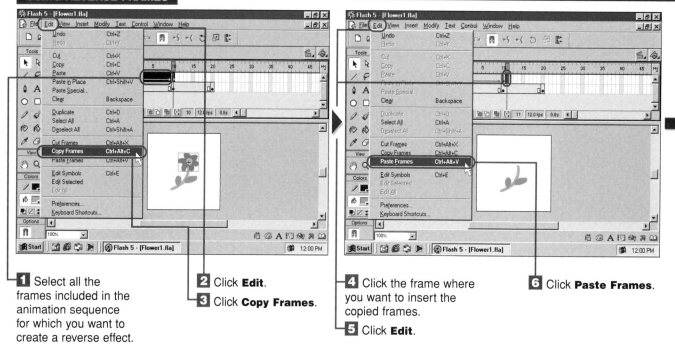

1 Select all the frames included in the animation sequence for which you want to create a reverse effect.

2 Click **Edit**.

3 Click **Copy Frames**.

4 Click the frame where you want to insert the copied frames.

5 Click **Edit**.

6 Click **Paste Frames**.

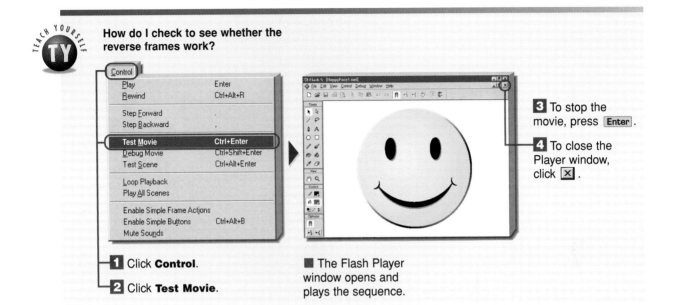

How do I check to see whether the
reverse frames work?

Control
Play   Enter
Rewind   Ctrl+Alt+R

Step Forward   .
Step Backward   ,

Test Movie   Ctrl+Enter
Debug Movie   Ctrl+Shift+Enter
Test Scene   Ctrl+Alt+Enter

Loop Playback
Play All Scenes

Enable Simple Frame Actions
Enable Simple Buttons   Ctrl+Alt+B
Mute Sounds

3 To stop the
movie, press **Enter**.

4 To close the
Player window,
click **×**.

1 Click **Control**.

2 Click **Test Movie**.

■ The Flash Player
window opens and
plays the sequence.

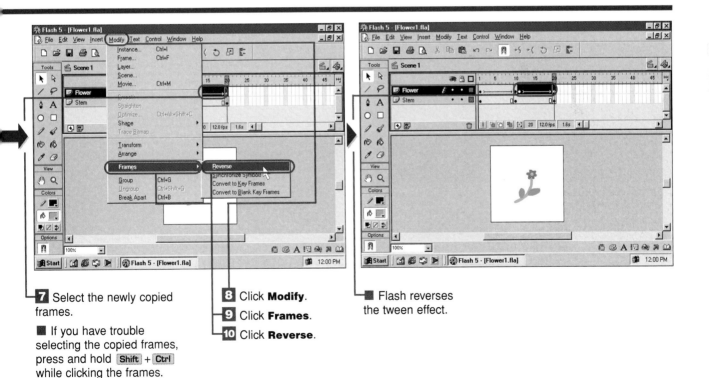

7 Select the newly copied
frames.

■ If you have trouble
selecting the copied frames,
press and hold **Shift** + **Ctrl**
while clicking the frames.

8 Click **Modify**.

9 Click **Frames**.

10 Click **Reverse**.

■ Flash reverses
the tween effect.

SAVE AN ANIMATION AS A MOVIE CLIP

You can save an animation sequence as a movie clip that you can use again elsewhere in your movie.

SAVE AN ANIMATION AS A MOVIE CLIP

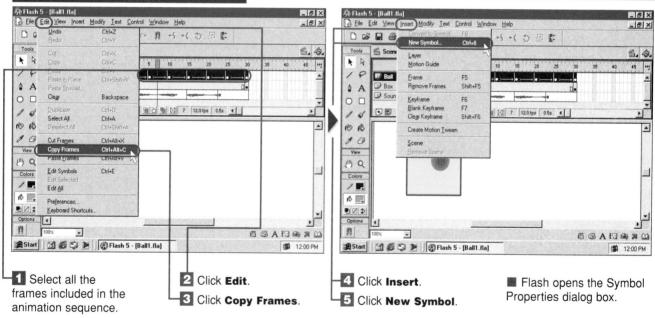

1 Select all the frames included in the animation sequence.

2 Click **Edit**.

3 Click **Copy Frames**.

4 Click **Insert**.

5 Click **New Symbol**.

■ Flash opens the Symbol Properties dialog box.

How do I place a movie clip in my movie?

You can place movie clips into your project just as you place any other item saved in the Flash Library:

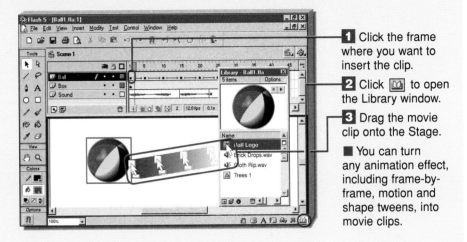

1 Click the frame where you want to insert the clip.

2 Click 🔲 to open the Library window.

3 Drag the movie clip onto the Stage.

■ You can turn any animation effect, including frame-by-frame, motion and shape tweens, into movie clips.

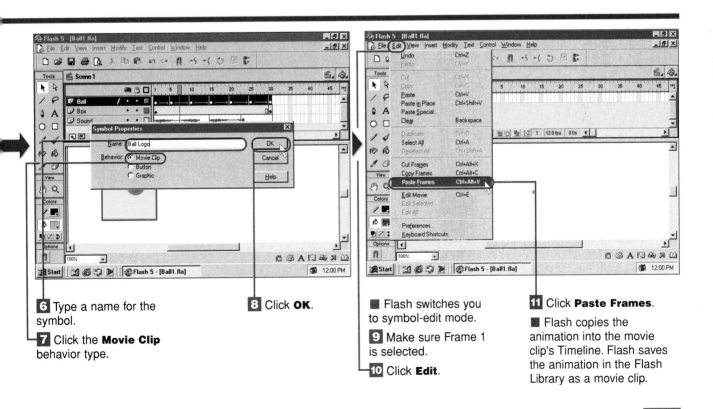

6 Type a name for the symbol.

7 Click the **Movie Clip** behavior type.

8 Click **OK**.

■ Flash switches you to symbol-edit mode.

9 Make sure Frame 1 is selected.

10 Click **Edit**.

11 Click **Paste Frames**.

■ Flash copies the animation into the movie clip's Timeline. Flash saves the animation in the Flash Library as a movie clip.

Shape-Changing

Animated

CHAPTER 10

Creating
Interactive Buttons

Do you need to create an interactive button for your Flash project? Learn all about buttons and how to create them in Flash.

PLAY MOVIE

Assign Action

FLASH
BUTTONS

UNDERSTANDING FLASH BUTTONS

A popular way to enable users to interact with your Flash movies is through the use of *rollover buttons*. You might create a simple button that changes in appearance when the user rolls the mouse pointer over it, and changes appearance again when the user clicks it. Buttons are commonly employed on Web pages. You can create buttons in Flash that are static or animated.

BUTTONS ARE SYMBOLS

Buttons are a type of Flash symbol that are assigned button *behaviors*. The behaviors are based on what happens when the mouse pointer interacts with the button. You can assign Flash actions to a button that trigger an action such as Get URL or Load Movie.

See Chapter 12 to learn more about assigning Flash actions.

BUTTON FRAMES

When you create a button in Flash, the button comes with its own Timeline and four distinct frames: Up, Over, Down, and Hit. The four frames make up a mini-movie clip of the button's behavior.

UP FRAME

The Up frame is used to display what the inactive button looks like. This is the frame the user sees when the mouse pointer is not hovering over the button. By default, the Up frame has a keyframe added.

OVER FRAME

The Over frame displays what the button looks like when the mouse pointer moves or "rolls" over the button. For example, you might make the button turn bright red or emit a sound when the user pauses the mouse pointer over it, thereby alerting the user that the button is now active.

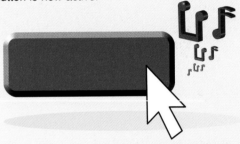

DOWN FRAME

The Down frame displays what the button looks like when a user has clicked it.

HIT FRAME

The Hit frame defines the button area or boundary as a whole. This frame is often the same size and shape as the image in the Over and Down frames. The Hit frame differs from the other button frames in that it is not actually seen by the user.

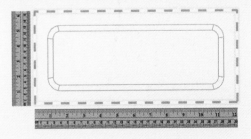

CREATE A BUTTON SYMBOL

When you create a button in Flash, it includes a Timeline with four frames: Up, Over, Down, and Hit. You must assign an image or action to each of the four button states. A button can be any object or drawing, such as a simple geometric shape the user can easily identify and click.

See the Section "Understanding Flash Buttons" to learn more about button basics.

CREATE A BUTTON SYMBOL

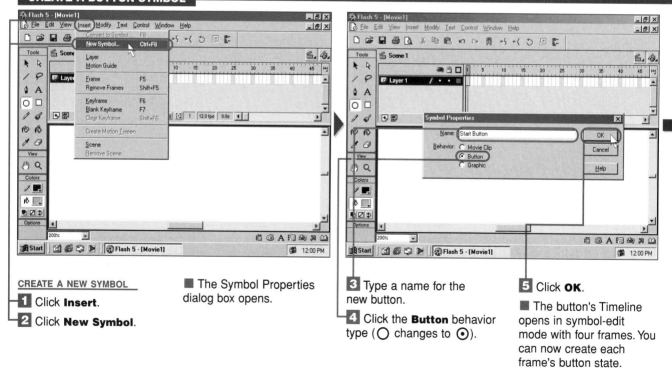

CREATE A NEW SYMBOL

1 Click **Insert**.

2 Click **New Symbol**.

■ The Symbol Properties dialog box opens.

3 Type a name for the new button.

4 Click the **Button** behavior type (○ changes to ⊙).

5 Click **OK**.

■ The button's Timeline opens in symbol-edit mode with four frames. You can now create each frame's button state.

TEACH YOURSELF

Does Flash have premade buttons I can use?

Flash has two common libraries, one with buttons, the other with sounds. To display the button library:

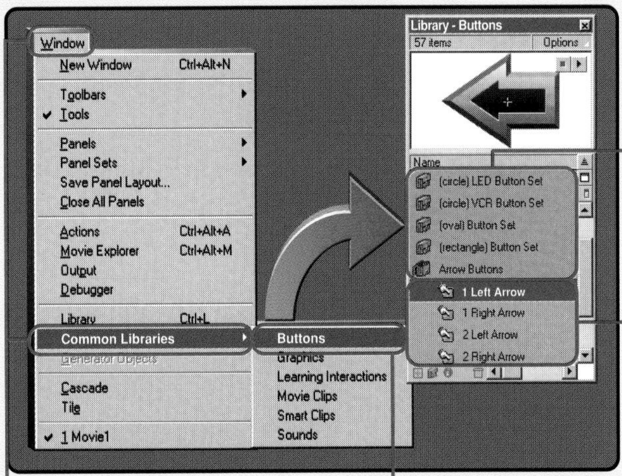

1 Click **Window**.

2 Click **Common Libraries**.

3 Click **Buttons**.

■ The Buttons Library window appears.

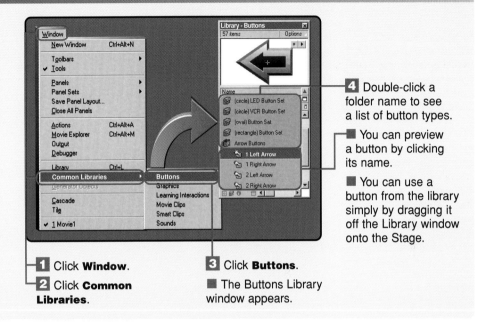

4 Double-click a folder name to see a list of button types.

■ You can preview a button by clicking its name.

■ You can use a button from the library simply by dragging it off the Library window onto the Stage.

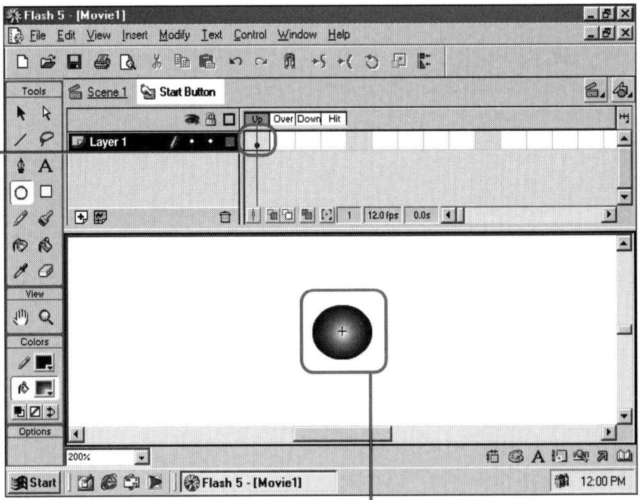

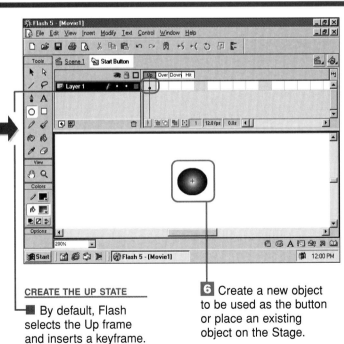

CREATE THE UP STATE

■ By default, Flash selects the Up frame and inserts a keyframe.

6 Create a new object to be used as the button or place an existing object on the Stage.

Note: See Chapter 2 to learn more about using the Flash drawing tools.

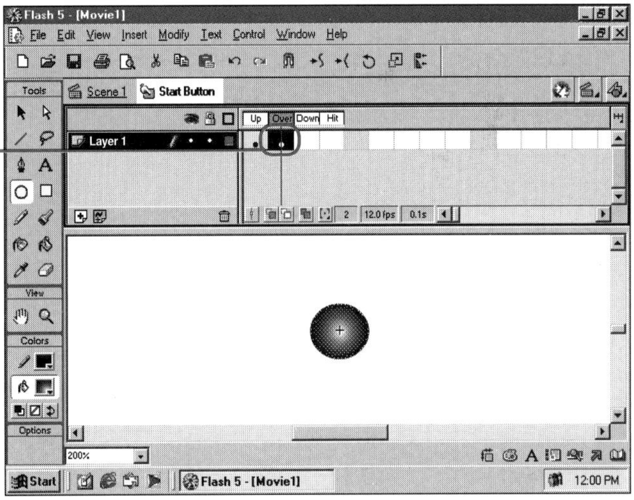

CREATE THE OVER STATE

7 Click the **Over** frame.

8 Press F6 to insert a keyframe into the frame.

Note: See Chapter 8 to learn more about frames.

CONTINUED

You can draw a new object with the Flash drawing tools, or you can use an imported graphic as a button. Simple geometric shapes always make good buttons. If you duplicate the same object in each button frame, you can make minor changes to make the button differ in each state. For example, you can change the color, scale, or shape for each keyframe.

See Chapter 2 to learn more about drawing with the Flash tools or see Chapter 7 to learn more about importing graphics.

CREATE A BUTTON SYMBOL (CONTINUED)

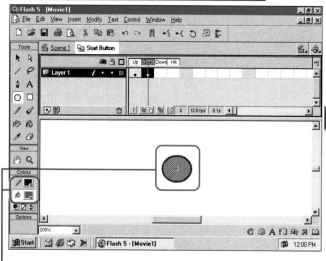

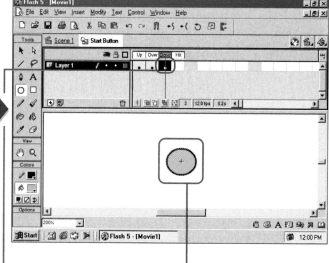

■ Flash duplicates the object you placed in the Up keyframe.

■ You can make minor changes to the object.

■ In this example, the object's fill color changes to alert the user that the button is active.

Note: See Chapter 3 to learn more about editing objects.

CREATE THE DOWN STATE

9 Click the **Down** frame.

10 Press F6 to insert a keyframe into the frame.

■ Flash duplicates the object you placed in the Over keyframe.

■ You can edit the object, if desired. For example, you might add a sound to the frame, or a short animation.

How do I preview a button?

In symbol-edit mode, click the button's Up frame, then press **Enter**. Watch the Stage as Flash plays through the four button frames. Any changes made to frames appear during playback.

You can preview the button in movie-edit mode. Press **Ctrl** + **E** (Windows) or **⌘** + **E** (Mac) to return to movie-edit mode. Press **Ctrl** + **Alt** + **B** to activate the button on the Stage and move the mouse pointer over the button and click it to see the rollover capabilities.

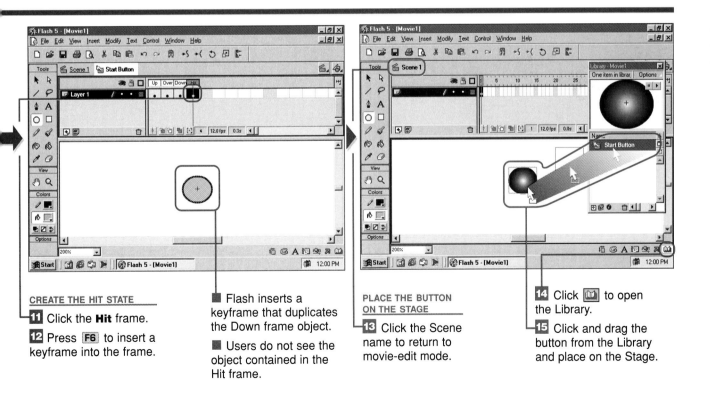

CREATE THE HIT STATE

11 Click the **Hit** frame.

12 Press **F6** to insert a keyframe into the frame.

■ Flash inserts a keyframe that duplicates the Down frame object.

■ Users do not see the object contained in the Hit frame.

PLACE THE BUTTON ON THE STAGE

13 Click the Scene name to return to movie-edit mode.

14 Click 🗔 to open the Library.

15 Click and drag the button from the Library and place on the Stage.

CREATE SHAPE-CHANGING BUTTONS

While a simple geometric shape makes a good button, you might want something a bit more exciting. You can change the object used for each button state. For example, an ordinary circle shape button might become a flower when the user rolls over it with the mouse.

See the Section "Create a Button Symbol" to learn more about creating buttons.

CREATE SHAPE-CHANGING BUTTONS

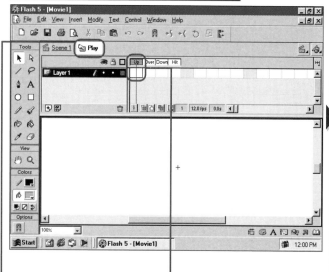

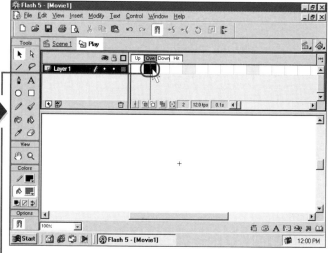

CREATE A NEW BUTTON

1 Create a new button symbol and Flash immediately switches you to symbol-edit mode and the button's name appears at the top of the Timeline.

Note: See the Section "Create a Button Symbol" to learn how to create a new symbol.

■ Flash selects the Up frame by default when you switch to symbol-edit mode.

2 Click the **Over** frame.

How do I view a newly created button in movie-edit mode?

You must create buttons in symbol-edit mode. When you finish, you do not see the button symbol unless you place an instance of the symbol onto the Flash Stage. To do so:

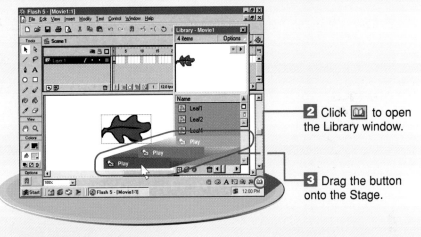

2 Click 📖 to open the Library window.

3 Drag the button onto the Stage.

1 Press Ctrl + E (Windows) or ⌘ + E (Mac) to return to movie-edit mode.

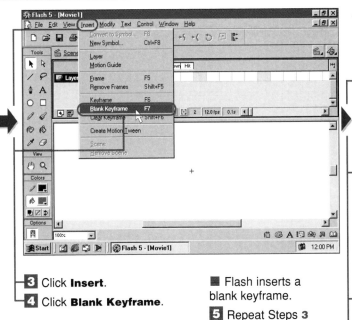

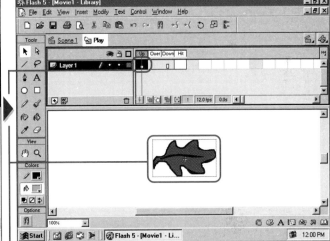

3 Click **Insert**.

4 Click **Blank Keyframe**.

■ Flash inserts a blank keyframe.

5 Repeat Steps **3** and **4** to add blank keyframes to the Down and Hit frames.

CREATE THE UP STATE

6 Click the **Up** frame to select it.

7 Create a new object or place an existing object on the Stage to be used as the inactive button state.

Note: See Chapter 2 to learn more about using the Flash drawing tools or see Chapter 6 to learn how to use symbols and instances.

CONTINUED ▶

CREATE SHAPE-CHANGING BUTTONS

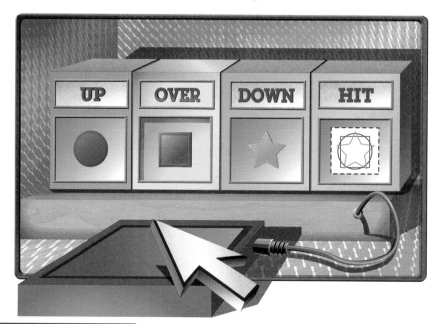

If a button's image stays the same for all four frames in the button Timeline, users cannot distinguish between its active and inactive states. Changing the button's image for each state gives users some idea of the button's status. They can see a difference when the mouse pointer hovers over a live button or when they click the button.

CREATE SHAPE-CHANGING BUTTONS (CONTINUED)

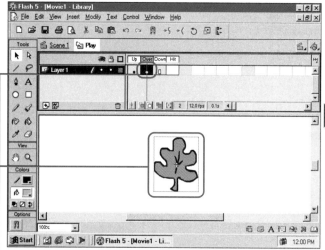

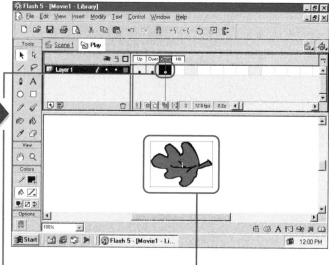

CREATE THE OVER STATE

8 Click the **Over** frame to select it.

9 Create a new object or place an existing object on the Stage to be used as the active button state. The object must differ from the object placed in the Up frame.

Note: See Chapter 2 to learn more about using the Flash drawing tools or see Chapter 6 to learn how to use symbols and instances.

CREATE THE DOWN STATE

10 Click the **Down** frame to select it.

11 Create another new object or place an existing object on the Stage. Make this object differ from the other two objects used in the previous frames.

Why do I need to draw a shape in the Hit frame?

The Hit frame defines the active area of the button, so it needs to be big enough to encompass the largest object in the other button frames. If you are having trouble guessing how large of an area to define, click 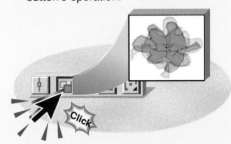 to see outlines of the shapes on all the other frames. Click 📋 again to turn the feature off. A user can click anywhere in the active button area, called the "hot" area, to activate the button. If the area is not defined properly, a user may click a portion of the button and not be able to interact with the button. Even though anything you draw in the Hit state is invisible to the user, the Hit frame's contents are essential to the button's operation.

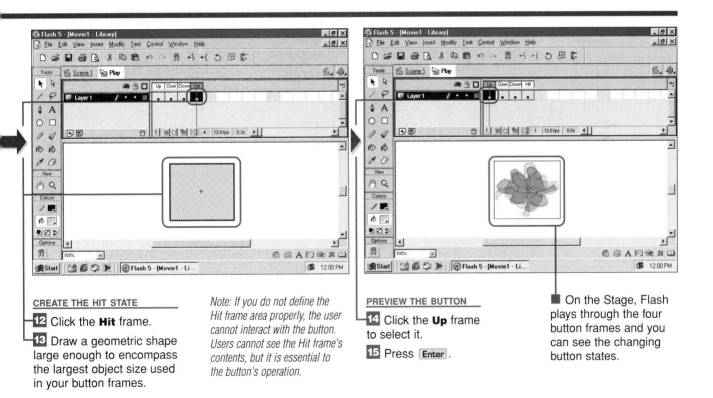

CREATE THE HIT STATE

12 Click the **Hit** frame.

13 Draw a geometric shape large enough to encompass the largest object size used in your button frames.

Note: If you do not define the Hit frame area properly, the user cannot interact with the button. Users cannot see the Hit frame's contents, but it is essential to the button's operation.

PREVIEW THE BUTTON

14 Click the **Up** frame to select it.

15 Press [Enter].

■ On the Stage, Flash plays through the four button frames and you can see the changing button states.

CREATE AN ANIMATED BUTTON

You can create impressive animation effects for buttons. For example, you might make a button glow when the mouse pointer hovers over it, or animate the button with a cartoon that includes sound. Flash makes it easy to place movie clips into your button frames.

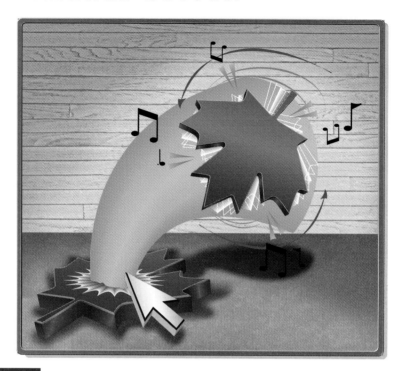

See Chapters 8 and 9 to learn how to create animations and movie clips in Flash.

ADD AN ANIMATION STATE

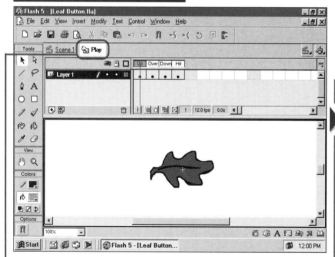

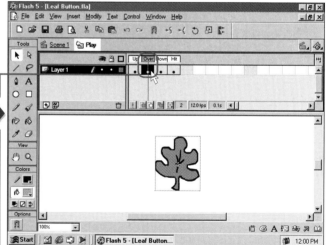

INSERT A MOVIE CLIP

1 Open the button to which you want to add an animation in symbol-edit mode. The button's name appears above the Timeline.

Note: See the section "Create a Button Symbol" to learn how to create a button.

2 Click the frame to which you want to add an animation, such as the Up, Over, or Down frame.

Note: The Hit frame is not seen by the user, so it is not useful to animate the frame.

216

**Can I add sounds
to button frames?**

You can add sound
clips to button frames
the same way you
add movie clips. Try
adding a sound from
Flash's Sound Library:

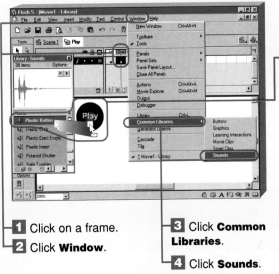

5 In the Sounds Library,
click the sound clip and drag
it out to the button area on
the Stage. A sound wave
appears in the frame.

■ You can press `Enter` to
test the button sequence.
See Chapter 11 to learn
more about adding sounds
to frames.

1 Click on a frame.

2 Click **Window**.

3 Click **Common
Libraries**.

4 Click **Sounds**.

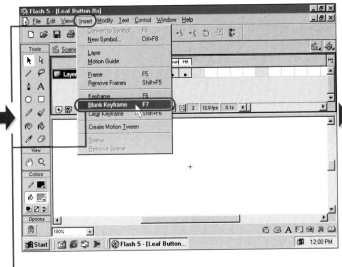

3 Click **Insert**.

4 Click **Blank Keyframe**.

■ Flash inserts a blank
keyframe.

*Note: If the frame already has
an object, press* `Shift` + `F6`
*to clear the existing keyframe
and object.*

5 Click 🖳 to open
the Library window.

6 Click the movie clip
that you want to insert.

*Note: See Chapter 6 to learn
how to use the Flash Library.
See Chapters 8 and 9 to learn
how to create animations and
movie clips in Flash.*

CONTINUED ➡

CREATE AN ANIMATED BUTTON

You can add an animation frame to any button state. For example, you might want the user to see a spinning leaf when the button is inactive, or you might want the leaf object to spin only when the user rolls over the button with the mouse. You might play the animation when the user actually clicks the mouse button. The only frame you do not want to animate is the Hit frame because its contents are not visible to the user.

ADD AN ANIMATION STATE (CONTINUED)

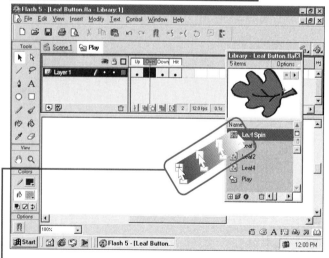

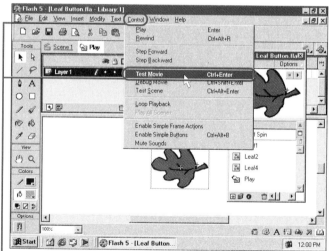

7 Click and drag the movie clip from the Library window and place it on the Stage where the button appears.

TEST THE MOVIE CLIP

1 Click **Control**.

2 Click **Test Movie**.

■ The Flash Player window opens.

How do I preview the animated button in movie-edit mode?

When you press `Ctrl` + `Alt` + `B` to preview a button's rollover capabilities in movie-edit mode, any movie clips you added to button frames do not run. Instead, you see the first frame of the movie clip. To see the fully animated button, click **Control** and then click **Test Movie**.

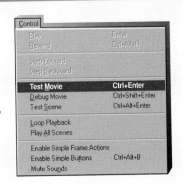

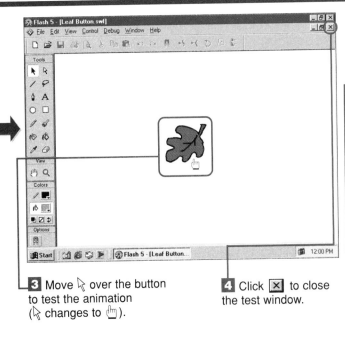

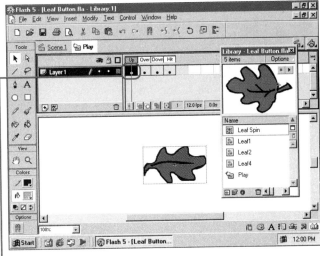

3 Move ⬚ over the button to test the animation (⬚ changes to ⬚).

4 Click ⌧ to close the test window.

TEST ALL BUTTON STATES

1 Click the **Up** frame to select it.

2 Press `Enter`.

■ On the Stage, Flash plays through the four button frames including the animation effect.

Buttons already utilize built-in actions, such as moving immediately to the Down frame when a user clicks the button. You can add other Flash actions to your buttons. For example, you can add a Play action to a button so that a movie clip starts playing when the user clicks the button, or a Stop action that enables the user to stop the movie.

See Chapter 12 to learn more about assigning actions.

ASSIGN A BUTTON ACTION

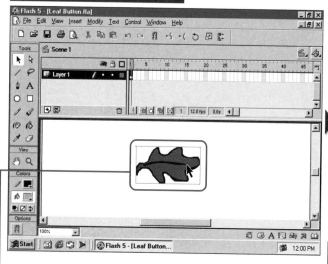

ADD AN ACTION TO A BUTTON

1 Click the button to switch to symbol-edit mode.

Note: See the Section "Create a Button Symbol" to learn how to create a button.

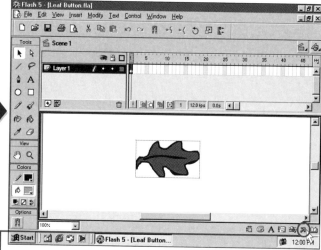

2 Click 🔊.

■ The Object Actions dialog box opens.

Why am I unable to select my button on the Flash Stage?

If Flash displays the button animation sequence when you move your mouse pointer over the button on the Stage, this means that you have left the Enable Simple Buttons feature active. Press `Ctrl` + `Alt` + `B` to disable the feature. Now you can click the button to select it.

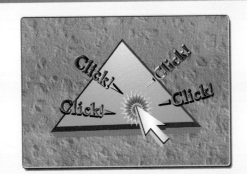

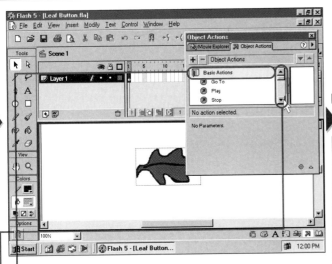

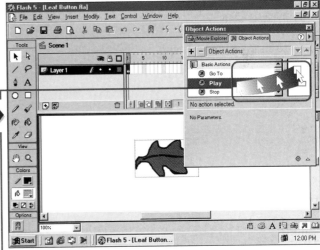

3 From the Object Actions Toolbox list, click **Basic Actions**.

4 Scroll through the list of actions and locate the one you want to apply.

Note: See Chapter 12 to learn how to work with Flash actions.

5 Click and drag the action from the list and drop it in the Actions list box.

■ You can also double-click the action name to immediately place it in the Actions list box.

CONTINUED ▶

ASSIGN BUTTON ACTIONS

Flash actions are simplified programming scripts that instruct Flash how to perform a certain task, such as loading a movie or stopping a sound clip. Using a basic programming language, actions include command strings to spell out exactly what action Flash must perform. You can assign actions to button states. Most button actions require input from the user, such as moving the mouse over the button, or clicking the button. You don't have to know programming in order to use Flash actions.

See Chapter 12 to learn more about Flash actions and how you can put them to use.

See Chapter 12 to learn more about Flash actions and how you can put them to use.

ASSIGN A BUTTON ACTION (CONTINUED)

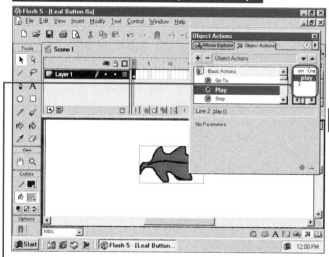

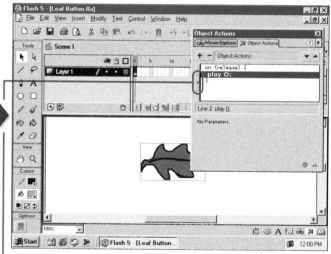

■ Flash adds the necessary action components to the Actions list.

Note: See Chapter 12 to learn how to work with Flash actions.

■ To see the Actions list in full size, you can click ▯.

How do I edit an action assigned to a button?

You can perform edits to your button actions in the Object Actions box. Click the line you want to edit in the Actions list. Depending on the action, a variety of parameters appear at the bottom of the box. You can make changes to those parameters, if necessary. To remove an action component from the Actions list, click the line you want to delete and then click ⊟. To add an action, click ⊞ and then click another action.

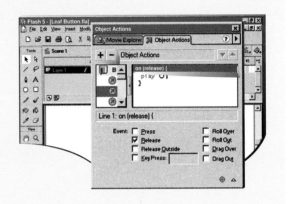

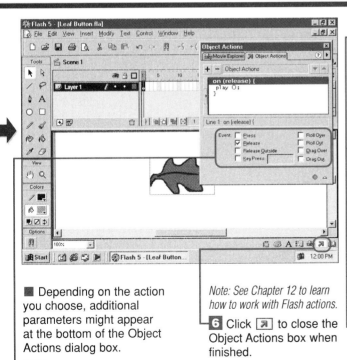

■ Depending on the action you choose, additional parameters might appear at the bottom of the Object Actions dialog box.

■ You can change any parameter settings, as necessary.

Note: See Chapter 12 to learn how to work with Flash actions.

6 Click 🔳 to close the Object Actions box when finished.

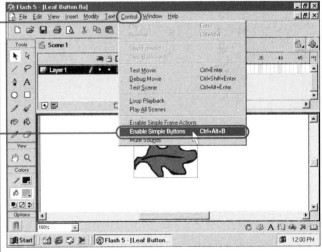

TEST A BUTTON ACTION

1 Click **Control**.

2 Click **Enable Simple Buttons**.

■ You can now move ▷ over the button and click to see the associated action.

CHAPTER 11

Adding Sounds

Does your animation need some sound? In this chapter, you learn how to add sound files to your animation frames and control how they play.

INTRODUCING FLASH SOUNDS

Adding sound to your Flash projects is like adding icing to a cake. With sounds, you can help convey your message and give your movies a polished edge. Sounds can be as simple as a short sound effect clip, or as complex as coordinating background music.

For more definitions concerning sounds, see the Appendix.

DIGITAL SOUNDS

Although sounds are invisible, they are made of waves that vary in size, or time, and volume. For computer usage, sounds are transformed into mathematical equations called *digital sampling*. Digital sounds are visually represented as *waveforms*.

DIGITAL QUALITY

Digital quality is measured by how many samples exist in a single second of the sound, called the *sampling rate*. Sampling rates are expressed in *kilohertz* (kHz). The higher the rate, the larger the file size, and the clearer the sound. A smaller sampling results in a smaller file size. When planning sounds for your Flash movie, remember that larger sound clips take longer to download.

TYPES OF SOUNDS

All sounds you add in Flash, whether music or sound effects, fall into two categories: *event driven* and *streamed*. Event driven sounds are triggered by an action in your movie and must be downloaded completely before playing. Streamed sounds are downloaded as needed, and start playing even if the rest of the clip is not yet loaded.

SYNCHRONIZING SOUNDS

You can synchronize sounds to match the frames in your Flash movie. Flash offers four sync options—event, stream, start, stop—based on what you want the sound to do, such as make an animation sequence play along with a sound track.

SOUND FILE FORMATS

You can import WAV, AIF, MP3, and QuickTime file formats into Flash. You can export audio used in your Flash movies as MP3 format, or you can compress it as ADPCM, MP3, or RAW.

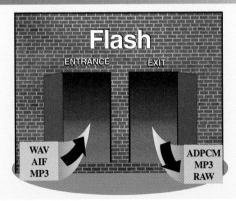

IMPORT A SOUND CLIP

Although you cannot record sounds in Flash, you can import sounds from other sources for use with movies and other projects. For example, you might download an MP3 file off the Internet and add it to a movie, or import a saved recording to play with a Flash button. Flash supports popular sound file formats, such as WAV and AIF.

Sound Clips

IMPORT A SOUND FILE

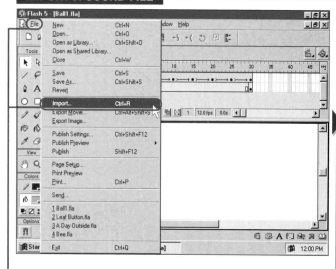

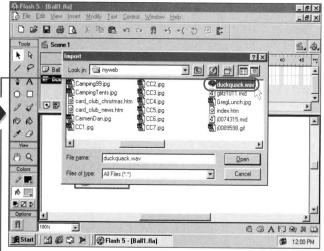

1 Click **File**.

2 Click **Import**.

■ The Import dialog box opens.

3 Click the sound file you want to import.

Does Flash have any sounds I can use?

Flash has several common libraries from which you can borrow items: one includes sounds. To display the sound library:

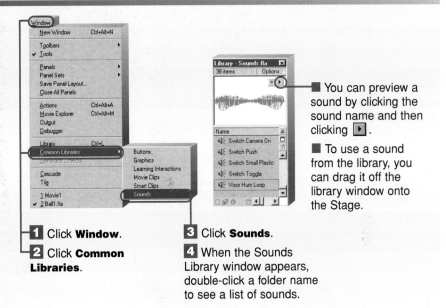

■ You can preview a sound by clicking the sound name and then clicking ▶.

■ To use a sound from the library, you can drag it off the library window onto the Stage.

1 Click **Window**.

2 Click **Common Libraries**.

3 Click **Sounds**.

4 When the Sounds Library window appears, double-click a folder name to see a list of sounds.

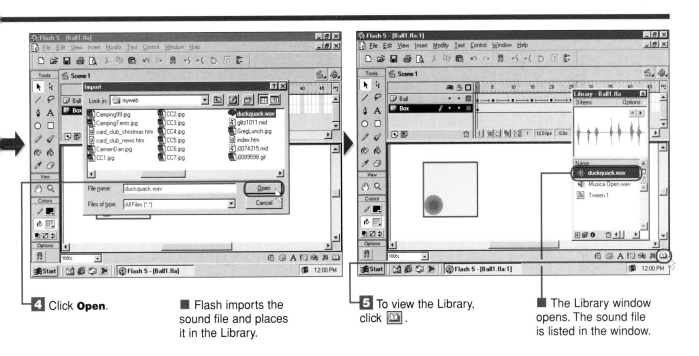

4 Click **Open**.

■ Flash imports the sound file and places it in the Library.

5 To view the Library, click 📖.

■ The Library window opens. The sound file is listed in the window.

ADD A SOUND LAYER

Flash helps organize your movie by allowing you to place sound clips in another layer. This makes it easier to find sound files quickly and edit them as needed. Flash allows for multiple sound layers in your movie.

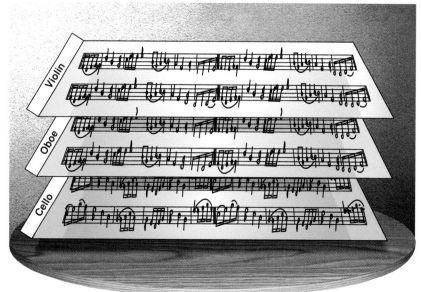

See Chapter 5 to learn more about working with Flash layers.

ADD A SOUND LAYER

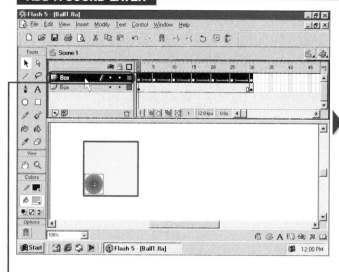

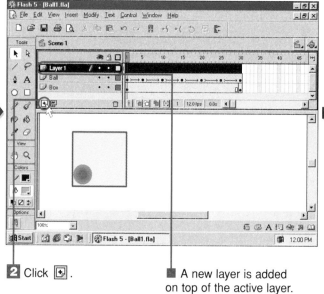

1 Click the layer you want to appear beneath the added layer.

■ Flash always adds a new layer to the Timeline directly above the active layer.

2 Click ⊞.

■ A new layer is added on top of the active layer.

Can I make a soundtrack layer?

There is no such thing as a soundtrack layer in Flash, but you can organize multiple sound layers and place them visually under a mask layer and name the mask layer Sound track. By placing all of your sound layers beneath a labeled mask layer, you can quickly see the organization of sound files in your Flash movie.

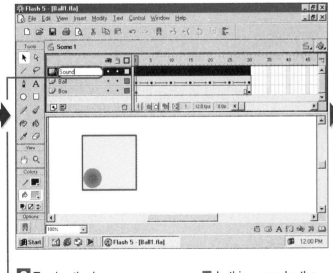

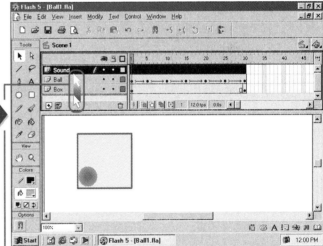

3 To give the layer a distinct name, double-click the default layer name.

4 Type a name that identifies this layer as a sound layer.

■ In this example, the layer is labeled "Sound."

5 Press **Enter**.

■ Flash saves the new name of the layer.

■ To make the sound layer easy to find, you can drag the layer to the top or bottom of the Timeline layer stack.

ASSIGN SOUNDS TO FRAMES

You can enliven any animation sequence with a sound clip whether you add a single sound effect or an entire sound track. Like graphics, sound files are saved as instances that can be inserted into frames on the Timeline and used throughout your movie. Sounds are represented as waveforms in Flash frames.

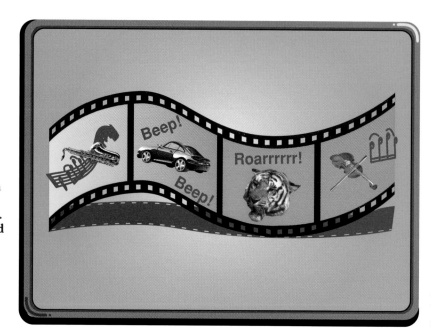

See Chapter 8 to learn more about frames.

ASSIGN A SOUND TO A FRAME

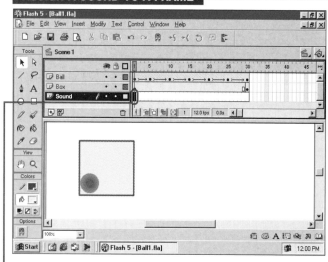

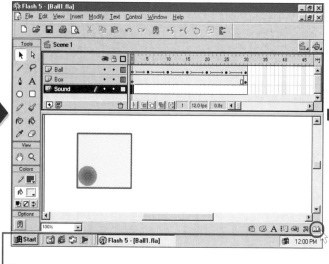

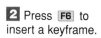 Click the frame to which you want to add a sound.

■ To keep your sounds organized, you can add the sound to a specially named layer dedicated to sound clips (see the Section "Add a Sound Layer.")

2 Press F6 to insert a keyframe.

3 Click 🖳.

■ The Library window opens.

What is a waveform?

When you drag a sound from the Library onto the Stage, there is no visual representation of the sound. Instead a waveform image of vertical lines representing the digital sampling of the sound appears in the Timeline frame.

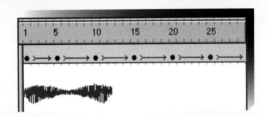

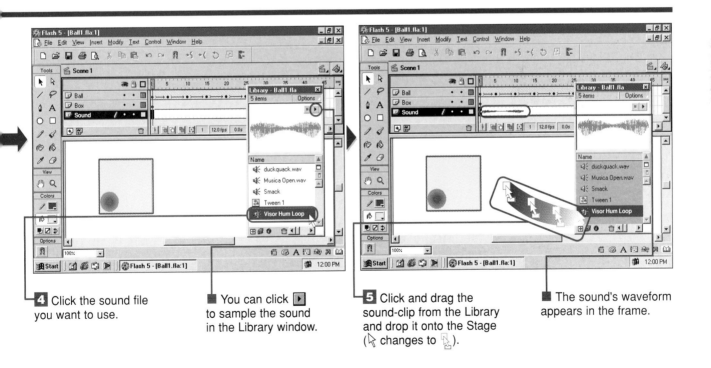

4 Click the sound file you want to use.

■ You can click ▶ to sample the sound in the Library window.

5 Click and drag the sound-clip from the Library and drop it onto the Stage (⟍ changes to ⟍).

■ The sound's waveform appears in the frame.

ASSIGN SOUNDS TO BUTTONS

You can apply sounds to page buttons to help people know how to interact with the buttons or just to give the buttons added flair. For example, you might add a clicking sound that the user hears when he or she clicks a button.

See Chapter 10 to learn more about creating interactive buttons.

ASSIGN SOUNDS TO BUTTONS

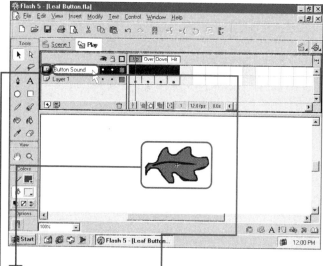

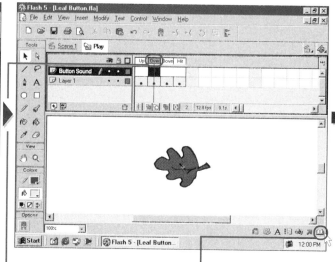

1 Open the button to which you want to add a sound in symbol-edit mode.

Note: See Chapter 10 to learn more about creating buttons.

2 Add a layer to the button Timeline.

Note: See Chapter 5 to learn more about Flash layers.

3 Double-click on the layer name and type a name for the layer.

Note: See the Section "Add a Sound Layer" to learn how to add and name a layer.

4 Click the frame to which you want to add a sound.

■ You can add a keyframe, if the frame does not already have one.

Note: See Chapter 8 to learn how to add keyframes.

5 Click 📖 to open the Library window.

Note: See Chapter 6 to learn how to use the Flash Library.

234

To which button frame should I assign a sound?

The most practical frames to use when assigning sounds are the Over and Down frames, but you can assign sounds to any button frame. For example, you might want the button to beep when the user rolls over the button with the mouse pointer. This alerts the users to the button. To do this, assign a sound to the Over frame. You might also want the button to make another type of sound when the user actually clicks it; assign a sound to the Down frame.

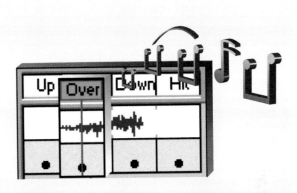

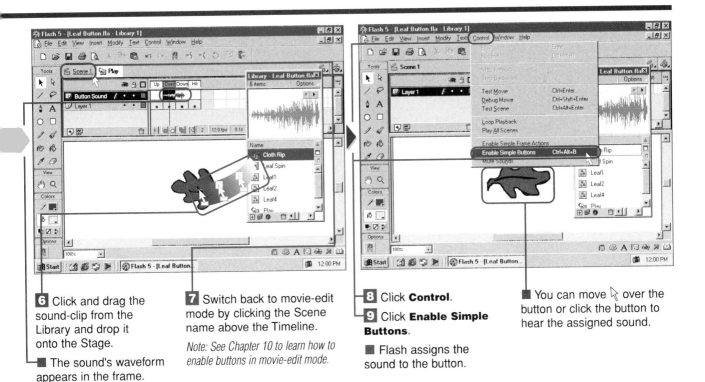

■ **6** Click and drag the sound-clip from the Library and drop it onto the Stage.

■ The sound's waveform appears in the frame.

■ **7** Switch back to movie-edit mode by clicking the Scene name above the Timeline.

Note: See Chapter 10 to learn how to enable buttons in movie-edit mode.

■ **8** Click **Control**.

■ **9** Click **Enable Simple Buttons**.

■ Flash assigns the sound to the button.

■ You can move ▷ over the button or click the button to hear the assigned sound.

CREATE EVENT SOUNDS

You can assign an event-driven sound to be triggered by an action in your Flash project. Event sounds play in their entirety, and must be completely downloaded before they begin playing. Event sounds also play in their own Timeline. By default, all sounds you add are treated as Event sounds unless you specify another type.

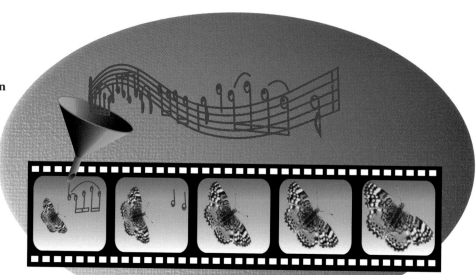

See the Section "Assign Sounds to Frames" to learn more about assigning sounds.

CREATE EVENT SOUNDS

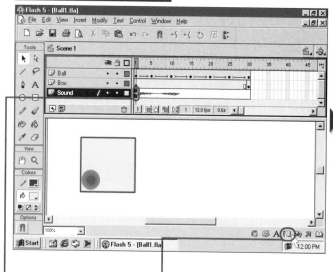

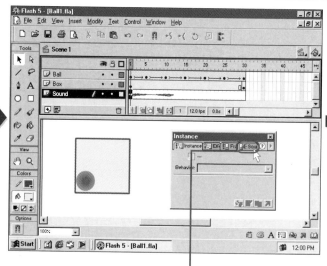

TURN A SOUND INTO AN EVENT SOUND

1 Click the frame containing the sound you want to change.

Note: See Chapter 8 to learn how to work with Flash frames and the Section "Assign Sounds to Frames" to learn how to add a sound clip.

2 Click 🔲 .

■ The Instance panel opens.

3 Click the **Sound** tab.

Can I overlap event sounds, or start two sounds simultaneously?

By default, any sound you assign to a frame is an event sound until you change it to something else. Although you can only insert one sound per frame, you can use multiple layers to play sounds at the same time or to overlap them. For example, you might place one event sound in a sound layer labeled Sound 1 and assign the sound to frame 1. You can create a second layer and name it Sound 2, and place yet another sound in frame 5. Both sounds will play together when you play the movie.

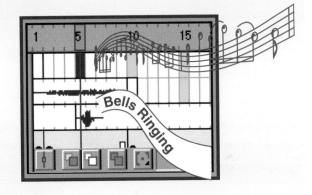

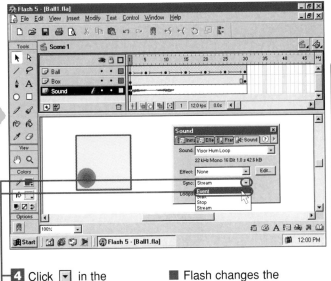

-4 Click ▼ in the Sync box.

-5 Click **Event**.

■ Flash changes the sound into an event sound.

TEST THE SOUND

-1 Click the first frame in your movie.

-2 Press Enter.

■ The movie plays. When the movie reaches the selected frame, the sound plays.

Note: See Chapter 13 to learn how to play Flash movies.

237

ASSIGN START SOUNDS

You can use the Flash Start sound control to start a new instance of a sound even if it's already playing from an earlier instance in your movie. The Start sound command is handy when you want to synchronize a sound with your animation.

See the Section "Introducing Flash Sounds" to learn more about sound types.

ASSIGN START SOUNDS

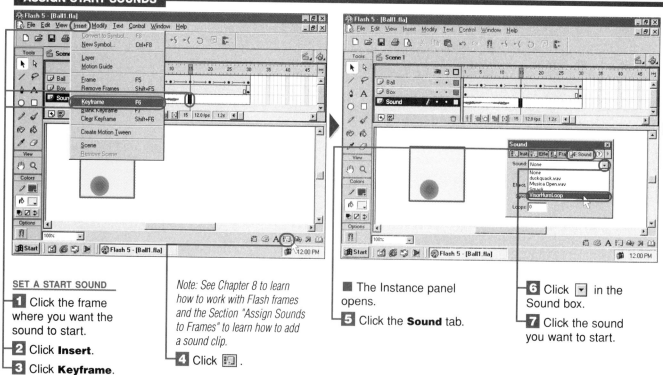

SET A START SOUND

1 Click the frame where you want the sound to start.

2 Click **Insert**.

3 Click **Keyframe**.

Note: See Chapter 8 to learn how to work with Flash frames and the Section "Assign Sounds to Frames" to learn how to add a sound clip.

4 Click 🔲 .

■ The Instance panel opens.

5 Click the **Sound** tab.

6 Click ▼ in the Sound box.

7 Click the sound you want to start.

How can I control the sound's volume?

You can find volume effects controls in the Sound panel. Click ▼ in the Effect box to view the settings you can select. For example, to make the sound fade in, click the Fade In setting. Learn more about editing sounds in the Section "Edit Sounds."

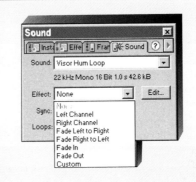

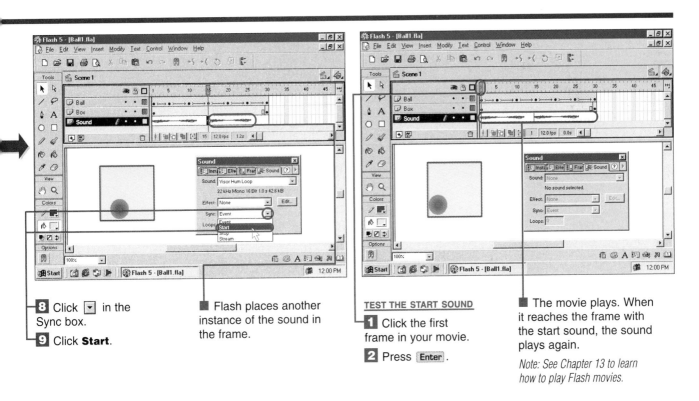

■ **8** Click ▼ in the Sync box.

■ **9** Click **Start**.

■ Flash places another instance of the sound in the frame.

TEST THE START SOUND

1 Click the first frame in your movie.

2 Press Enter.

■ The movie plays. When it reaches the frame with the start sound, the sound plays again.

Note: See Chapter 13 to learn how to play Flash movies.

ASSIGN STOP SOUNDS

If you want to stop a sound before it reaches the end, you can insert a Stop sound command. For example, if your animation ends on a particular frame, but your sound clip goes on much longer, you can put a Stop command in the frame to end the sound.

See the Section "Assign Start Sounds" to learn how to add a start sound to your movie.

ASSIGN STOP SOUNDS

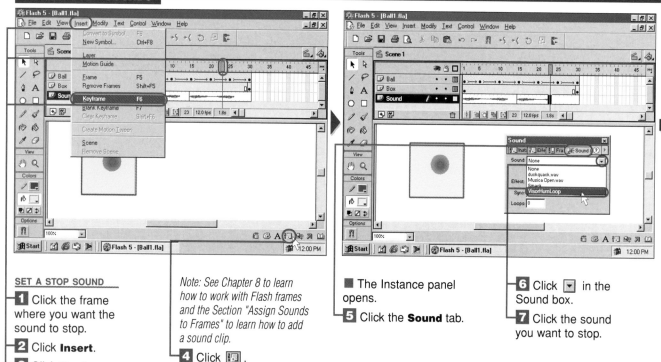

SET A STOP SOUND

■1 Click the frame where you want the sound to stop.

■2 Click **Insert**.

■3 Click **Keyframe**.

Note: See Chapter 8 to learn how to work with Flash frames and the Section "Assign Sounds to Frames" to learn how to add a sound clip.

■4 Click [🔢].

■ The Instance panel opens.

■5 Click the **Sound** tab.

■6 Click [▼] in the Sound box.

■7 Click the sound you want to stop.

Does the Stop command have to be in the same layer?

You can place a Stop command on any layer to stop the sound. The command immediately stops any playback of the sound regardless of where the sound is assigned.

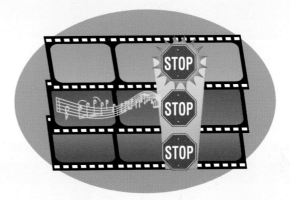

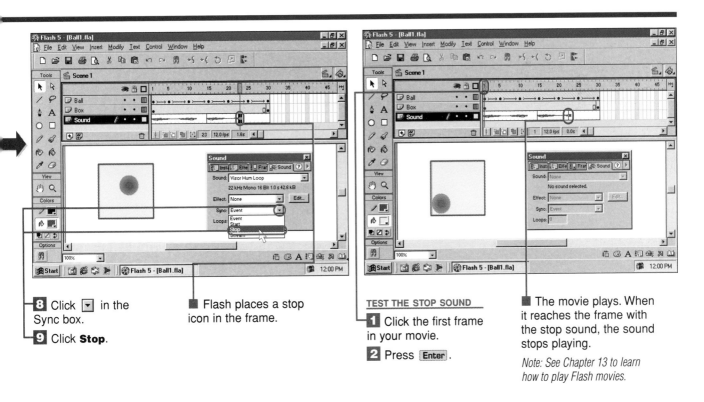

8 Click ▼ in the Sync box.

9 Click **Stop**.

■ Flash places a stop icon in the frame.

TEST THE STOP SOUND

1 Click the first frame in your movie.

2 Press [Enter].

■ The movie plays. When it reaches the frame with the stop sound, the sound stops playing.

Note: See Chapter 13 to learn how to play Flash movies.

ASSIGN STREAMING SOUNDS

You can use Streaming sounds for Flash movies you place on Web pages. The sound starts streaming as the page downloads, so the user does not have to wait for the entire file to finish downloading. The frames are synchronized with the sound, so if the sound is a bit slow downloading, the frames slow down as well. Streaming sounds are good for long sound files, such as a musical sound track.

See Chapter 12 to learn more about assigning actions.

ASSIGN STREAMING SOUNDS

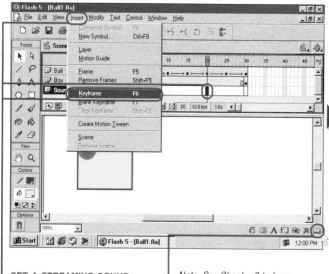

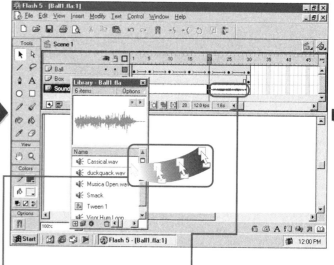

SET A STREAMING SOUND

1 Click the frame where you want to start the streaming sound.

2 Click **Insert**.

3 Click **Keyframe**.

Note: See Chapter 8 to learn how to work with Flash frames and the Section "Assign Sounds to Frames" to learn how to add a sound clip.

4 Click  .

■ The Library window opens.

5 Click and drag the sound you want to use from the Library and drop it on the Flash Stage.

■ The sound's waveform appears in the frame.

**What do I do if my
streaming sound gets
cut off too soon?**

Try switching the units
from seconds to frames:

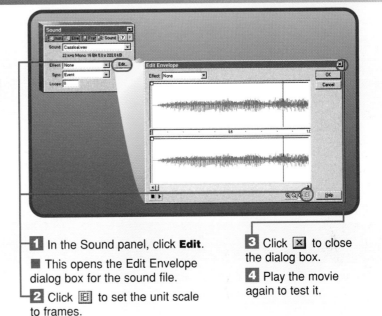

━1 In the Sound panel, click **Edit**.

■ This opens the Edit Envelope
dialog box for the sound file.

2 Click ▦ to set the unit scale
to frames.

3 Click ⊠ to close
the dialog box.

4 Play the movie
again to test it.

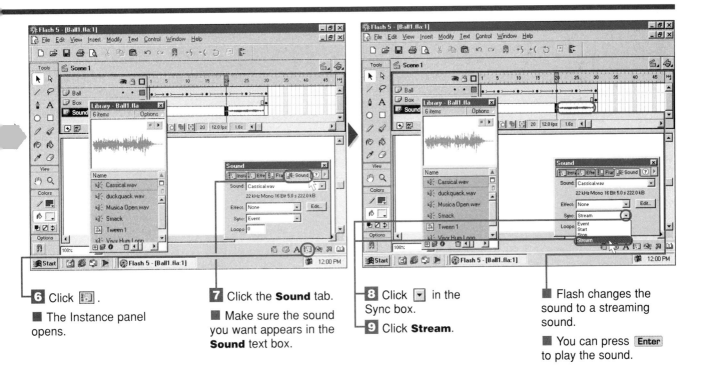

━6 Click ▦ .

■ The Instance panel
opens.

7 Click the **Sound** tab.

■ Make sure the sound
you want appears in the
Sound text box.

━8 Click ▼ in the
Sync box.

━9 Click **Stream**.

■ Flash changes the
sound to a streaming
sound.

■ You can press Enter
to play the sound.

LOOP SOUNDS

You can make a sound play over and over again with the Loop command. Looping means to play the sound repeatedly, as many times as you like.

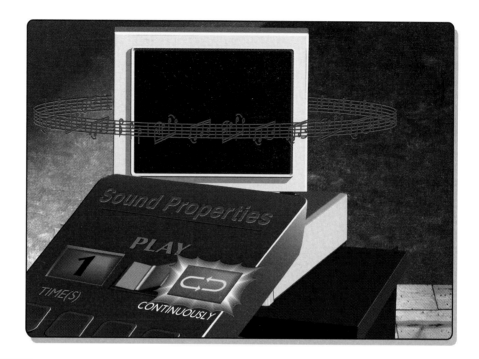

SET A LOOPING SOUND

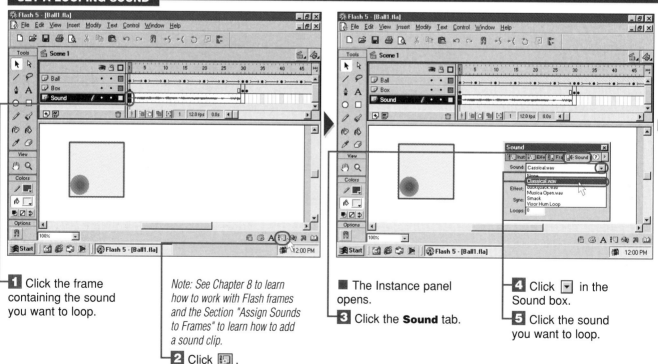

1 Click the frame containing the sound you want to loop.

Note: See Chapter 8 to learn how to work with Flash frames and the Section "Assign Sounds to Frames" to learn how to add a sound clip.

2 Click ▣.

■ The Instance panel opens.

3 Click the **Sound** tab.

4 Click ▾ in the Sound box.

5 Click the sound you want to loop.

What if I want the sound to loop forever?

If you have set a streaming sound, you can set the loop to a high number, like 30 or 40. Flash does not loop the sound that many times, but the sound keeps looping until the end of the movie.

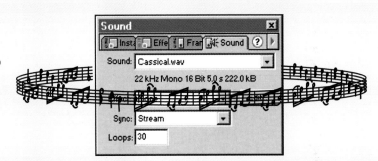

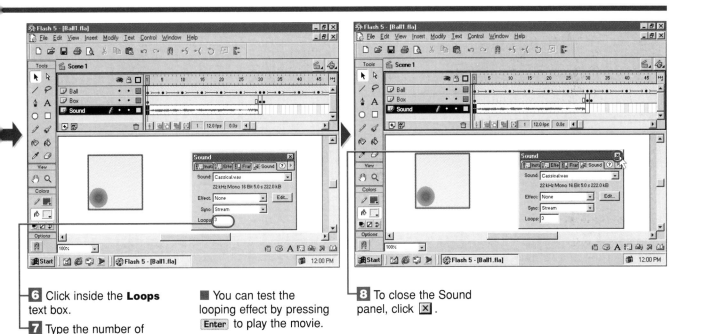

6 Click inside the **Loops** text box.

7 Type the number of times you want the sound to loop.

■ You can test the looping effect by pressing Enter to play the movie.

Note: See Chapter 13 to learn how to play Flash movies.

8 To close the Sound panel, click ☒.

EDIT SOUNDS

Flash comes with some handy volume controls that you can use to fade sounds in or out, or make sounds move from one speaker to another in a stereo set up.

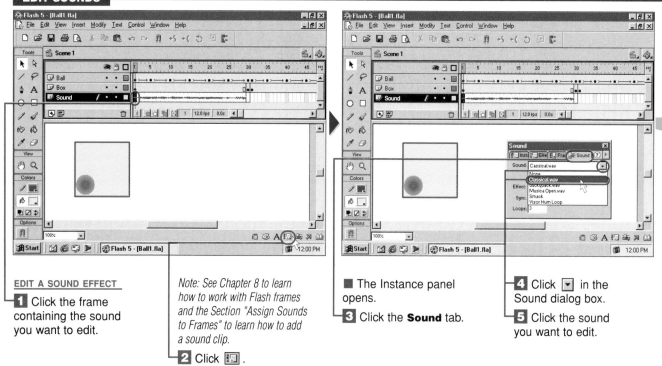

EDIT A SOUND EFFECT

■1 Click the frame containing the sound you want to edit.

Note: See Chapter 8 to learn how to work with Flash frames and the Section "Assign Sounds to Frames" to learn how to add a sound clip.

■2 Click 🔲 .

■ The Instance panel opens.

■3 Click the **Sound** tab.

■4 Click ▼ in the Sound dialog box.

■5 Click the sound you want to edit.

246

Can I create a custom sound?

Flash is not designed to be a sound-editing program, although you can tinker with a few additional editing controls.

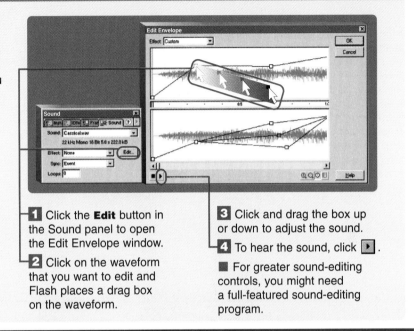

1 Click the **Edit** button in the Sound panel to open the Edit Envelope window.

2 Click on the waveform that you want to edit and Flash places a drag box on the waveform.

3 Click and drag the box up or down to adjust the sound.

4 To hear the sound, click ▶.

■ For greater sound-editing controls, you might need a full-featured sound-editing program.

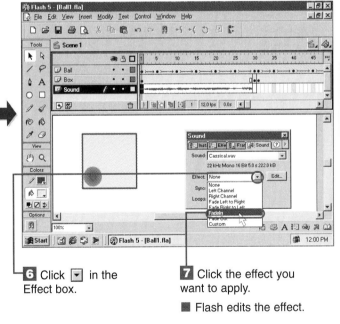

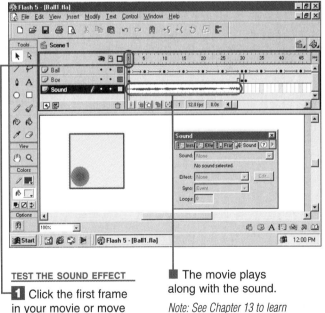

6 Click ▼ in the Effect box.

7 Click the effect you want to apply.

■ Flash edits the effect.

TEST THE SOUND EFFECT

1 Click the first frame in your movie or move the playback head to the start of the Timeline.

2 Press Enter.

■ The movie plays along with the sound.

Note: See Chapter 13 to learn how to play Flash movies.

SET AUDIO OUTPUT FOR EXPORT

You can control how sounds are exported in your Flash files. You can find options for optimizing your sound files for export in the Publish Settings dialog box. Options include settings for compressing your sounds in ADPCM, MP3, or RAW format. By default, Flash exports sounds in MP3 format using a bit rate of 16 Kbps. MP3 is the emerging standard for distributing audio on the Internet.

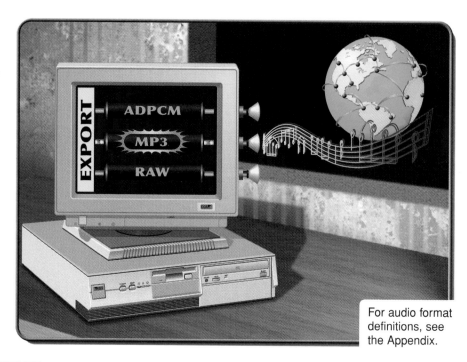

For audio format definitions, see the Appendix.

SET AUDIO OUTPUT FOR EXPORT

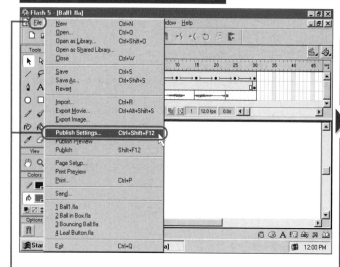

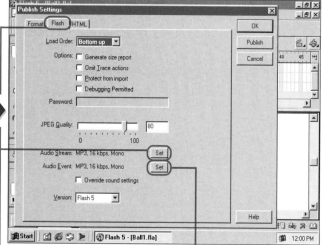

1 Click **File**.

2 Click **Publish Settings**.

■ The Publish Settings dialog box opens.

3 Click the **Flash** tab.

4 Click the **Set** button corresponding to the audio type you want to control.

■ To control the export quality of streaming sounds, you can click the Audio Stream **Set** button.

■ To control the export quality of event sounds, you can click the Audio Event **Set** button.

■ Clicking either Set button opens the Sound Settings dialog box.

248

What is a good bit rate for MP3?

The higher the bit rate you set, the better the quality of your audio. MP3 is a very efficient compression format, so you can set the bit rate high and still maintain a small file size. This is one of the reasons MP3 is fast emerging the standard of choice for distributing sounds on the Internet, especially on Web pages. For large music files, a setting of 64 Kbps is good. For speech or voice files, 24 or 32 Kbps is acceptable. To set near CD quality, use a setting of 112 or 128 Kbps. 16 Kbps is suitable for simple button sounds, or larger audio sounds where quality is not crucial.

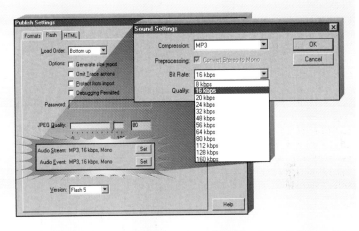

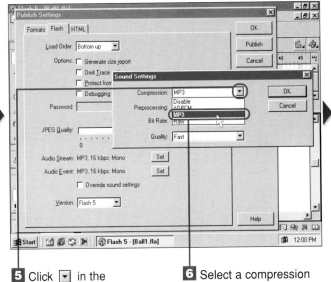

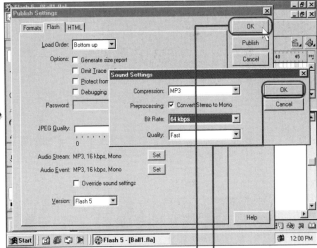

5 Click ▾ in the **Compression** box.

6 Select a compression format to apply.

■ Depending on the format you select, the remaining options in the Sound Settings dialog box change to reflect settings associated with your selection.

■ You can make changes to the remaining settings as needed.

7 Click **OK** in the Sound Settings dialog box.

8 Click **OK** to exit the Publish Settings dialog box.

CHAPTER 12

Adding Flash Actions

Do you need to add some user controls to your animation? In this chapter, you learn how to add interactive Flash actions to frames.

INTRODUCING FLASH ACTIONS

You can add interactivity to your Flash movies by assigning frame actions. An *action* is a behavior assigned to a frame, such as turning off a sound or stopping a movie. The occurrence that triggers the action is called an *event*. An event might be a click of a button or reaching a certain frame in your movie. The result of the action is the *target*, the object that is affected by the event.

WHAT EXACTLY ARE ACTIONS?

You can use actions to tell Flash to perform certain tasks, or *actions*. For example, the Go To action tells Flash to jump to a specified frame in the movie's Timeline and start playing that frame. The Stop action tells Flash to stop playing the movie. You can use actions to allow users to interact with your movie. For example, you might place a button in your movie that a user can click to stop the movie.

HOW DO ACTIONS WORK?

Flash actions work like macros and scripting commands found in programming languages. When you assign an action, Flash adds it to a list of actions for that particular frame. This list is called an *action list*. Flash then executes the actions in the list based on the order that they appear.

WHAT ARE EVENTS?

An event triggers an action in your movie. Flash categorizes three types of events: mouse events (also called *button actions*), keyboard events, and frame events (also called *frame actions*). For example, a mouse event occurs when a user interacts with a button, such as moving the mouse pointer over the button or clicking on the button. Keyboard events occur when a user presses a keyboard key and are typically assigned to buttons. Frame events are placed in keyframes in your movie and trigger actions that occur at certain points in the Timeline.

WHAT ARE TARGETS?

A *target* is the object affected by the action. Targets are directed toward the current movie (called the *default target*), other movies (called the *Tell Target*), or a browser application (called an *external target*). For example, you might place a button in your movie that, when clicked, opens a Web page. You direct most of your frame actions toward the current movie, which is the default target.

ADD ACTIONS TO FRAMES

You can use the Frame Actions box to add actions to your movie. Frames can include multiple actions, but you can only assign an action one frame at a time. You add actions to the frame's *action script*, a list of actions associated with the frame. Flash performs the actions in the order they appear in the list.

See Chapter 5 to find out more about Flash layers.

ADD ACTIONS TO FRAMES

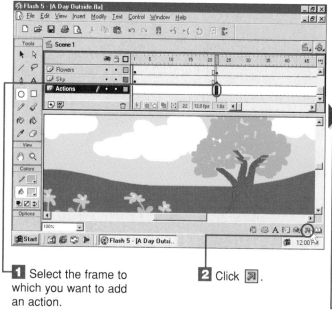

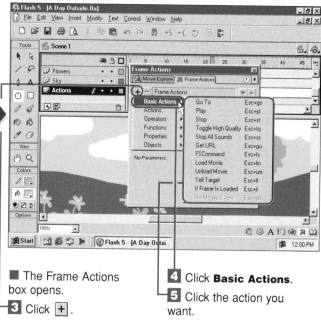

1 Select the frame to which you want to add an action.

Note: You can only insert actions into keyframes.

2 Click .

■ The Frame Actions box opens.

3 Click **+**.

4 Click **Basic Actions**.

5 Click the action you want.

See the Section "Introducing Flash Actions" to find out more about actions.

How do I organize actions in my movie?

To help you clearly identify actions you assign to frames, consider creating a layer specifically for actions in your movie. This technique makes finding the action you want to edit easier. To add a layer to the

Timeline, click 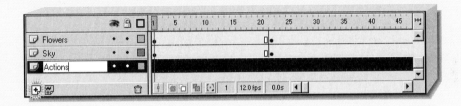. A new layer appears above the current layer. You can rename the layer, or move it to another position in the layer stack. See Chapter 5 to find out more about moving and positioning Flash layers.

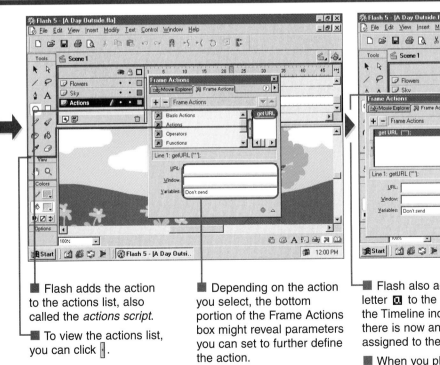

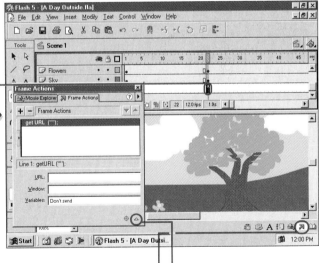

■ Flash adds the action to the actions list, also called the *actions script*.

■ To view the actions list, you can click ▮.

■ Depending on the action you select, the bottom portion of the Frame Actions box might reveal parameters you set to further define the action.

■ Flash also adds a tiny letter ▣ to the frame in the Timeline indicating there is now an action assigned to the frame.

■ When you play the movie, Flash carries out the frame action you assigned.

■ To view the entire actions list, you can click ▣. You can click the button again to collapse the actions list.

■ To close the Frame Actions box, you can click ▣.

ASSIGN GO TO ACTIONS

You can assign a Go To
action that tells Flash to
start playing a particular
frame in your movie. The
Go To action includes
parameters you can
define to play a specific
frame. You can use the
Go To action with frames
or buttons.

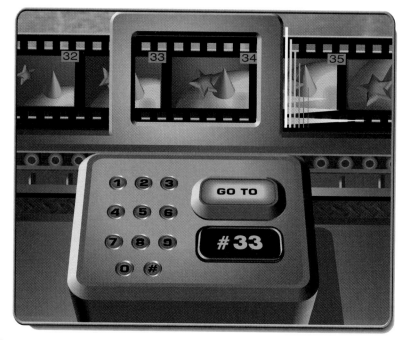

See the Section
"Introducing Flash
Actions" to find
out more about
frame actions.

ASSIGN GO TO ACTIONS

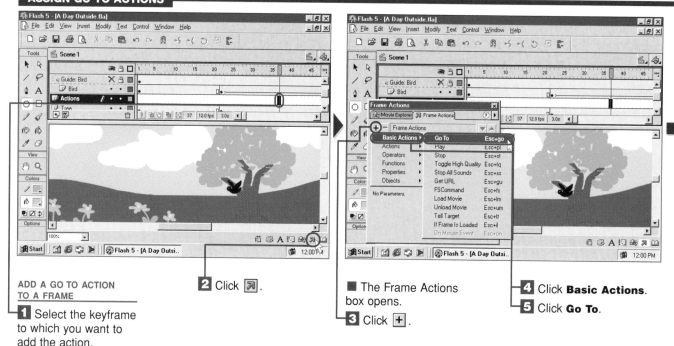

**ADD A GO TO ACTION
TO A FRAME**

1 Select the keyframe
to which you want to
add the action.

2 Click 🔊 .

■ The Frame Actions
box opens.

3 Click ➕ .

4 Click **Basic Actions**.

5 Click **Go To**.

Can I reference a scene in the Go To parameters that I have not created yet?

You can plan ahead and reference scenes you have not yet created in your movie. If the scene still is not available when you play the movie, Flash ignores the Go To command because it does not reference a legitimate frame in your movie.

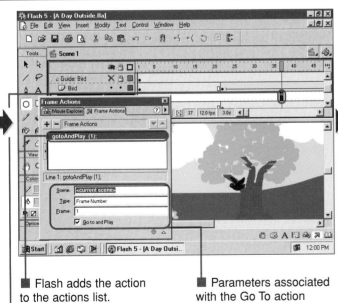

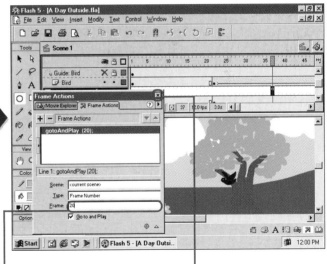

■ Flash adds the action to the actions list.

■ Flash also adds a tiny letter **a** to the frame in the Timeline indicating there is now an action assigned to the frame.

■ Parameters associated with the Go To action appear at the bottom of the box.

6 Type the number of the frame you want to go to in the **Frame** text box.

■ When you play the movie, Flash follows the frame action you assigned.

■ To close the Frame Actions box, click **✕**.

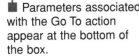

CONTINUED

ASSIGN GO TO ACTIONS

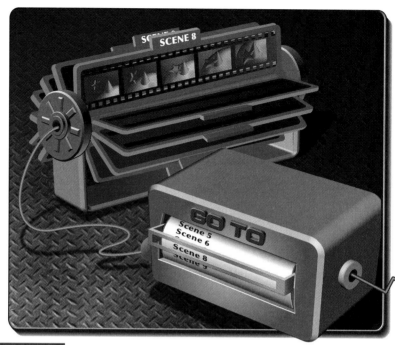

You can also reference scenes in a Go To action. You can specify a scene name in the Go To action parameters. When you assign a Go To action, Flash follows the instruction during the course of playing the movie and jumps to the scene you referenced. If you edit your movie later, such as add or delete frames or entire scenes, be sure to update any Go To actions to reference the correct frames or scenes.

See the Section "Assign Frame Labels" to find out more about labels, or see Chapter 8 to discover how to create scenes.

ASSIGN GO TO ACTIONS (CONTINUED)

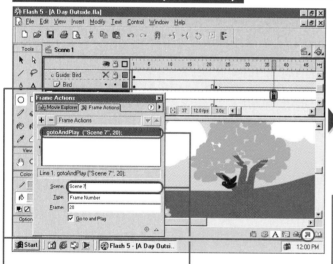

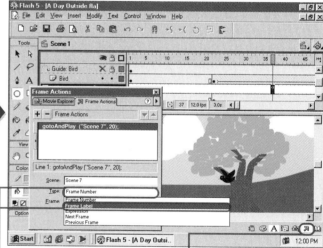

ADD A GO TO ACTION TO A SCENE

1 Select the keyframe to which you want to add the action.

2 Click .

3 Click inside the Scene text box and type the scene name.

■ As you type, Flash fills in the parameters in the actions list.

■ To go to a specific label, you can click in the Type text box.

4 Click **Frame Label**, then type the label into the Frame text box.

See the Section "Assign Frame Labels" to find out more about organizing action frames.

■ When you play the movie, Flash follows the frame action you assigned.

■ To close the Frame Actions box, click .

Can I test my action out on the Stage?

You cannot see Flash actions by playing the movie on the Flash Stage. You must open the Flash Player window to view how your actions affect the movie.

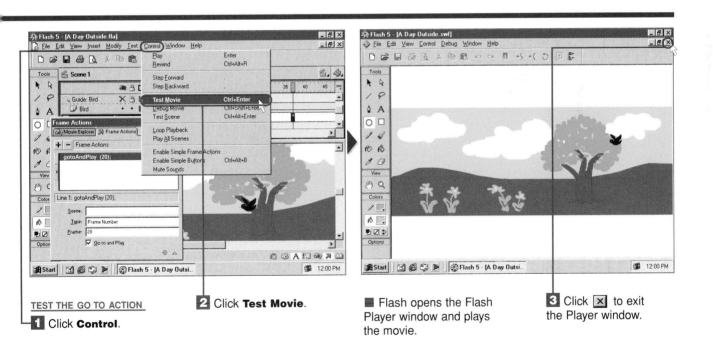

TEST THE GO TO ACTION

1 Click **Control**.

2 Click **Test Movie**.

■ Flash opens the Flash Player window and plays the movie.

3 Click ☒ to exit the Player window.

ASSIGN STOP AND PLAY ACTIONS

You can assign a Stop action to stop a movie from playing, or you can assign a Play action to play it again. For example, perhaps one of the keyframes in your movie is text heavy and you want to allow the user to read the text. You can create a button and assign a Stop action that allows the user to stop the movie and assign a Play action to another button that allows the user to play the movie again.

From the legendary Titanic, to the Edmund Fitzgerald, many large ships have been swallowed by the sea over the years. This Web page takes you on a tour of the ocean floor, where many shipwrecks still remain. Grab your life jacket and enter the site to find out more about some infamous nautical disasters!

See the Section "Introducing Flash Actions" to find out more about frame actions.

ASSIGN STOP AND PLAY ACTIONS

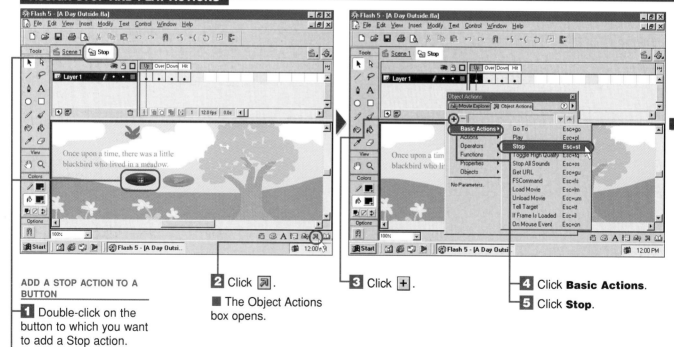

ADD A STOP ACTION TO A BUTTON

1 Double-click on the button to which you want to add a Stop action.

■ Flash opens the button in symbol-edit mode.

2 Click 🗗.

■ The Object Actions box opens.

3 Click ➕.

4 Click **Basic Actions**.

5 Click **Stop**.

What is the difference between frame actions and object actions?

Actions can be applied to frames or buttons. Frame actions are assigned to frames and control how a movie plays. Button actions, as demonstrated in the steps in this section, are assigned to buttons and require input from the user. For example, a Stop action assigned to a button enables the user to stop a movie by clicking on the button to which the action is assigned. You can assign Stop and Play actions to frames or buttons, but remember that button actions require user input in order to carry out the action. To assign a Stop action to a frame rather than a button, simply click the frame to which you want the action assigned and follow Steps **2** through **5** in this section. To

assign a Play action to a frame, follow Steps **9** through **12** in this section. To learn more about assigning frame actions, see the Section "Add Actions to Frames."

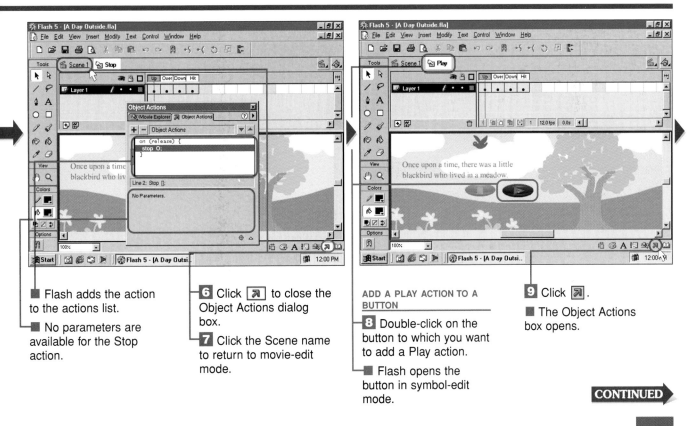

■ Flash adds the action to the actions list.

■ No parameters are available for the Stop action.

6 Click 🗷 to close the Object Actions dialog box.

7 Click the Scene name to return to movie-edit mode.

ADD A PLAY ACTION TO A BUTTON

8 Double-click on the button to which you want to add a Play action.

■ Flash opens the button in symbol-edit mode.

9 Click 🗷.

■ The Object Actions box opens.

CONTINUED ▶

ASSIGN STOP AND PLAY ACTIONS

Stop and Play are two of the most commonly used actions, and are used for both button actions and frame actions. They act much like the controls found on a VCR or CD player. You can use the Play action to start a movie you have previously stopped with the Stop action.

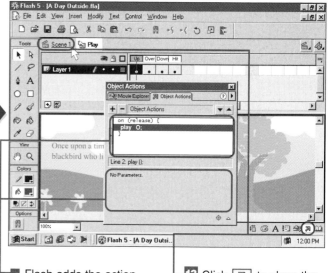

10 Click ➕.

11 Click **Basic Actions**.

12 Click **Play**.

■ Flash adds the action to the actions list.

■ No parameters are available for the Play action.

13 Click 🔟 to close the Object Actions dialog box.

14 Click the Scene name to return to movie-edit mode.

Can I resize the type in the actions list?

If you have trouble reading the small type in the actions list, you can resize it. To do so, perform these steps:

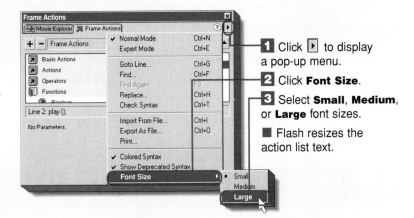

■1 Click ▶ to display a pop-up menu.

■2 Click **Font Size**.

■3 Select **Small**, **Medium**, or **Large** font sizes.

■ Flash resizes the action list text.

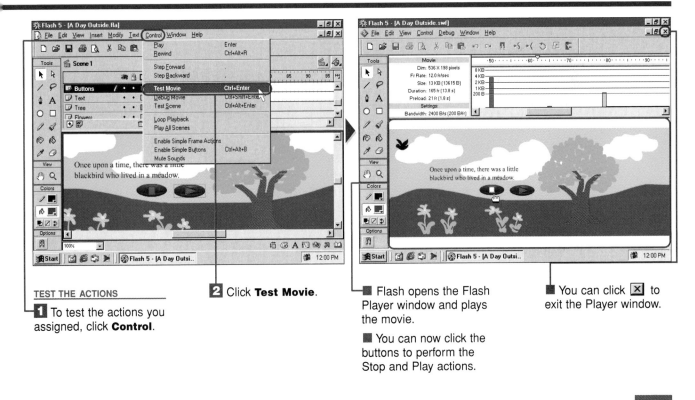

TEST THE ACTIONS

■1 To test the actions you assigned, click **Control**.

■2 Click **Test Movie**.

■ Flash opens the Flash Player window and plays the movie.

■ You can now click the buttons to perform the Stop and Play actions.

■ You can click ☒ to exit the Player window.

LOAD A NEW MOVIE

You can use the Load Movie action to start a movie file within your current movie. The Load Movie action can replace the current movie with another you have previously created, or play the loaded movie on top of the current movie as if it were another layer.

See the Section "Introducing Flash Actions" to find out more about frame actions.

LOAD A NEW MOVIE

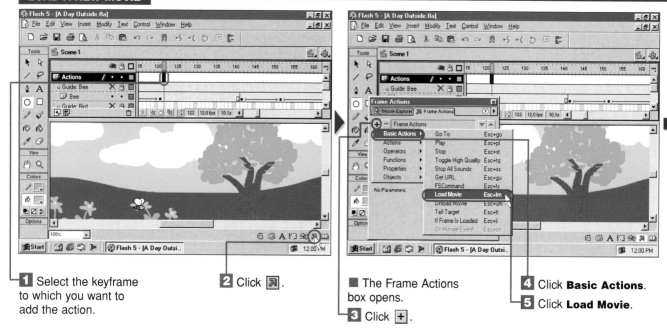

1 Select the keyframe to which you want to add the action.

2 Click 🔊.

■ The Frame Actions box opens.

3 Click ⊞.

4 Click **Basic Actions**.

5 Click **Load Movie**.

Can I open the movie in a separate browser window?

Another way you can load a new movie file to play is to use the Get URL action. This action opens the new movie in a separate browser window. Follow the same steps shown in this section, but select the Get URL action instead of the Load Movie action. In the parameters, type the following:

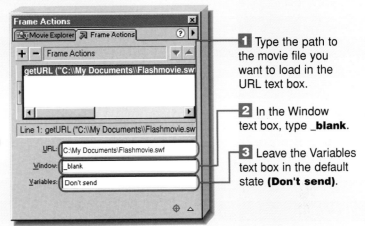

1 Type the path to the movie file you want to load in the URL text box.

2 In the Window text box, type **_blank**.

3 Leave the Variables text box in the default state **(Don't send)**.

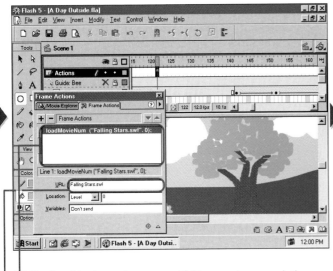

■ Flash adds the action to the actions list.

6 Click in the URL text box and type the name of the movie file you want to load.

■ You can type a relative path, which includes just the filename and extension, or you can enter an absolute path to the movie. An absolute path includes the drive and folder where the file is located.

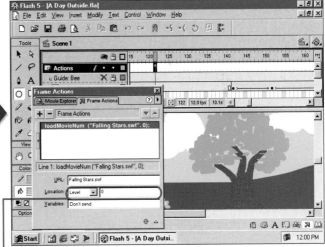

■ Select a location parameter for your movie.

■ Leave the Location level set to 0 if you want the new movie to replace the current movie.

■ To make the new movie play on top of the current movie, type 1 or higher in the Location level text box.

■ You can test the action by playing the movie in the Flash Player window.

See the section "Assign Go To Actions" to find out how to test an action.

CHANGE ACTION ORDER

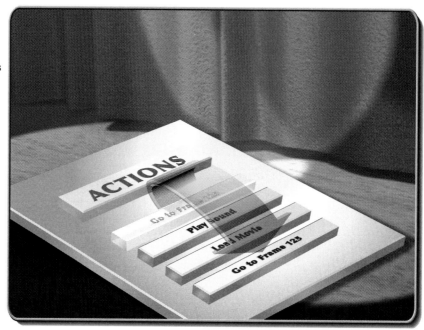

You can change the order of your actions list. When you add more than one action to a frame, Flash executes the actions in the order they appear in the actions list. You can reorder the actions as necessary.

See the Section "Add Actions to Frames" to find out more about assigning actions.

CHANGE ACTION ORDER

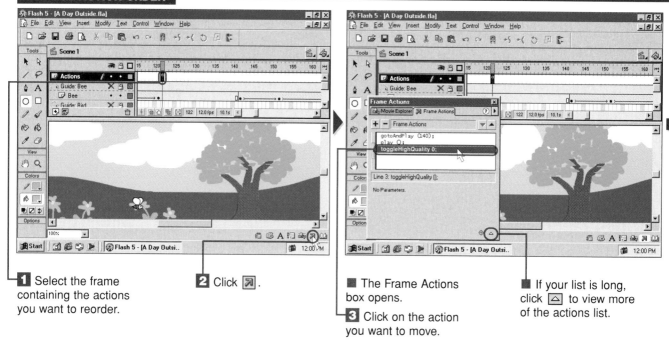

1 Select the frame containing the actions you want to reorder.

2 Click 🗷.

■ The Frame Actions box opens.

3 Click on the action you want to move.

■ If your list is long, click △ to view more of the actions list.

How do I delete an action?

To remove an action from
the actions list in the
Frame Actions box, first
select the action. Next,
click the — button. Flash
removes the action from
the list.

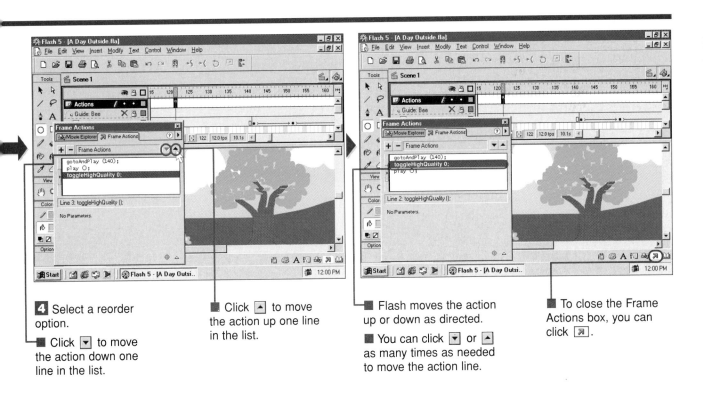

4 Select a reorder
option.

■ Click ▼ to move
the action down one
line in the list.

■ Click ▲ to move
the action up one line
in the list.

■ Flash moves the action
up or down as directed.

■ You can click ▼ or ▲
as many times as needed
to move the action line.

■ To close the Frame
Actions box, you can
click ⊠.

ASSIGN FRAME LABELS

You can keep your frames and actions organized if you use labels. If you assign a label to a keyframe, the label appears when you move the mouse pointer over the label flag. If you assign a label to a keyframe that starts tween animation, the label appears across the in-between frames in the Timeline. You can also use the label name in action parameters, such as the Go To action.

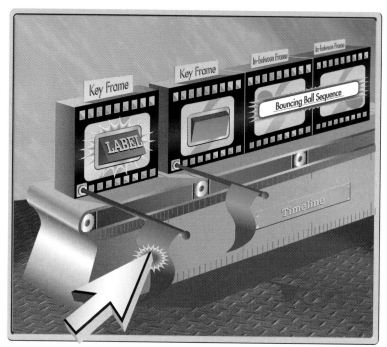

See the Section "Add Actions to Frames" to find out more about assigning actions.

ASSIGN FRAME LABELS

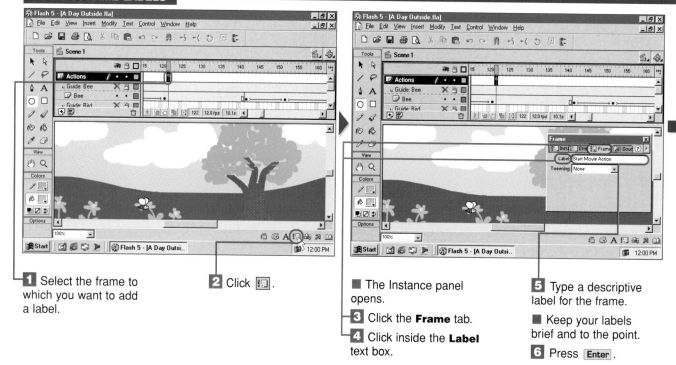

1 Select the frame to which you want to add a label.

2 Click 🔲.

■ The Instance panel opens.

3 Click the **Frame** tab.

4 Click inside the **Label** text box.

5 Type a descriptive label for the frame.

■ Keep your labels brief and to the point.

6 Press Enter.

What if I cannot see my label flags?

You can resize the frames in your Timeline to make them easier to see. Click the ⊞ button, then click **Large**. Flash resizes your Timeline to show large frames.

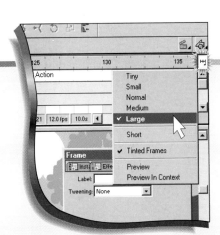

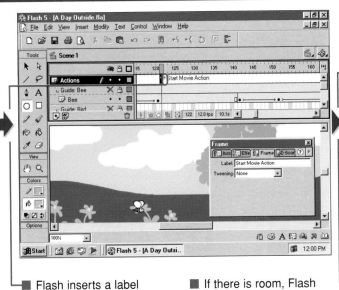

■ Flash inserts a label flag in the frame.

■ If there is room, Flash displays the label across the frames.

■ If you cannot see the label text, move the ⍜ over the label flag and pause (⍜ changes to ⍦).

■ Flash displays the label name.

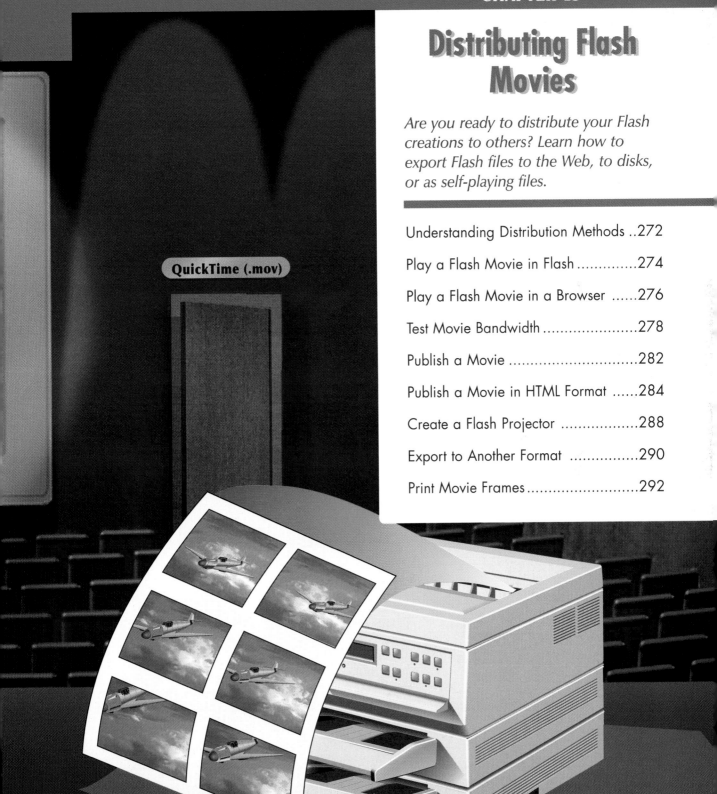

CHAPTER 13

Distributing Flash Movies

Are you ready to distribute your Flash creations to others? Learn how to export Flash files to the Web, to disks, or as self-playing files.

QuickTime (.mov)

You can distribute your Flash projects to an audience in several ways. You might publish a Flash movie to a Web page, or save it as a QuickTime movie to send to another user via e-mail, or deliver the movie as a self-playing file.

START WITH AN AUTHORING FILE

When you create content in Flash, you start by creating an *authoring file*. The authoring file is where you draw and animate your movie's content. This file contains all the elements that make up your movie, such as bitmap objects, sounds, symbols, buttons, text, and so on. The authoring file can be quite large in file size. Authoring files use the .fla file extension.

CREATE AN EXPORT FILE

After you create the authoring file and get it working just the way you want, you can turn it into an export file, an actual Flash movie. The process of exporting or publishing compresses the file contents, making it easier for others to view the file. The resulting file is uneditable, so you cannot change its contents. Flash movie files use the .swf file extension.

DISTRIBUTE AS A FLASH MOVIE

When you distribute a movie as a movie file, Flash assigns it a .swf file format, which requires the Flash Player plug-in to view.

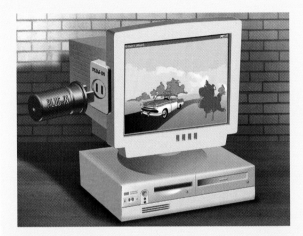

DISTRIBUTE TO A FLASH PROJECTOR

Another way to distribute your movie is to turn it into a *projector*. A projector is a stand-alone player that runs the movie without the need of another application.

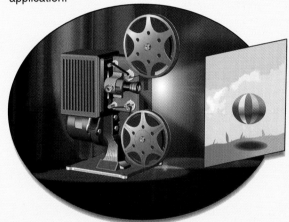

PUBLISHING FLASH MOVIES ON WEB PAGES

The Flash Publish feature can help you publish your movies on the Web. It exports your movie as a Flash Player (.swf) file and creates an HTML file that displays the movie in a Web browser.

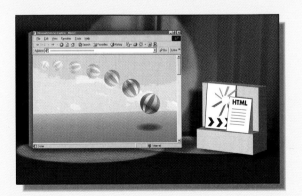

DISTRIBUTING TO OTHER FILE FORMATS

You can export your movies into other file formats, such as QuickTime or Windows AVI. You can even export your movie as a series of GIF or PNG images.

PLAY A FLASH MOVIE IN FLASH

You can use the Flash
Player to play your Flash
movies. You can play
movies from within Flash 5,
or outside the confines
of the Flash 5 program
window by using the Flash
Player window. The Flash
Player is installed when you
install Flash 5 onto your
computer.

PLAY A FLASH MOVIE IN FLASH

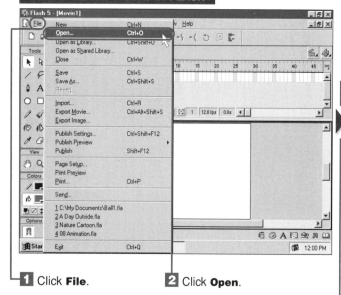

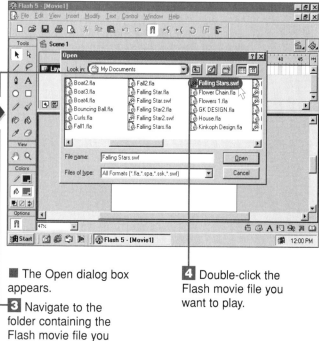

1 Click **File**.

2 Click **Open**.

■ The Open dialog box
appears.

3 Navigate to the
folder containing the
Flash movie file you
want to play.

4 Double-click the
Flash movie file you
want to play.

274

Can I control how the movie plays?

The Flash Player window has a few tools you can use to control how the movie plays. Click the **Control** menu to see the available commands. For example, by default, the Loop command is turned on. To deactivate the command, click **Loop**.

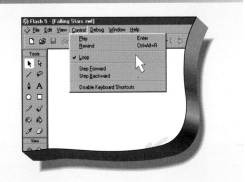

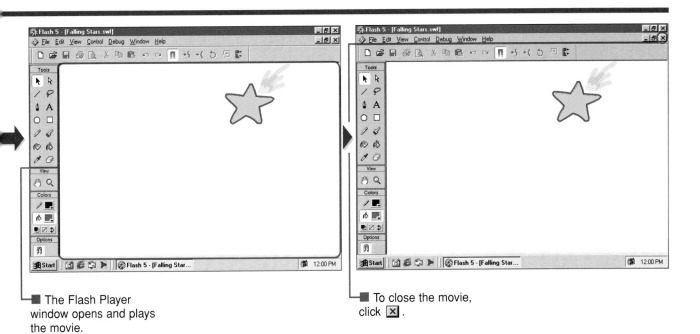

■ The Flash Player window opens and plays the movie.

■ To close the movie, click ☒ .

PLAY A FLASH MOVIE IN A BROWSER

You can play a Flash movie using the browser's Flash plug-in. Most browsers, such as Microsoft Internet Explorer and Netscape Navigator, include the Flash Player plug-in program for playing SWF files.

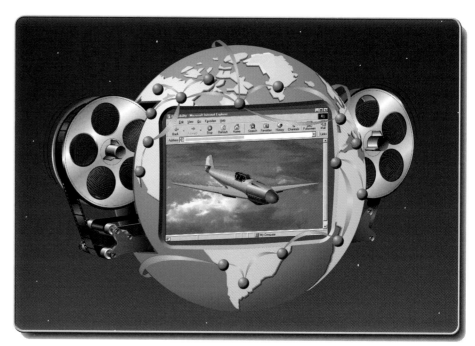

PLAY A FLASH MOVIE IN A BROWSER

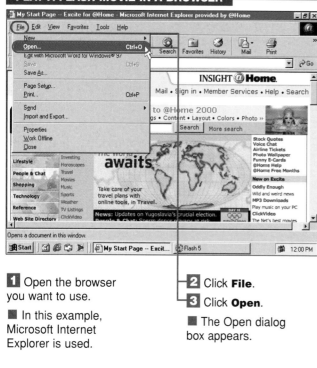

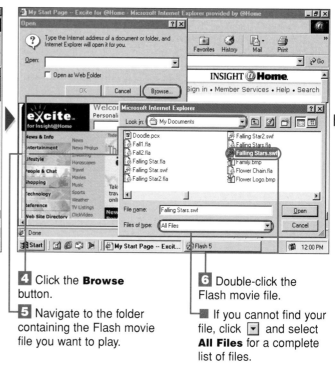

1 Open the browser you want to use.

■ In this example, Microsoft Internet Explorer is used.

2 Click **File**.

3 Click **Open**.

■ The Open dialog box appears.

4 Click the **Browse** button.

5 Navigate to the folder containing the Flash movie file you want to play.

6 Double-click the Flash movie file.

■ If you cannot find your file, click ▾ and select **All Files** for a complete list of files.

How do I open another movie to play in the Flash Player window?

As long as you have the Flash Player window open, you can view other Flash movies as well. To view another movie, perform the following steps:

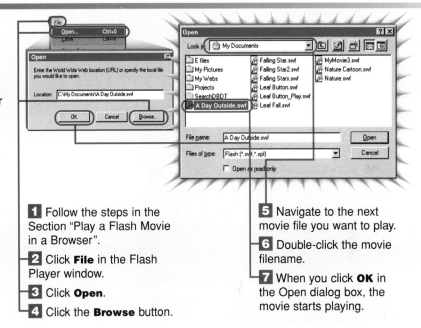

1 Follow the steps in the Section "Play a Flash Movie in a Browser".

2 Click **File** in the Flash Player window.

3 Click **Open**.

4 Click the **Browse** button.

5 Navigate to the next movie file you want to play.

6 Double-click the movie filename.

7 When you click **OK** in the Open dialog box, the movie starts playing.

7 Click **OK**.

■ The Flash Player window opens and the movie begins playing.

■ To close the movie, click ⊠.

TEST MOVIE BANDWIDTH

You can use the Bandwidth Profiler to help you determine which movie frames might cause problems during playback on the Web. File size and the user's data-transfer rate determines how smoothly and quickly your movie downloads and plays. You can test six different modem speeds, and gauge which frames use the most bytes to see exactly where your movie might slow down during playback.

TEST MOVIE BANDWIDTH

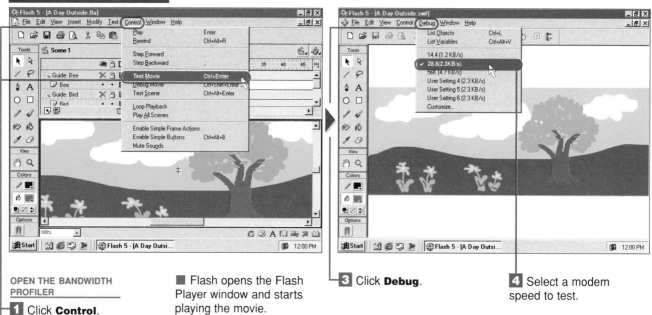

OPEN THE BANDWIDTH PROFILER

1 Click **Control**.

2 Click **Test Movie**.

■ Flash opens the Flash Player window and starts playing the movie.

3 Click **Debug**.

4 Select a modem speed to test.

278

Can I customize the download speed I want to test?

To customize the modem speed, perform the following steps:

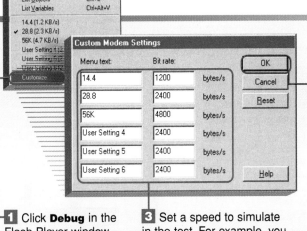

4 Click **OK** to save your changes.

1 Click **Debug** in the Flash Player window.

2 Click **Customize**.

■ Flash opens the Custom Modem Settings dialog box.

3 Set a speed to simulate in the test. For example, you can change an existing speed settings' bit rate by typing in another bit rate. Or you can enter a custom speed in a User Setting box and a bit rate to test for that speed.

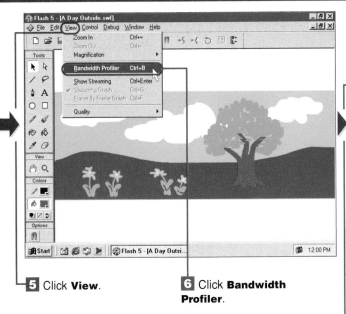

5 Click **View**.

6 Click **Bandwidth Profiler**.

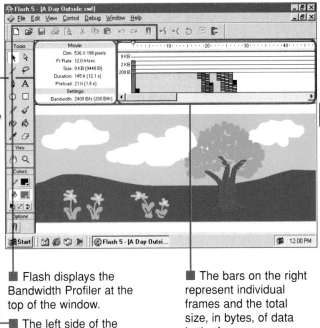

■ Flash displays the Bandwidth Profiler at the top of the window.

■ The left side of the Profiler shows information about the movie, such as file size and dimensions.

■ The bars on the right represent individual frames and the total size, in bytes, of data in the frame.

CONTINUED

TEST MOVIE BANDWIDTH

You can use two different views in the Flash Bandwidth Profiler to see how the frames play. A bar on the graph represents a frame. In Streaming Graph mode, the width of each bar shows how long it takes the frame to download. The default view is Streaming Graph mode. In Frame by Frame Graph mode, if the bar extends above the bottom red line of the graph, the Flash movie pauses to download the frame's data.

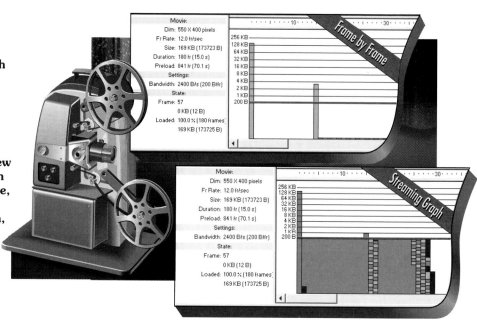

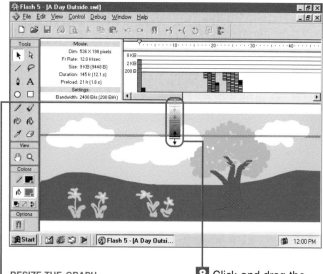

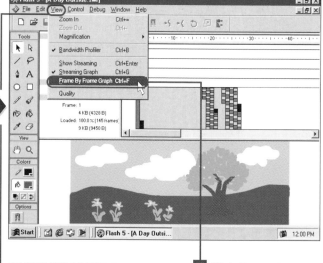

RESIZE THE GRAPH

7 To make sure you are viewing all the movie's information on the left side of the profiler, resize the profiler graph. Move the ▸ over the bottom border until the pointer turns into ↕.

8 Click and drag the border to resize the profiler graph.

■ Flash resizes the Bandwidth Profiler.

CHANGE THE GRAPH VIEW

9 To check which frames might be causing a slow down, switch to Frame by Frame Graph mode. Click **View**.

10 Click **Frame by Frame Graph**.

How do I view a specific frame in the profiler?

Use the scroll bar arrows ▽ to move left or right in the Profiler Timeline at the top of the Profiler graph. To view a specific frame, drag the playhead to the frame, or click the playhead where you want it to go.

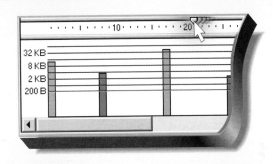

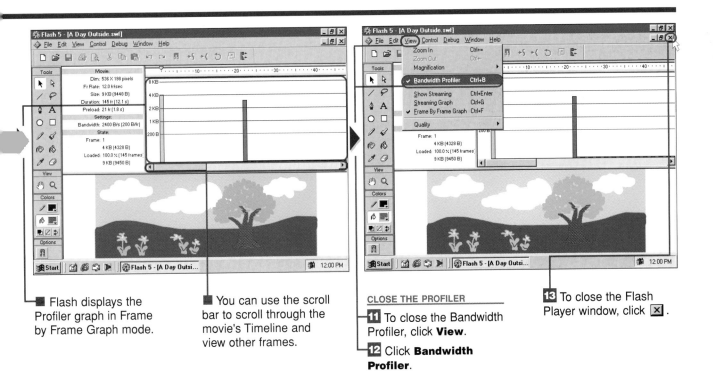

■ Flash displays the Profiler graph in Frame by Frame Graph mode.

■ You can use the scroll bar to scroll through the movie's Timeline and view other frames.

CLOSE THE PROFILER

11 To close the Bandwidth Profiler, click **View**.

12 Click **Bandwidth Profiler**.

13 To close the Flash Player window, click ☒ .

PUBLISH A MOVIE

You can use two phases to publish your Flash movie. First you prepare the files for publishing using the Publish Settings dialog box, then you publish the movie using the Flash Publish command. By default, Flash is set up to publish your movie as an SWF file for the Web, but you can choose to publish in other formats.

PUBLISH A MOVIE

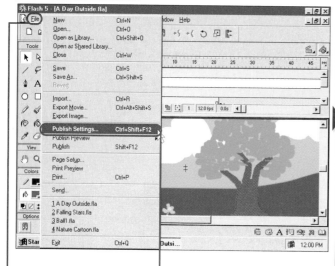

PREPARE FILES FOR PUBLISHING

1 Click **File**.

2 Click **Publish Settings**.

■ Flash opens the Publish Settings dialog box.

Note: If you have previously published your file, tabs from your last changes appear in the dialog box.

3 Click the **Formats** tab.

4 Click the Format option you want to use (☐ changes to ☑).

■ Depending on which format you select, additional tabs appear in the dialog box with options related to that format.

Can I preview a movie before I publish it?

Testing your movie often is a good idea, especially in a browser, to check how it plays. Flash has a feature that lets you preview a movie in a browser window before you publish the movie.

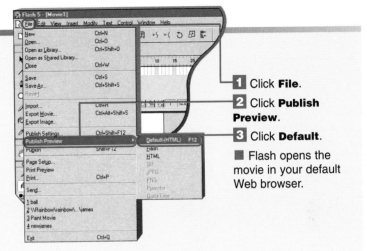

1 Click **File**.

2 Click **Publish Preview**.

3 Click **Default**.

■ Flash opens the movie in your default Web browser.

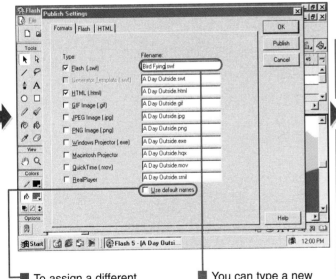

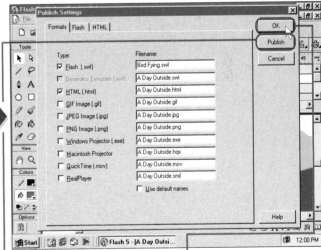

■ To assign a different filename other than the default supplied by Flash, you can click the **Use default names** option (☑ changes to ☐).

■ You can type a new filename in the format's text box.

■ Flash publishes your files to the My Documents folder unless you specify another folder and file name path in the file name text box.

5 When you are ready to publish the movie using the settings you selected, click **Publish**.

■ Flash generates the necessary files for the movie.

6 Click **OK** to save the settings and close the Publish Settings dialog box.

PUBLISH A MOVIE IN HTML FORMAT

You can save a movie in HTML format. In response, Flash creates an HTML page that displays your movie along with the SWF movie file. Flash generates all the necessary HTML code for you, including the tags needed to view your page in both Microsoft Internet Explorer and Netscape Navigator. You can then upload the HTML document to your Web server.

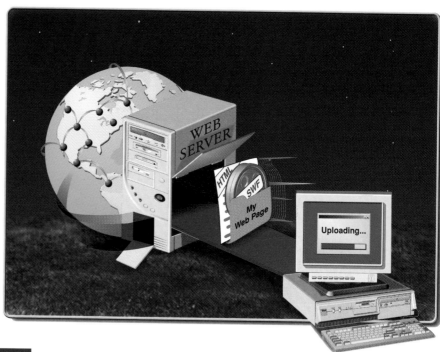

PUBLISH A MOVIE IN HTML FORMAT

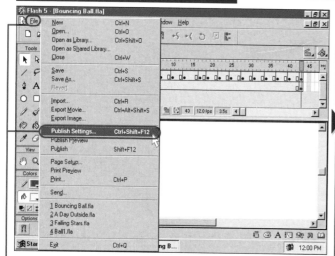

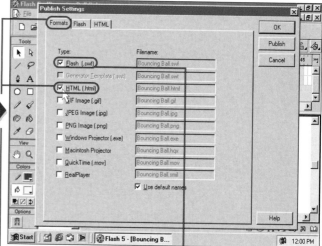

1 Click **File**.

2 Click **Publish Settings**.

■ Flash opens the Publish Settings dialog box.

Note: If you have previously published your file, tabs from your last changes appear in the dialog box.

3 Click the **Formats** tab.

4 Click **HTML** format.

■ Flash automatically selects the Flash format (.swf) for you.

Note: The Flash and HTML formats are selected by default the first time you use the Publish Settings dialog box. See the Section "Publish a Movie" to find out more about publishing Flash movies.

What HTML tags does Flash insert into the HTML document?

The Publish feature inserts the tags necessary for playing a Flash movie file in the browser window, including the OBJECT tag needed for Microsoft's Internet Explorer browser and the EMBED tag needed for Netscape's Navigator browser. Flash also inserts the IMG tag for displaying the movie file in another format, such as animated GIF or JPEG. The OBJECT, EMBED, and IMG tags create the movie display window used to play the Flash movie.

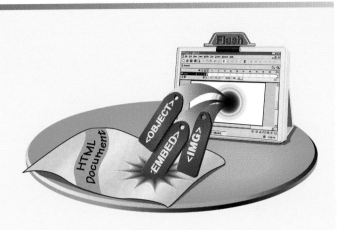

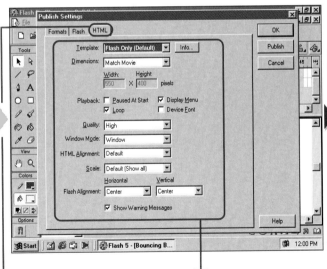

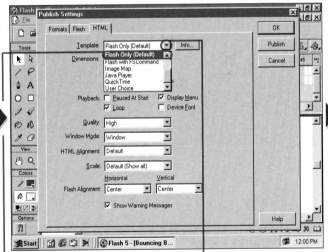

5 Click the **HTML** tab.

■ Flash displays options associated with generating a Web page, such as playback options and movie dimensions.

6 Select any options you want to apply.

■ The default Flash Only template allows other Flash users to view your movie. Those without the Flash plug-in cannot view the movie.

■ You can click ▼ in the Template box and select another template from the list.

CONTINUED

PUBLISH A MOVIE IN HTML FORMAT

You can use the options in the Publish Settings dialog box to specify exactly how you want your movie to appear in the browser window. You can set alignment, dimensions, and even playback options. Any changes you make to the settings override any previous settings for the file.

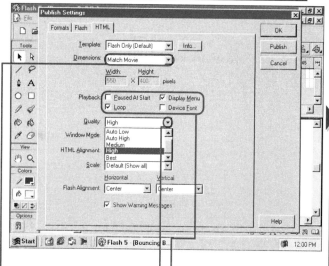

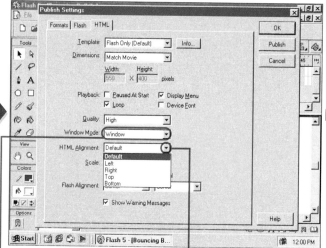

■ You can click the 🔽 in the Dimensions box to set width and height attribute values for the movie-display window—the area where the Flash plug-in plays the movie.

■ You can click the **Playback** options to control how the movie plays on the Web page (☐ changes to ☑).

■ You can click the 🔽 in the Quality box to view options for controlling the image quality during playback.

■ You can click the 🔽 in the Window Mode box and select options for playing your movie on a regular, opaque, or transparent background (Windows browsers only).

■ You can click the 🔽 in the HTML Alignment box and change the alignment of your movie as it relates to other Web page elements.

How do I make my movie full-size in the browser window?

To make your Flash movie appear full-screen size in the browser window, perform the following steps:

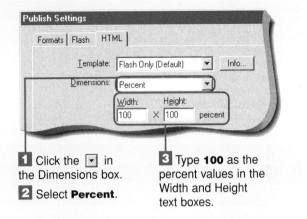

1 Click the ▾ in the Dimensions box.

2 Select **Percent**.

3 Type **100** as the percent values in the Width and Height text boxes.

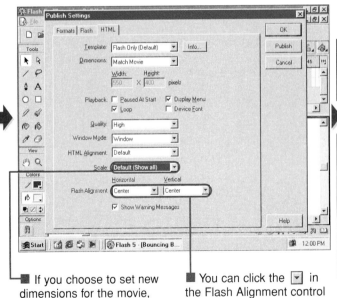

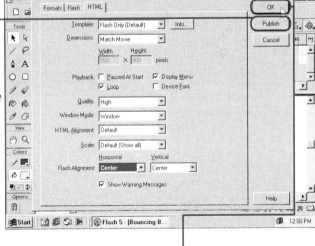

■ If you choose to set new dimensions for the movie, you can click the ▾ in the Scale box to rescale movie elements to fit the new size.

■ You can click the ▾ in the Flash Alignment control boxes and designate how the movie aligns in the movie window area.

7 When you are ready to publish the movie using the settings you selected, click the **Publish** button.

■ Flash generates the necessary files for the HTML document.

8 Click **OK** to save the settings and close the Publish Settings dialog box.

CREATE A FLASH PROJECTOR

You can create a Flash movie that plays in its own Flash Player window without the benefit of another application, which means that anyone you give the file to does not need to install Flash Player. When you publish the movie as a Windows Projector or Macintosh Projector format, Flash publishes the movie as an executable file (.exe).

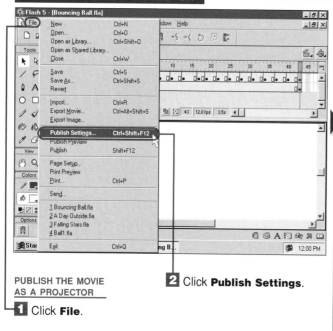

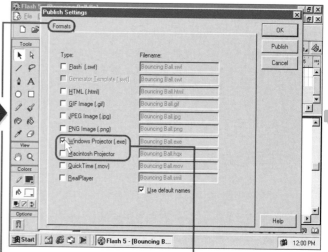

PUBLISH THE MOVIE AS A PROJECTOR

1 Click **File**.

2 Click **Publish Settings**.

■ Flash opens the Publish Settings dialog box.

Note: If you have previously published your file, tabs from your last changes appear in the dialog box.

3 Click the **Formats** tab.

4 Select either **Windows Projector** or **Macintosh Projector** as the format (☐ changes to ☑).

■ You can deselect the Flash and HTML format check boxes (☑ changes to ☐).

Can I rename the movie file?

If you want a different name for the movie, deselect the **Use default names** check box (☑ changes to ☐), then type another name next to the movie format to which you are saving.

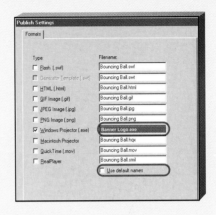

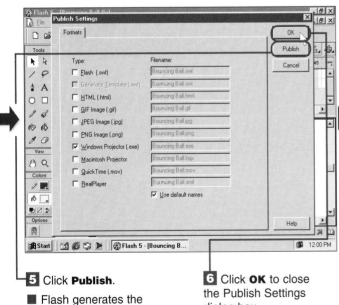

5 Click **Publish**.

■ Flash generates the necessary files for the movie and saves the movie with an .exe file extension.

6 Click **OK** to close the Publish Settings dialog box.

PLAY THE MOVIE

■ You can test the movie by double-clicking its name.

■ In this example, the file is opened via Windows Explorer.

■ The Flash Player window opens and plays the movie.

EXPORT TO ANOTHER FORMAT

You can easily export a Flash movie into another file format for use with other applications. For example, you might save your movie as a Windows AVI file or as a QuickTime file.

EXPORT TO ANOTHER FORMAT

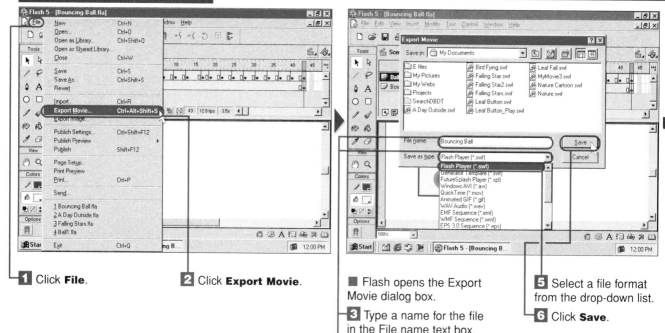

1 Click **File**.

2 Click **Export Movie**.

■ Flash opens the Export Movie dialog box.

3 Type a name for the file in the File name text box.

4 Click the ▼ in the Save as type box.

5 Select a file format from the drop-down list.

6 Click **Save**.

What is the difference between exporting a movie and publishing a movie?

When you publish a movie, you can publish to Flash (SWF), Generator Template, HTML, GIF, JPEG, PNG, Windows Projector, Macintosh Projector, QuickTime, and RealPlayer formats. When you export a movie, you can save the file in over a dozen different file formats, such as Windows AVI or Animated GIF. Some of the formats and options are the same between the two features, but when you publish a movie as opposed to exporting it, Flash saves information about the movie's Publish settings along with the movie file. When you export a movie, you are saving it to a single format.

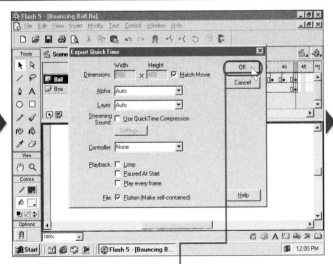

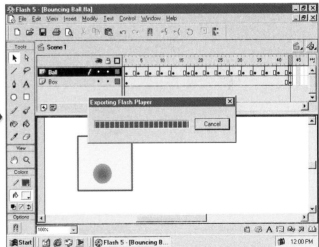

■ Depending on the file type you selected, an additional Export dialog box opens with options for size, sound, and video format.

■ You can make any selections necessary.

7 Click **OK**.

■ Flash exports the movie to the designated file type.

■ Depending on the file type, another dialog box, such as the Video Compression dialog box, might open first. Make any selections necessary, and click **OK** to continue exporting the file.

Note: Interactive elements you include in your Flash movies might not export to other file formats properly.

Some of your Flash projects might require you to print out a frame or series of frames. For example, you might print out frame content to show a storyboard of the movie. You can use the Page Setup dialog box to specify a layout for the storyboard, then use the Print dialog box to specify which pages to print.

PRINT MOVIE FRAMES

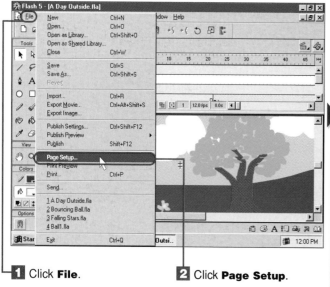

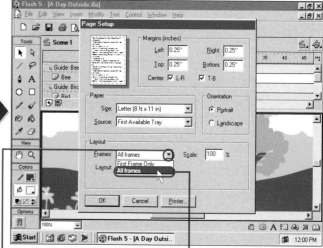

1 Click **File**.

2 Click **Page Setup**.

■ The Page Setup dialog box opens.

3 Click the ▼ in the Frames box.

4 Click **All frames**.

■ You can use the First Frame Only option if you want to print just the first frame of the movie.

Can I preview before I print?

You can preview exactly how the frames and layout appear on the printed page using the Flash Print Preview feature. Click 🗓 to open the Print Preview window. Click the **Print** button to print the frames, or click the **Close** button to return to the Flash window.

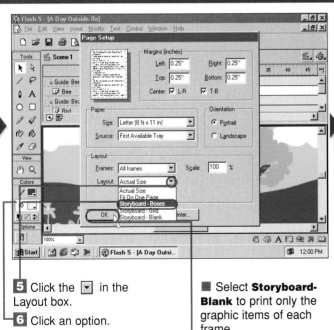

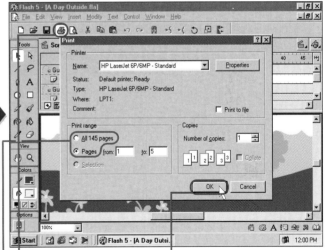

5 Click the 🔽 in the Layout box.

6 Click an option.

■ Select **Storyboard-Boxes** to storyboard the frames in boxes on the printed page.

■ Select **Storyboard-Grid** to print the frames in a grid pattern.

■ Select **Storyboard-Blank** to print only the graphic items of each frame.

7 Click **OK**.

■ The Page Setup dialog box closes.

8 Click 🖨.

■ The Print dialog box opens.

9 Select a Print Range option (○ changes to ◉).

■ You can click **All pages** to print the entire movie.

■ Alternately, you can click **Pages** and type a range of pages you want to print.

10 Click **OK**.

■ Flash prints the specified pages and layout.

WEB GRAPHIC AND ANIMATION TERMS

If you are new to the world of Web graphics and animation, this collection of terms will come in handy as you learn how to use Flash.

action: An interactive task triggered by a Flash event, such as clicking a Web page button. Flash actions can include playing a specific movie or sound, or opening a Web page.

ADPCM (Adaptive Differential Pulse-Code Modulation): An audio compression format that converts sound into binary data, used for transferring sound through fiber-optic telephone lines. ADPCM was a primary format for earlier versions of Flash.

aliasing: Refers to a bitmap graphic's edges, particularly in curved lines, that appear jagged instead of smooth.

animation: Making static images appear to move by placing images onto a series of frames. The content of each frame varies slightly from the preceding one so that when the frames are played, the illusion of movement occurs.

antialiasing: Smoothing the jagged edges of a bitmap image.

authoring file: The Flash file in which you create the content, animation, and interactivity that will become a Flash movie. The authoring file uses a *.fla* file extension.

bandwidth: The amount of data that can flow through a network connection, measured in bits per second (bps). Higher bandwidths allow faster data transmissions. When applied to the Web, bandwidth commonly measures the amount of time it takes a Web page to download.

bitmap graphic: A graphic type in which the image is displayed as pixels. Each pixel stores the location and color for that pixel, measured in bits. Bitmap graphics are quite common on the Web. Also called *raster graphic*.

broadband: A high-speed, high capacity transmission channel carried on coaxial or fiber-optic cable networks. Broadband channels utilize a higher bandwidth than regular phone line connections.

browser compatibility: Refers to the different ways Web browsers interpret HTML. When designing Web pages, Web designers must factor in differences between browser programs and test pages for compatibility across browsers.

button: A graphic the user can click to perform an action. You can create interactive buttons for Web pages using Flash.

DHTML: Dynamic HyperText Markup Language, DHTML is the next generation of HTML language used to create and display Web pages. DHTML gives Web designers and developers greater control of Web page elements, such as positioning and layering.

dithering: If your computer encounters colors it cannot normally display, it simulates those colors by mixing other colors.

editable text fields: A third type of text block you can insert onto the Flash Stage, editable text fields enable you to customize information displayed on a Web page or collect information from users.

event: An interactive occurrence that causes a Flash action to happen, such as clicking a Web page button that starts a movie.

export: To turn Flash content into an optimized, playable movie file. You can export into .swf (Flash movie), .avi (Windows AVI), and .mov (QuickTime) movie formats.

fills: A graphical way of adding color or pattern inside a shape.

Flash Projector: An executable copy of your Flash movie that needs no player or plug-in to view. Use the Projector to distribute your movie via disk or CD-ROM.

Flash Standalone Player: An executable player application you can use to open a Flash movie for viewing.

frame: A unit within the Flash Timeline where you can insert graphics or sound for use in animation.

frame-by-frame animation: The most common form of animation, each frame displays a slight variation from the previous frame, creating the illusion of movement when played back. Animators also call this *cel animation*, a term carried over from the days of painting animation on transparent sheets (called *cels*).

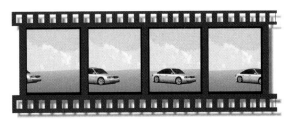

WEB GRAPHIC AND ANIMATION TERMS

frame rate: The speed, measured by frames per second (fps), at which frames are played.

guide layer: A backdrop for a Flash movie layout. Guide layers are not exported with the movie's contents.

instance: A copy of a Flash symbol. Every time you place a symbol from the Flash library onto the Stage, you insert an instance of that symbol.

keyframe: A frame you insert in your movie to define a change in animation.

layers: An organizational tool for arranging parts of a drawn object, creating a sense of depth.

Library window: Stores reusable elements in your Flash movie.

loop: To play an animation or sound a specified number of times.

mask: Conceal an area or space from view.

modifier: Additional tools you can use to customize the selected tool or feature you want to apply.

motion tweening: Tweening the size, position, and rotation of a symbol between two defined points of a movie.

movie file: When creating Flash movies, content is created in an authoring file, then exported into a movie file, which uses an *.swf* file extension. The authoring file's content is compressed and optimized to be played as a movie file.

MP3 (MPEG-1 Audio Layer 3): Fast becoming the standard for digital audio on the Internet, MP3 audio compression format significantly reduces the size of sound files by reducing the amount of redundant coding without reducing audio quality. MP3 is the default audio format for Flash 5 movies.

onion skinning: A feature that allows the Flash animator to see multiple-frame outlines of the animation sequence.

panel: A window that offers additional controls for working with a Flash element.

playhead: Indicates which frame you are viewing in the Timeline.

RAW (Raw PCM): An older audio format, RAW is not very useful for Internet distribution of audio files. It creates larger sound files than ADPCM or MP3 audio file formats.

sample: In digital sampling, a linear representation of a sound.

sample rates: The number of samples that exist in each second of a sound file.

scenes: You can break up parts of a Flash movie into managable scenes for greater control over content.

shape tweening: Morphing one shape into another between two defined points in a movie.

smoothing: Controlling the edges of a selected area of color.

stacking order: Flash layers are placed one on top of the other in a stacking order. You can control which layer appears first by changing the order of the stack.

static frame: Repeats the content of the previous frame.

streaming content: The process of viewing or hearing parts of a broadcast file while the remainder of the file is still being downloaded.

symbol: A reusable Flash object you can reinsert throughout your movie. Symbols are stored in the Flash Library.

target: The specified object that will be affected by a Flash interactive event.

tweening: The process of allowing Flash to calculate changes to an animation between two defined points.

vector graphics: A type of graphic format that uses mathematical equations to draw the image.

INDEX

INDEX

INDEX

INDEX

reuse bitmaps, 131
reverse sequence of frames in animations, 200-201
rollover buttons. *See* buttons
rotate
    bitmap fills, 135
    objects, 64
    symbols, in animation, 174-177
rounded rectangles, draw, 43
rulers, display or hide, 22

S

sampling rate of sounds, overview, 226
save
    animations, as movie clips, 202-203
    color sets, 73
    files, 10
    gradients, 71
scale objects, 60-61
scenes
    assign Go To actions to, 258
    create, 164-165
    rearrange, 165
    switch between, 165
search for help information, 24-25
select
    fills, 53
    frames, in Timeline, 160
    objects
        part of, 53
        using Arrow tool, 50-51
        using Lasso tool, 52-53
    zoom percentage, 19
shape hints
    delete, 199
    use in animations, 196-199
shape recognition feature, in Flash, 29
shape tween
    create, 192-195
    vs. motion tween, 193
shape-changing buttons, create, 212-215
shapes
    add strokes, 62-63
    for Brush tool, select, 45
    fill using Paint Bucket tool, 46-47
    of fills, change, 58-59
    of lines, change, 56
    morph, 192-195
    oval, draw, 42-43
    rectangles, draw, 42-43
    use hints when morphing, 196-199

shortcuts, keyboard, hide Timeline using, 15
size
    of Bandwidth Profiler graph, change, 280
    of Brush tool, change, 44
    of frames in Timeline, change, 147, 261
    measurement units, change, 17
    of movies, set
        for browser windows, 287
        for Stage, 142-143
    of Stage, change, 16-17
    of symbols, animate by changing, 182-185
    of text, change, 87
        in action list, 263
    of text boxes, change, 93
smooth lines, 40
Snap tool, use, 23
sound clips. *See* sounds
sounds
    add layer to movie, 230-231
    assign to buttons, 217, 234-235
    assign to frames, 232-233
    customize, 247
    edit, 246-247
    event, create, 236-237
    file formats, 227
    import to Library, 228-229
    Library, use, 229
    loop, 244-245
    overview, 226-227
    preview in Library, 233
    set output for export, 248-249
    start, assign to frames, 238-239
    stop, assign to frames, 240-241
    streaming, assign to frames, 242-243
    volume, control, 239
speed
    of animations, adjust, 159
    download, test for movies, 278-281
    of movies, set, 142-143
    of tweened animation, set, 190-191
spin symbols, in animation, 178-180
stack
    layers, 104-105
    objects, 78-79
Stage
    align objects with, 81
    levels, 28
    move objects on, 54
    overview, 6
    size, change, 16-17
    turn on grid lines, 23
    zoom out or in, 18-19

INDEX